THE NORWEGIAN ELKHOUND

THE   NORWEGIAN   ELKHOUND

by Nina P. Ross

Doral Publishing, Inc.
Wilsonville, Oregon
1995

Published by Doral Publishing, Inc.
8560 Salish Lane #300, Wilsonville OR 97070-9612.
Order through Login Publishers Consortium, Chicago, Illinois.

Printed in the United States of America.

Edited by Luana Luther.
Cover design by Douglas Hewitt.
Cover photograph of Tortasen's Torris taken by owner Frank Christiansen, September 1992, in Malm, Norway.

Library of Congress Number: 93-74007
ISBN:0-944875-39-4

Ross, Nina P.
        The Norwegian elkhound / by Nina P. Ross.
        -- Wilsonville, Or. : Doral Pub., 1995.

        p. : ill. ; cm.

        Includes bibliographical references and
index.
        ISBN 0-944875-39-4

        1. Norwegian elkhounds.   I. Title.
SF429.N6R   636.753 dc20
                                       93-74007

dedicated to
the Norwegian Elkhound Association of America
for its continuing efforts to preserve the
beauty and character of the breed

Preface

As a child
Sitting on the front porch with my mother
I often wondered if we saw the same velvety red rose
Or if to her the rose was some other color—
Maybe green, blue, or a color I had never before imagined.

As a student
Sitting in an English literature class with my peers
I often wondered how the teacher knew what Shakespeare meant
In the play we were studying—
Because that's not what it meant to me.

As a gardener
Digging in the hard red clay of the South
I often wondered why some people were repulsed
By the sweet smell of honeysuckle on a warm sticky evening—
While others doused themselves in its perfume.

As an observer
Sitting ringside at a dog show
I often wondered why the dogs were all so different
In the ring with their breeders of record—
When they all claimed to follow the same standard.

—**Author**

ACKNOWLEDGMENTS

Acknowledgment and appreciation is given to all those who graciously supplied photographs, information and articles:

The American Kennel Club
Frank Christiansen
Joe Corona
Glenna C. Crafts
Lynn and Donna Davenport
Patricia Craige Trotter
David Gleaves
Jakob Petter Holsing
Richard and Bette Isacoff
Per Lovold
Elizabeth A. Parmer
Stewart Nelson Photography
Norwegian Elkhound Association of America and
        Regional Club Members
Orthopedic Foundation for Animals
Donald Rotier

TABLE OF CONTENTS

Chapter 1. History 1

Chapter 2. Spotlighting Kennels.. 21

Chapter 3. Norwegian Elkhound Standards 59

Chapter 4. Structure and Function 71

Chapter 5. Breeding with a Purpose...................................... 87

Chapter 6. Raising a Litter of Puppies 99

Chapter 7. Showing in Conformation 109

Chapter 8. Training a Norwegian Elkhound 123
           Elkhounds in Obedience by Donald Rotier

Chapter 9. The Elkhound as a Hunting Dog 143
           Hunting with Gray Elkhounds in Norway by Frank Christiansen

Chapter 10. Basic Concepts of Genetics 159

Chapter 11. Buying and Caring for a Puppy 173

Chapter 12. Norwegian Elkhound Kennels: 1970s-1990s 187

Chapter 13. NEAA National Specialty Winners 207

Chapter 14. In Conclusion 221

Bibliography 227

Glossary 229

Appendixes 239
      Illustrations
      Alphabetical Listing of American Kennels and Owners
      Norwegian Elkhound Association of America: Regional Clubs
      Norwegian Elkhound Breeder/Judges
      Orthopedic Foundation for Animals:
      Norwegian Elkhound Registration Numbers

Index 295

CHAPTER ONE
HISTORY

The Norwegian Elkhound is a handsome silver-gray dog native to Scandinavia. Although he is medium-sized, he has the energy, stamina and agility to keep a mighty moose at bay. His trademark of distinction is his silvery tail carried snugly up over his back in a tight curl. A black muzzle and black prick ears add to his distinguished appearance. He is, by his own demeanor, an aristocrat among Northern dogs.

Although the Elkhound is easy going, reliable, intelligent and eager for praise, he is staunch, dignified and independent. His innate intelligence gives him an independent disposition often mistaken for stubbornness. At times he seems intent on having his own way, but, in the end, serves as a devoted companion and guardian to all who win his respect.

The Norwegian Elkhound is a mold unto himself with every physical part expressing a purpose. His wedge-shaped head, his compactness and squareness of body, harsh coat, tightly curled tail are nature's requirements for a hunting dog in foreboding terrain where stamina supersedes speed. His pureness is shown in his high prepotency, always producing get with a strong inheritance of Elkhound characteristics, namely the tightly curled tail, prick ears and haughty disposition.

In his homeland, the Gray Elkhound is indispensable as a hunter of big game, being bred to track moose over the rugged country in rigorous subarctic climate and to keep his prey at bay, waiting for his master to make the kill. His versatility is utilized in much the same way in Europe, the United States and Canada. The popularity of the breed in the United States led to the organization of the Norwegian Elkhound Association of America (NEAA) in 1930 and subsequent recognition by the American Kennel Club (AKC).

English Ch. Llychlyn Morgan.

Evidence reveals that the Norwegian Elkhound roamed the woods in the rolling valleys tucked between the fjords and cliffs of Norway for more than six thousand years. The rugged Kjolen mountains are home to the moose or *elg* for which he was named. It was here that his saga through the centuries began. At first he was in competition with prehistoric man in his search for game. Later, as man and dog came to know each other they worked as a team in their quest for food.

Archaeologists have uncovered traces of an early people who roamed and lived off the valleys and waters of the rugged land that was rich with game and fish. These migratory people, referred to as *Veidefolket* or gypsies, were accompanied by wild dogs thought to be the forerunners of the Norwegian

Malm, Norway.

Elkhound. At that time the dogs were referred to as *Torvmosehund.*

VIKING PERIOD

The Viking period followed. The Vikings were bold and daring Norsemen who traveled the seas, sailing in large, skillfully designed pirate ships made of oak. The ships were manned by as many as 60 rowers. Although the first raids were initiated by the Norwegians as early as 793 A.D., the Danes and Swedes sometimes participated in joint ventures with them. During other incursions, the Danes and Swedes pillaged on their own or in direct opposition to the Norwegians. Pictures of the Vikings often show them wearing helmets adorned with horns—no doubt a tongue-in-cheek portrayal. The sea rovers had direct physical contact with their victims, making it highly unlikely that they would intentionally provide convenient handles for their opposition, a sure way to turn the tide of battle.

Sagas tend to romanticize the tyrants by picturing them as devoted family men who, before going to sea, planted crops in the rugged north country and returned in time for the harvest. While they were gone, as the stories go, their wives, children and the elderly took care of the farms with the help of dogs. Dogs were prized possessions of the Vikings, serving as comrades, guardians and hunters at home and on the farm. The dogs were as rugged and bold as the Vikings themselves. Traces of the dogs' existence indicate they bore physical features similar to the Elkhound of today.

The Vikings' sea travels took them to Greenland well before Erik the Red's explorations from 982 to 985. In 986, Erik deposited a load of colonists in Greenland. The Norse inhabited Greenland from 986 to 1480 and some as yet questionable evidence points to their existence there beyond 1500. Archaeologists continue to fight the elements and mosquitoes in their quest for remnants of Norse habitation in the Arctic areas, including Canada where artifacts attest to a prior existence of Norse settlements.

Erik the Red was from Norse-Icelandic stock, a hardy race of hunters and farmers who settled along the southwest coast of Greenland during the Viking explorations. Their descendants were lured by the abundance of seals and whales in the area. They survived by sealing, whaling and gathering anything that would help them survive in the icy world of fjords and ice floes, not unlike their native Scandinavia. In direct opposition to the Viking ancestors, these Scandinavians lived as Christians beginning in the 12th Century, importing their own resident bishop from Norway.

The expansive conquests by the Vikings resulted in settlements in Scotland, Ireland and the north of England, including York where they replaced the Picts, an earlier population. Their forays continued and were vented on much of Europe. Spain, Italy, France and Germany felt their scourge. Many Vikings remained in the countries they ravaged and became citizens, one of several factors that brought the Viking Age to a close around 1066. Other factors include the population growth in Europe; improving defense strategies on land and sea; declining slave trade; the spread of Christianity; and the fact that many victimized countries were using Viking mercenaries against the Viking marauders, causing a final meshing of a social fabric that ultimately enveloped the Vikings and brought an end to the terror.

The Jorvik Viking Centre in northern England used evidence of archaeology from the Coppergate Dig to recreate Viking York, one of the greatest commercial cities in Europe. The 10th

Century city lies buried deep below its modern counterpart. The dogs depicted in the ancient city were of the Border Collie type rather than Spitz.

Archaeologists in Viking Scotland have found evidence of the remains of dogs in burial graves. They surmised that the dogs were Terrier and Welsh Corgi types.

Three Viking ships were discovered and excavated in Norway: *Tune* in 1867; *Gokstad* in 1880; and the *Oseberg* in 1904. More recently, others have been discovered, excavated and restored in numerous locations in Scandinavia. Their remains provide a key to the artistry of the shipwrights during the Viking Age—building ships sturdy enough to withstand the ravaging storms of the North Sea, yet lightweight enough to be hauled over long distances of land.

BURIAL SHIPS

Viking ships were often used as burial ships. The dead were placed in special burial chambers that were furnished with their earthly possessions: furniture, tools, clothing, jewelry, food,

Viking Ship: Oseberg.

horses, oxen and dogs. The skeletons of at least 12 horses and six dogs were found outside the *Gokstad*. The ships were laded with rocks and mired in a blue clay that kept them well preserved over the centuries.

Persistent study and research by osteologists and archaeologists have categorized the dog bones found at burial sites into three sizes: small, medium and large. The results of their tedious work infer a strong resemblance to an elkhound-type breed of dog that still exists today in Scandinavia in sizes similar to the early skeletal remains.

ARTIFACTS

Research by Professor Brinchmann at the Museum of Bergen in Norway attests to the Elkhound's primal existence. Brinchmann analyzed bones as well as other relics of the Stone Age found in Viking burials. He concluded that the bones were dog skeletons, a testament to the value man placed on his dog in that early era. Artifacts unearthed from a grave at Valloby leave little doubt as to the existence of elkhound-like dogs in Norway before the time of Christ.

Other relics and dog bones have been found in southwest Norway, further evidence of the Elkhound's ability to acclimate, whether to the subzero temperatures of Norway's bleak Arctic interior, family life on a farm or to the rough waters of the North Sea.

CHRISTIANITY

After the arrival of Christianity in Norway and the passing of the Viking period in all its infamous glory, not much is recorded about the Elkhound. The country itself suffered from the ravages of man and nature. Many people migrated to other parts of Scandinavia and to Finland. As the centuries passed, deadly plagues took their toll and the country was left with few inhabitants.

Gradually groups of homeless people from surrounding countries began to filter back into Norway, accompanied by Elkhounds to help them hunt big game in the rugged woods and deep snow. Many of these people, who were of Finnish descent, settled in a deeply forested area between Oslo and Ringerike called *Krokskogen*. They used their Elkhounds to hunt large birds as well as big game.

SNORRI STURLUSON

The Norse, like the Greeks during the time of Homer, were poets and story tellers, preserving much of Scandinavian history in saga form. The clergy and scholars of Iceland, a country discovered and inhabited by the Norse, wrote many manuscripts of sagas as the storytellers related the tales to them. Two important manuscripts, the *Elder Edda* in poetry and the *Younger Edda* in prose, deal with religion and philosophy. The two *Eddas* have been translated into modern languages and are studied all over the world.

The *Prose* or *Younger Edda* was compiled by Snorri Sturluson who lived from 1178 to 1241. Sturluson was a rich man who was president of the Icelandic Parliament or Althingi. Although many writers of the time were clerics, Sturluson, a politician, captured the mythology and heroic stories of Norway and the Vikings in saga and poetic form. Ironically enough, he was murdered, an odious act mandated by a king of Norway.

WOLF PERIOD

A more recent period in Norse history, equally as bleak, was the 20-year stretch between 1825 and 1845 known as the *Wolf Period.* During this period, thousands of hungry wolves swarmed through Scandinavia, killing much of the farm stock, including many dogs. The Elkhound is credited with helping rid the country of the wolves by his ingenuity and fearless fighting. Time and re-telling have turned the story into a legend.

The saga preserving the history of the Wolf Period portrays the Elkhound as its hero. The saga gives the exact time of the incident, the night of February 14, 1842. For years that night was known as *Graabine,* or Wolf Night.

WOLF NIGHT, A SAGA

Dogs and livestock were barricaded in sheds at night to protect them from the wolves. Fanarok, an Elkhound known for his leadership capabilities, had just bedded down in the straw when he heard the cries and screams of his beloved little brother Purven, the runt of the litter. Somehow Purven had been off playing when the others were closed in for the night. Purven didn't stand a chance against the wolves and was slain.

Fanarok vowed to avenge Purven's death. With mournful howls he sent the message to farm after farm throughout Norderhove Valley. The next night, as he sat alone on the ice in the middle of Lake Juveren, the wolves began their approach. Suddenly, with the wolves at his heels, Fanarok streaked to the slough at the other edge of the lake where eight strong Elkhounds lay waiting. The din from the ensuing encounter between wolves and dogs attracted additional hungry wolves as well as farmers with clubs and weapons.

The raging farmers encircled the small lake and began closing in on the surprised wolves, retaliating for 20 years of torment. The subsequent fight lasted most of the night. By morning, Norway was rid of wolves, and the Elkhound again had proved his worth as hunter, family guardian and protector.

GAMLE BAMSE GRAM
The wolves did in fact kill off most of the game in the woods of Norway, leaving one small herd of moose in Osterdalen and Hedmarken. Sadly, too, only a few Elkhounds were spared.

Gamle Bamse Gram.

Breeders and hunters searched the secluded valleys in an effort to find the better Elkhounds and, over a period of years, re-established their bloodlines.

In 1865, a puppy destined to become the cast for today's Norwegian Elkhound was whelped. He was called *Gamle Bamse Gram* and was owned by a well-known sportsman of the time, Consul Jens Gram of Ask, Ringerike. The earliest recorded pedigrees are traced back to 1865, many of them including Gamle Bamse Gram.

CONFORMATION SHOWS IN NORWAY

In 1877, the Gray Elkhound began his career in conformation shows in Norway where the first benched show was held. Breeders of Elkhounds believed then as they do now that an Elkhound must be proven as a hunting dog before he can be shown in a conformation show. There were 124 hunting dogs entered in the first show in Norway. Fifteen of them were Elkhounds. The second show was held in 1880. The entry increased to 180, including 28 Elkhounds.

A group of Norwegian hunters and sportsmen established the *Norsk Dyrehundklub* in 1899 and began to formulate the breed standard for the Elkhound. The breed standard, completed in 1906, has undergone several revisions, the latest in 1950. The club changed its name to the *Norsk Elghundklub* in 1949.

DOGS OF NORWAY

Among the first Elkhounds to be exhibited in Norway were Bamse, exhibited by Arne Omsted; Kandix, owned by J. C. Hals; Fin, owned by H. Solberg; Nero, owned by J. Skagnaes; Skram, owned by O. H. Waagaard; Lars Suseg's Pasop and Bring; and T. Lier's Max and Fin. The first Gray Elkhound champion in Norway was Sara, bred by Ole Blegeberg and whelped in 1912. She earned her championship in 1916.

Senny II, bred by Gullick Rua of Jondalen, became the foundation stock for one of Norway's most notable kennels, T. Hemsen's *Glitre Kennels*. Glitre dogs can be traced back in almost every Elkhound pedigree because of Hemson's extensive breeding and exporting of Elkhounds to other countries. A few of the outstanding Elkhounds carrying the Glitre name were Ch. Skrub av Glitre, Ch. Rugg av Glitre, Ch. Heika av Glitre, Bjonn and Bob av Glitre, Boy, Jern and Ch. Trond av Glitre. The

Tortasen's Jakko.

Norwegian Elkhound owned by President Herbert Hoover was Ronnie av Glitre.

Other kennels in Norway contributing to the preservation of the Gray Elkhound are as follows: Elgstolen, owned by Erik Enberg; Fjeldheim, by E. A. Cappelin Smith; Gjetemyra, by Hans Christiansen; Homanskogen, by Victor Jensen; Kalagerasen, by Peder Kalager; Lifjell by Hans Fosse; Skromtefjell by Sven Mjearum; Sokomdal, by A. and S. Furuseth; Stavsetras by Charles Stavseth; Suteras, by O. C. Svae; Tortasen by Jakob Petter Holsing; and Vardetoppen by Harald Sjaastad.

Elkhound kennels in Norway during the period 1930-1960 were considered large if they had three or four bitches. Present-day kennels seldom have more than two bitches. Owners breed mainly to supply hunting dogs for themselves and their friends. Commercial breeding of Elkhounds in Norway is virtually non-existent.

Several owners of Gray Elkhound kennels in Norway have come to America to judge Elkhounds at specialties and other AKC point shows. The kennels and their owners are as follows:

Elglia Kennels of Johnny Aarflot; Tallo Kennels of Olav Campbell and his son Ralf Campbell; Tortasen Kennels of Jakob Petter Holsing; and Jarlsberg Kennels of Gerd Berbom who also resided in England. Several of these kennels are still in existence and many pedigrees of Elkhounds in America carry their names.

Successful long-time breeders of Norwegian Elkhounds in many countries have helped preserve the natural beauty of the Elkhound, his innate intelligence and ruggedness, through carefully thought out breeding programs. The Norwegian Elkhound remains, therefore, a comrade, a guardian and a hunter, much like his ancestors who first roamed the frigid lands of Scandinavia.

ELKHOUND BREEDS

The Norwegian Elkhound of the United States is the same as the Gray Elkhound of Norway. However, the Norwegian Elkhound of Norway is the *svart* or Black Elkhound. The Black Elkhound tends to be smaller than the gray and has a lighter build, similar to the Buhund. The dense, sleek, shiny black coat of the *svart* consists of an outer coat of short black hair and a woolly undercoat. White markings on his feet and a small blaze on his chest are permissible. The Black Elkhound was registered as a separate breed in 1903. He is used for hunting moose or bear. He works silently on leash, leading the hunter to the game. At one time, the Black Elkhound had dwindled in numbers almost to the point of extinction. However, concerned breeders are working to preserve the breed. Several of the breed have been imported by kennels in the United States. The Black Elkhound is slightly smaller than the Gray Elkhound but makes up for it with stamina and hunting ability.

Other elkhound breeds used for moose hunting in Scandinavia are as follows: Jamthund, an elkhound from Jamtland, Sweden; Karelsk bjornhund, the Karelian Bear Dog from Finland; Ostsibirsk Laika, an East Siberian Laika from Russia; Vestsibirsk Laika, a West Siberian Laika from Russia; Russisk-Europeisk Laika, the Russian-European Laika from Russia; and Finsk-Karels Laika, the Finnish-Karelian Laika from Russia.

In Finland, the red Finnish Spitz, known as the *Barking Bird Dog*, is a smaller, lighter-boned breed. It was accepted into regular classes by the AKC in 1988 after having been shown in

Comparing Black and Gray Elkhounds.

the Miscellaneous class. The Finnish Spitz shown on the following page is Ch. Kitsuna's Ella Spitzgerald NT389852 (Am. Can. Ch. Jayenn's Kekselias x Ch. Jayenn's Quetsch Kaiku), a female, whelped 05-21-88, from the Kitsuna, Reg., kennel. Breeder-owners are Richard and Bette Isacoff. The *Bear Dog*, or the black and white Karelian, has a disposition that is not conducive to being a companion dog, although it is fearless in its quest for the hunt.

The Buhund, a smaller dog, is 17 3/4 inches at the withers with bitches being a little less. The breed may be wheaten, reddish-yellow or black in color with a preference toward solids. Buhunds often have a white blaze and white feet. They are natural herders of sheep, cattle or even poultry.

Finnish Spitz, the barking bird dog.

THE ELKHOUND IN SWEDEN

The Swedish Elkhound Club serves as the parent club for Elkhound breeders and sportsmen. The Elkhound in Sweden developed much the same way as the Elkhound in Norway, although it is a taller, rangier version of the Norwegian Elkhound. Its head type and expression are different and light markings on the nose are usual. Even though Swedish breeders developed the *Jamthund* to contend with the deep snow of the later hunting season in Sweden, the Elkhound is firmly established as a

Swedish Jamthund.

companion and a hunter. Both the Gray Elkhound and the Jamthund are recognized by the Swedish Kennel Club. The latest addition to the Elkhound family in Sweden is the Swedish White Elkhound.

SWEDISH WHITE ELKHOUND
The Swedish Elkhound Association and The Swedish Kennel Club approved the White Elkhound in 1993. It is a variation of the Swedish Jamthund and the Gray Elkhound, Norway's national dog, which is known as the Norwegian Elkhound in the United States. The White Elkhound tends to be larger than a Gray Elkhound and is built more like the Jamthund. It is a clear white color and is 56 cm. for dogs and 53 cm. for bitches.

An entry of 110 White Elkhounds was evaluated by Norwegian judge Frank Christensen in Sweden in July 1993. Shows in Scandinavia tend to be more informal than shows in America. The dogs are not *stacked* while being judged.

A few of the successful kennels in Sweden are: Alterdalen, owned by Tage Oman and Runar Lundstrom; Bergasen, by Gunnar Svensson; Bransian, by Rune Jarlestad; Gardetorpet,

*Swedish
White Elkhound.*

by Robert Carlsson; Nickas, by Birger Ericsson; Skogsmarken, by Sven Klasson and Klas Karlsson; and Stavholmen, owned by K. H. Lundin. Many top-winning Elkhounds have been produced in Sweden. As with other countries, there is considerable importing and exporting of Elkhounds among Swedish breeders.

BRITISH ELKHOUND CLUB

Although there were other Elkhounds in England at the time, a dog named *Foerdig* became the first Norwegian Elkhound to be registered in the English Kennel Club stud book. Whelped in 1874 and belonging to Major Godfrey Faussett, he was the first Elkhound to win in a show, thus qualifying him for entry in the stud book. Milly, the first bitch to qualify, was entered in the stud book in 1879. She was bred by Mrs. Baillie Hamilton.

Early on, the Elkhounds bred in England were more rugged than they are now. Almost all Elkhounds with English bloodlines can be traced back to Foerdig, Senny II of the Glitre Kennel, Jaeger, a Swedish import, Ch. Woden, his sister Gerda and his offspring, Astrid, Christina and Norga.

In 1923, nearly 50 years after Foerdig was registered, the British Elkhound Society was formed. By that time, approximately 90 Elkhounds had been registered in England. In 1924, an English translation of the Norwegian breed standard was published. It was replaced in 1927 and revised periodically to conform to the British interpretation of the ideal Elkhound. The British Elkhound Club remains the guiding force in the preservation and promulgation of the Elkhound in England.

A few of the kennels in England are: Elkhome, owned by M. Basher; Eskamere, by A. Heward; Fourwents, by Joyce E. Winter; Friochan, by Kitty C. Heffer; Garrowby, by Viscountess Halifax; *of the Holm,* by W. F. Holmes; Jotsoma, by W. Carey; Kinburn, by Kincaid Lennox; Lillabo, by E. M. Langman; Lofoten, by the Iorns; Mindas, by M. Parkes; Ravenstone, by A. M. Lovell; Thingvollr, by M. Hutchinson; Torden, by Harburn; Tortawe, by the D. H. Griffiths; and Trulsmoi, by R. M. Kennett.

SCOTLAND

The Norwegian Elkhound is well established in Scotland. Fanciers formed the Elkhound Association of Scotland in 1948. Its first show was held in 1949. While many Elkhounds were brought from England, others were imported from Sweden and

Norway. Familiar names include Inverailort Kennels of Mrs. C. H. T. Cameron-Head, Mrs. Laughton Swanney, Mrs. M. M. Thompson, Mr. McGregor, Mrs. J. MacLennan, Mr. & Mrs. K. Wallace and Dr. and Mrs. Arthur Sneeden.

ELKHOUNDS IN CANADA
Canada has vast mountainous areas of land reminiscent of Scandinavia. Although these areas are ideal hunting ranges for Norwegian Elkhounds, the Canadian Fish and Wildlife Agency, under the auspices of the Canadian government, has put stringent controls on hunting with dogs in an effort to protect the existence of big game. Nevertheless, Canadians have played an important role in the advancement of the Elkhound in North America.

Like the United States, most of the Norwegian Elkhounds in Canada have pedigrees that can be traced back to imports from other countries. There are many active kennels of which the following are just a few: Elvlund, owned by E. Kennedy; Glitnir, by Lorna Dell; Hirtzlheim, by D. and D. Hirtle; Houndhaven, by J. and T. Whiting; Karin Kennels, by Barbara A. Innes; Melreva, by Estelle R. Matthews, formerly of Scotland; Stormfjell, by J. and G. McCorkell; Torr Kennels, owned by W. R. Torrance; Vakker-Lund, by John Terelly; Valgtor, by H. O. Swanson; Vigeland, by Norman A. Vig; Vikinghund, by D. R. Galloway; and Yokipi Kennels of British Columbia, owned by Jack Spence.

NORWEGIAN ELKHOUND ASSOCIATION OF AMERICA
In 1913, three Elkhounds were imported from Norway to the United States. Koik, Bimba and Laila, owned by Gottlieb Lechner of Idaho, became the first three Elkhounds to be registered by the American Kennel Club (AKC). Between 1914 and 1921, 11 were registered. There were no registered imports between 1913 and 1922, although 12 were imported from Norway and registered during the next seven years.

Eighty-nine Elkhounds were registered with the AKC in 1934 and an additional 150 were registered in 1935. NEAA was formally organized in 1934; however, the AKC did not approve its constitution and bylaws until 1936. Chairman of the committee to draft the constitution and bylaws was Bayard Boyesen of Vindsval Elkhounds. NEAA's first president was Mr. David Wooley and Mr. Lawrence Litchfield was elected Secretary-Treasurer.

NEAA began a tradition of inviting foreign judges to judge at its specialty shows. Mr. Johnny Aarflot from Norway was the first and returned on numerous other occasions to judge. Foreign judges to date include Aarflot, 1962; Miss Gerd Berbom, Norway, 1965; Olav Campbell, Norway, 1968; Aarflot, 1971; Olaf Roig and Oivind Asp, Norway, 1974; Dr. Jesper Hallingby, Norway, 1976; Dr. Arthur E. T. Sneeden, Scotland, 1978; Mrs. Mary Jarman, England, 1980; Baroness Susan Van Boetzelaer, Holland, 1982; Jakob Petter Holsing, Norway, 1984; Oyvind Dahl, Norway, 1990; Mrs. Ann Heward, England, 1992; and Rolf Frostad, Norway, 1994.

NEAA actively recruits Norwegian Elkhound breeders, owners, exhibitors and friends of the Elkhound to belong to its organization. Its membership has grown from 27 members in 1935, 240 in 1967, to 428 in 1994. Through the years, the association has contributed to the welfare of purebred dogs in general and the Norwegian Elkhound in particular. It provided subsidies to the Cornell Research Laboratory for Diseases of Dogs. It publishes educational literature for distribution to judges and other interested parties in the form of a pamphlet entitled *Interpretive Comments*. It supplied the fundamentals for an AKC video, *The Norwegian Elkhound*. And, to stay current with the AKC policies and issues concerning purebred dogs, it sends a delegate to the AKC meetings in New York. The primary function of the NEAA is to preserve the uniqueness of the Elkhound.

NEAA serves as an umbrella organization for regional Norwegian Elkhound clubs. The regional clubs are encouraged to work closely with NEAA in their contributions to the continuing concern for the Elkhound. In addition, one of the regional clubs hosts each national specialty; therefore, the location changes with each specialty. The first national specialty was held April 7/8, 1962, in conjunction with the International Club of Chicago. The judge was Herr Johnny Aarflot of Norway. There were 73 entries.

NORWEGIAN ELKHOUNDS IN THE UNITED STATES

The first Norwegian Elkhound to finish a championship in the United States was Ch. Grimm of Lifjell, a Norwegian import, finishing in 1926, shortly after the Elkhound was admitted to regular classes from the Miscellaneous class. He was owned by Walter Channing of Brixton Kennels in Dover, Massachusetts.

One of the first Elkhound Kennels in America was Vindsval, started in 1924 by Bayard Boyesen in Winchester, New Hampshire. He imported Glitre Elkhounds from Norway. Other early kennels include Stonewall, owned by Barbara Thayer Hall; Pitch Road, owned by A. Wells Peck; Narvikwood, owned by F. Wood and V. Hubbard; Bjorn-Lass, owned by Edith S. Kozak; and Stonylea, owned by L. F. Smith.

SUMMARY

The Norwegian Elkhound, like the Scandinavians he accompanied through history, survived the ruggedness of the north country. His role in the colorful sagas of time—real and inventive—earned him the title of national dog of Norway.

In the United States, the Norwegian Elkhound, a medium-sized gray dog, was imported from his native Scandinavia. He is characterized by a silvery tail that he carries high over the center of his back in a tight curl. The identical breed of dog is called the *Gray Elghound* in Scandinavia.

Elkhound is the term given to a group of Nordic dogs in Scandinavia. Included in the group are the Gray Elkhound, Black Elkhound, White Elkhound, Jamthund, Karelian Bear Dog, Finnish Spitz and the Buhund. The Black Elkhound is called *Norwegian Elkhound* in Norway.

There are few kennels with more than two bitches in Norway where the Elkhounds are used for hunting. However, many large kennels exist in the United States, Canada and England where the Elkhound is used as a companion dog and show dog as well as for hunting.

Camalot Tyra Av Vinsteren.

CHAPTER TWO
SPOTLIGHTING KENNELS

Many kennels were established during the short time between the acceptance of the Norwegian Elkhound into regular classes by the AKC and the 1950s. Pedigrees of today's Elkhounds still reflect the influence of the untiring efforts of those pioneers in the breed. As time passed, many new kennels were established to carry on with the preservation of the breed, many of them making a pronounced impact. Several of the breeding kennels are noted here.

CAMALOT
Some people find a good dog, are bitten by the bug and dive into the dog game big time. Not so with Mari Misbeek and her Camalot kennel. Mari was not satisfied with the Elkhounds she had purchased in the United States. Convinced that the best place to find the perfect Elkhound was in Norway, Mari studied the Norwegian language for a year and then took daughter and husband on a hunting trip to Norway. After searching for three weeks for the ideal Elkhound, the family returned home without an Elkhound but with a contract for litters from what she considered the best.

And so Camalot—CA for daughter Caren, MA for Mari and LOT from her husband's last name—became the *home of the Norwegian imports,* producing more than 50 champions.

Ch. Camalot Ruff's Trogan Av Bella HC111750 (Ruffs x Bella) was imported in 1974. Trogan produced nine champions out of six litters, including a son and daughter who were specialty winners, as was Trogan.

Trogan's littermate, Ch. Camalot Ruff's Tryste Av Bella HC111751 (Ruffs x Bella), was imported at the same time. Mari considered Tryste the foundation for Camalot. Not only did

Ch. Camalot Ruff's Trogan Av Bella.

Ch. Camalot Ruff's Tryste Av Bella.

Tryste produce nine champions out of four litters, but her get and grandchildren have been steady producers of winning Elkhounds.

Ch. Camalot's Trulle Av Bella HC300751 (Trogen x Bella) was whelped 03-05-75 and imported at the age of nine weeks. She was the 1976 NEAA specialty winners bitch.

Perhaps the best known Tryste daughter was Ch. Camalot Tryste's Totally Hot HC584824 (Ch. Vin-Melca's Nimbus x Ch. Camalot Ruff's Tryste Av Bella), whelped 11-04-78. She produced one litter sired by Ch. Camalot Bella's Trykk and two outstanding litters at the age of 8 1/2 and 9, sired by Ch. Camalot's Rebel Yell.

Ch. Camalot Bella's Trykk HC482800 (Trogen x Bella) was whelped in Norway on 02-15-77. He was imported to Camalot later that year along with littermates OTCH Camalot's Bella Tigra UD and Ch. Camalot's Tigger. Trykk, sire of 21 champions, won five specialties and won best of breed and Group I from the Veteran class at age 8 1/2.

Ch. Camalot's Total Celebration HD479363 (Ch. Camalot's Rebel Yell x Ch. Camalot Tryste's Totally Hot), herself a multiple specialty winner, continued the tradition set by the imports at Camalot by producing quality get who became specialty winners.

Ch. Camalot's Rebel Yell HD238900 (Ch. Camalot Trulle's Hot Stuff x Ch. Camalot Tryste's Til Eternity) sired 21 champions, including the 1990 NEAA specialty winners dog and the 1992 NEAA best in specialty winner.

Through the years, Camalot has been represented in the show ring by daughter Caren. At age 11, in her sundress and pigtails, Caren handled Ch. Camalot's Trulle Av Bella, age 15 months, to winners bitch at the 1976 NEAA specialty. Twenty years after the trip to Norway to look for the perfect dog, Caren showed Ch. Camalot's Final Deliberation HD794338 (Ch. Harka's Cinnabar, son of Trykk, by Ch. Camalot's Total Celebration)—an Elkhound Camalot considers one of the best.

CRAFDAL

Glenna Clark, whose parents operated the largest family-owned wholesale seed company in the U.S., was born in Clarkstown, Connecticut. She inherited the driving force to succeed from her parents, becoming a high achiever in everything she did. Her outstanding academic record led her to Vassar College where she was an avid sports enthusiast. As so many *and-they-lived-happily-ever-after* stories go, Glenna married her childhood sweetheart, Robert Crafts. During the ensuing years, three sons were born.

It was not until after the last of the children left home for college that Bob and Glenna acquired their first Elkhound—or, as it happened—their first three Elkhounds. First, there was Einar Haakonsson, known as Loki, from Maxine Endres. He was lonesome so his litter sister, Bamsi Haakonsdotter, joined him at the Crafts. Unfortunately, Bamsi was killed at 18 months of age. The Crafts leased her sister, Marta Haakonsdotter, who was bred to Dalgaard Viking and a litter of nine puppies was whelped June 7, 1955. Little did Glenna and Bob know that their pick from that litter—none other than Trygvie Vikingsson—was destined to pave the way to Elkhound stardom. The only female in the litter, Bamsi, remained with Tryg to form the awesome threesome. Yerta of Greenwood is also considered part of the Crafdal foundation stock.

The Crafts had never been to a dog show. But one Sunday afternoon six months later, they entered Tryg in a puppy match in Chagrin Falls, Ohio, where more than 100 puppies were entered. Needless to say, Tryg won Best In Show and the Crafts were hooked.

Tryg and his sister, Bamsi, won five point majors and Loki went Best of Breed at their first point show under breeder/judge

Ch. Camalot's Trulle Av Bella.   *Ch. Camalot Tryste's Totally Hot.*

Ch. Camalot Bella's Trykk.   *Ch. Camalot's Total Celebration.*

Ch. Camalot's Rebel Yell.

Caren with Ch. Camalot's Final Deliberation.

Int. Ch. Crafdal Trygvie Vikingsson.

Whelped June 7, 1955
Breeder-Owner: Glenna Crafts

CH. TRYGVIE VIKINGSSON	Dal-Gard Viking	Ch. Rodin of Halfred	Ch. Rolf of Lindvangen — Ch. Martin of the Hollow / Ch. Kari of Halfred
			Ch. Bamsi of Marris — Green Meadow Rodin / Helga II of Lindvangen
		Inga of Halfred	Ch. Marris Rogue — Green Meadow Rodin / Helga II of Lindvangen
			Jerva of Halfred — Lars of Lindvangen / Taska of Halfred
	Ch. Marta Haakonsdotter	Ch. Tari's Haakon	Ch. Fourwents Rugg av Aalesund (Eng.) — Syrak of the Holm / Olga av Aalesund
		Dal-gard Tari	Ch. Rolf of Halfred / Flicka of Stonewall
		Karen of Narvikwood	Ch. Dyre Vaa Tom — Bamse (Sweden) / Ch. Skail-Trixi (Sweden)
			Ch. Bamsi of Narvikwood — Ch. Dyre Vaa Trim / Ch. Astrid of Dyre Vaa

Pedigree: Int. Ch. Crafdal Trygvie Vikingsson.

Int. Ch. Crafdal Thor Mhor.   *Int. Ch. Crafdal Thor Mhor Thunder.*

Ch. Crafdal Tryg'n Thor's Tufsen.   *Ch. Crafdal Tryg'n Thor's Rollo.*

Ch. Crafdal Lillabo Kvinna.

Edna Mae Bieber in Hornell, New York, when they were just 13 months old. It was the first of many grand slams for the Crafts. The rest is an unbelievable fairy tale of success.

Among Tryg's accomplishments was siring more than 65 champion get, second only to his grandson Ch. Vin-Melca's Howdy Rowdy, as the Top Producing sire with 166 champion get. Tryg was sire of Ch. Vin-Melca's Vikina.

The Crafts moved to the Silver Lake area between Stow and Cuyahoga Falls, Ohio, and established their kennel on 10 acres of rolling land, just three miles from their home in Silver Lake. Glenna, who had spent many an hour on her soapbox lobbying against cramped kenneling and the debarking of dogs, was determined to cater to their well-being. A huge pond with a sandy beach on one end was added, allowing the dogs the choice of a refreshing dip even in the coldest of weather. The fenced runs were each large enough to accommodate a dog and a bitch or puppies. There was a house for the full-time kennel manager, food room and all the other necessities for successfully managing a kennel.

As is proper procedure, the Crafts applied to the AKC for a registered name for their kennel. Crafts Valley was their choice, but the request was denied. In 1958, the AKC granted permission to the Crafts to use CRAFDAL as their registered kennel prefix, and the prefix became synonymous with Norwegian Elkhounds.

To enhance an already successful line, the Crafts imported Elkhounds periodically, always for a reason—leg length, silver coloring, etc. Included were Friochan Rinta from Kitty Heffer, Irish American Champion Thor Mhor from Frank Matthews and from Edith Langman, Lillabo Kvinna and Lillabo Paula. Thor Mhor was bred to Tryg daughters. One such breeding produced Thunder, who went Best In Show from the classes at 11 months of age. Two other outstanding dogs, probably two of Crafdal's best, were Tufsen and Rollo. Tufsen is remembered as the dog used for the logo for one of the regional Elkhound clubs in California. As Glenna says: "He was born beautiful!"

Top-producing bitches included Friochan Rinta, Ch. Yerta of Greenwood, Ch. Crafdal Lillabo Kvinna, Ch. Crafdal Tryg's Vivla and Ch. Crafdal Tryg's Ruki.

Robert Crafts died September 20, 1969. A past president of NEAA, Bob was instrumental in inaugurating the first national specialty show. He is remembered as "one of God's most well-

NEAA 12th National Specialty. (L-R) John Prentiss, Dr. Nina Ross, Glenna Crafts, Paul E. Ross.

bred gentlemen, whether in or out of the ring," as written in a dedication to him in the October 23, 1971, NEAA 4th National Specialty Show catalog. He had been the exclusive handler of Tryg, who died just three weeks later. Glenna maintained the Crafdal line for several more years. Between the two of them, they finished more than 220 champions, with an additional 80 finished by other owners of Crafdal dogs. In 1972, after having sold and/or placed the remaining Elkhounds from Crafdal Farms, Glenna moved to Heron Haven, Little Cayman, British West Indies. At present she lives on her plantation in Delray Beach, Florida, not quietly, but still with a boundless energy and determination not unlike that of a young puppy—Norwegian Elkhound, that is.

KAMGAARD

Working quietly but striving for excellence in the age-old mountainous area of Eastern United States is Margaret Mott. Located in a secluded area by no means kept her from being well-known and respected among Elkhound fanciers in the United States and abroad. Her kennel name KAMGAARD uses the KAM from her maiden name, Kampish, and GAARD from Asgaard, the Eden of Norse mythology.

Mott's first involvement with Norwegian Elkhounds began when she was eight years old. Her father, who enjoyed hunting, saw a pair of Elkhounds and just had to have one. Crafdal Tryglik Tina (Am. Can. Ber. Ch. Crafdal Tryg's Troll x Am. Can. Ch. Crafdal Tryg's Teeka), her first show and breeding Elkhound, was purchased in 1963. All Kamgaard Elkhounds trace back to Tina. Of the 77 champions she has bred or owned, Mott said: "I have employed linebreeding primarily, inbreeding occasionally with an outcross every once in a while."

SBIS Ch. Kamgaard Kiss Me Kate CD, or Katie as she was called, was number one Brood Bitch at the 10th NEAA specialty in 1980. She was the dam of five champions from nine offspring. Katie was a striking example of correct breed type.

Like many breeders, Mott believes the backbone and true strength of her kennel lies in the bitches it has produced. Among her specialty and group-winning elite all girls' club are Ch. Kamgaard Tryglikk Kristiana (Bjorgulf Thor x Crafdal Tryglik Tina), Ch. Kamgaard Keepsake (SBIS Ch. Fredrika's Field Marshal x Ch. Kamgaard Bonnie Parker), Know It All, Kalliope, SBIS Am. Can. Ch. Kamgaard Kit'N' Kaboodle HC785374 (SBIS Am. Can. Ch. Norgren's Pith and Vinegar x Ch. Kamgaard Bonnie Parker), SBIS Ch. Kamgaard Kiss Me Kate CD HC407492 (BISS Ch. Vin-Melca's Huck Finn x Rafalc Gretel of Ravenstone), Am. Can. Ch. Kirkssted Kamgaard Kelly HD037987, Am. Can. Ch. Kamgaard Korniche, Am. Can. Ch. Kamgaard Kermette of Pelstad and Ch. Kamgaard Klear Skies Ahead HD861946 (Ch. Westwind American Storm x Ch. Ravenstone Rainbow), whelped 04-11-90.

Ch. Kamgaard Klear Impression HD504762 (Promises Big Deal x Tsiulikagta Ciara) was whelped 05-09-87. She carried the soundness and leg length Kamgaard strived for and achieved.

Ch. Kamgaard Kermett of Pelstad HD247022 was from a breeding between Ch. Kamgaard Kermit and Ch. Kamgaard Kount On Me. The offspring from this breeding proved to be another example of positive results from a carefully planned litter.

Two well-known producers of merit were the father and son team of Ch. Kamgaard Kingfish HC981582 (SBIS Ch. Kamgaard Kokomo Joe x Ch. Kamgaard Keepsake) and SBIS Am. Can. Ch. Kamgaard The Kissing Bandit HD115322 (Ch. Kamgaard Kingfish x Ch. Kamgaard Kissing Bug).

SBIS Ch. Kamgaard Knave of Hearts HD547045 was

SBIS Am. Can. Ch. Kamgaard
Kit N' Kaboodle.

Ch. Kamgaard Kingfish.

whelped 06-25-87. His sire and dam were SBIS Am. Can. Ch. Kamgaard The Kissing Bandit x SBIS Am. Can. Ch. Kamgaard Kit N' Kaboodle. Known for his pleasing disposition, Nathan was a Top Ten member in 1990 and won multiple specialties.

In 1984, SBIS Am. Can. Ch. Kamgaard Kit N' Kaboodle was exported to England in whelp to Kissing Bandit. She was followed several years later by Am. Can. Ch. Kirkssted Kamgaard Kelly, a Kingfish daughter, in whelp to Ch. Kamgaard Kavalier. The offspring from these two sharings helped create a new dimension to the breed in the United Kingdom.

Imports joining the ranks at Kamgaard were Rafalc Gretel of Ravenstone in 1973, Bella—from Norway—in 1974, Ravenstone Bestla and Bragi in 1975, Norsled Monika in 1976 and, in 1985, Ch. Kristina Karandor, Ch. Ravenstone Rainbow, Ravenstone Rolls Royce, Ravenstone Rounders, Ravenstone Regent Street and Ravenstone Rebel Yell. Am. Can. Ch. Kamgaard Korniche HD401453 was whelped 04-03-86. Her sire and dam were Ravenstone Rolls Royce x Am. Can. Ch. Kirkssted Kamgaard Kelly.

After almost 30 years at the drawing board, Mott is looking forward with eager anticipation to the next 30. She is working to integrate the offspring from some of the English exchange programs back into several of the older lines and predicts, "The best is yet to come!"

SBIS Ch. Kamgaard Kiss Me Kate CD.

Am. Can. Ch. Kirkssted Kamgaard Kelly.

Ch. Kamgaard Klear Impression.

Ch. Kamgaard Kermette of Pelstad.

*SBIS Am. Can. Ch. Kamgaard
The Kissing Bandit.*

*SBIS Ch. Kamgaard Knave of
Hearts.*

Ch. Kamgaard Klear Skies Ahead.

Am. Can. Ch. Kamgaard Korniche.

*Am. Ber. Ch.
Kamgaard
Kiss-Ka-Dee.*

VIKIRO KENNEL

What better name for a kennel owned and operated by Viki and Robert than Vikiro. And that is exactly what Victoria and Robert Lawton decided to call their Norwegian Elkhound kennel when they purchased their first show Elkhound in 1976. After studying the Elkhound and the breed standard for several years, the Lawtons purchased Bermarba's Elske Tara HC241486 (Ch. Vin-Melca's Huck Finn x Thornbeck Kynde), whelped 11-13-75. Tara became the foundation for their kennel.

Next to join Vikiro in an effort to maintain Norwegian and English lines in its breeding program was Ch. Camalot Tryste's Trinket HC400795 (Ch. Ravenstone Teodor x Ch. Camalot Ruff's Tryste av Bella), whelped 05-25-77. In 1980, Trinket reached the status of being a top-winning Elkhound bitch in the United States.

In 1979, a breeding between Norwegian import Ch. Camalot Ruff's Trogan av Bella and Bermarba's Elske Tara produced a litter of three brothers who were to become a pivotal influence in the Vikiro line. The brothers, Ch. Vikiro Tara's Adventurer HC678777, Ch. Vikiro Tara's Macho Man HC678776 and Ch. Vikiro's Silver Shadow HC678778 were whelped on 09-22-79.

Ch. Vikiro's Ravishing Ruby HC860450 (Ch. Vikiro Tara's Macho Man x Ch. Camalot Tryste's Trinket), whelped 07-01-81, was an example of the linebreeding Vikiro had planned. A repeat breeding in 1983 produced Am. Can. Ch. Vikiro's Jenuine Jade HC864121, whelped 05-15-83. Ch. Vikiro's Gold 'N' Sunshine HC869750 and Ch. Vikiro's Sapphire 'N' Ice HC846335 were also out of Macho Man and Trinket.

In 1982, Ch. Camalot Trulle's Belle Star HC767352 (SBIS Ch. Windy Cove Tara's Nimbusson x Ch. Camalot's Trulle av Bella), whelped 06-24-80, became part of the breeding program.

Ch. Vikiro Tara's Adventurer was bred to a Camalot-related bitch, Ch. Misty Tara Trogankhya Kodiak to produce SBIS Ch. Roundel's Gizmo of Vikiro HD162301 on 05-24-84. Gizmo was the 1988 NEAA National Specialty Best in Show winner. As a side note, winners bitch at the same specialty was Ch. Eidsvold Vala's Solveig HD231616, an Adventurer daughter.

Ch. Vikiro's This Gun for Hire HD273906, Ch. Vikiro Belle's Desert Moon HD253356, Ch. Vikiro's Silverado HD269716 and Ch. Vikiro Belle's Desperado HD248623, all from a litter by Ch.

Ch. Vikiro Tara's Adventurer.

Ch. Vikiro Tara's Macho Man.

Ch. Roundel's Gizmo of Vikiro.

Ch. Vikiro's This Gun for Hire.

Ch. Vikiro Ruby's Ghostdancer.

Vikiro Tara's Macho Man x Ch. Camalot Trulle's Belle Star, were whelped 04-01-85. Macho Man and Belle Star won the Stud Dog and Brood Bitch classes at the National Specialty. Ch. Vikiro's This Gun For Hire was a top winning Elkhound in 1988.

One of the last of the Ch. Vikiro Tara's Adventurer x Ch. Camalot's Trulle av Bella litters was whelped in 07-12-87, producing Ch. Vikiro Velvet Kisses Av Bona HD530657, a top producing bitch. The Lawtons decided to bring in Ch. Jo-Cala's The Gray Ghost to sire a litter with Ch. Vikiro's Ravishing Ruby. Ch. Vikiro Ruby's Ghostdancer HD273907 and Ch. Vikiro's Silver Silhouette HD274170 were the result. Although Silver Silhouette died at an early age, Ch. Vikiro Ruby's Ghostdancer proved to be a champion-producing brood bitch.

In a few short years, Vikiro produced 30 champions. The specialty wins, the quality Elkhounds, the discriminate breeding program have all played a part in making Vikiro a Norwegian Elkhound kennel of distinction.

VIN-MELCA KENNEL

Her parents set priorities, but Patricia Vincent set her own goals. It was understood that school work superseded training her dogs. There were always dogs and Patricia was always working with them, either grooming, obedience training or showing in conformation.

She obtained her first Elkhound, Ch. Ulf's Madam Helga, CD, from Joyce Creek Kennels in 1949. The dogs at Joyce Creek, all of them hunters, were used to hunt brown bear in the Dismal Swamp of North Carolina. Even at that young age she studied pedigrees and sought the advice of authorities in the breed. She bred her Elkhound to Ch. Carro of Ardmere, owned by the Wells Peck's Pitch Road Kennels. She kept a dog out of the resultant litter and named him Vin-Melca's Carro Again.

Priorities took precedent over her infatuation with dogs and she went off to college. In 1958, with college credentials in her pocket, she set forth to meet the next of her goals: to breed the most perfect Norwegian Elkhound the world has ever seen. She obtained an eight-week-old puppy bitch, Vin-Melca's Rebel Rouser (Ch. Koltorpets Paff x Loka) whom she called Vicki. Even though Vin-Melca's Carro Again had reached the upper limits of age for potency, Pat successfully bred him to Vicki.

With her natural eye for quality in dogs, coupled with

knowledge acquired from studying, observing and talking with knowledgeable people, she chose to keep a bitch from that litter. The bitch, Ch. Vin-Melca's Astridina, took her a giant step closer to her ultimate goal. Astridina was bred to Ch. Crafdal Trigvie Vikingsson, producing Ch. Vin Melca's Vikina and, from that point forward, in rapid succession, the models of perfection have continued to appear.

As it did for many young people in the '60s, California beckoned. Pat responded. With dogs in tow she relocated amid the awesome beauty of the Monterey Bay area where she met and married veterinarian Dr. John Craige. They settled in nearby Carmel where their house became home for Vin-Melca as well as a refuge for aspiring young people who spent their summers learning about dogs. It provided a workshop for aspiring judges who wanted to learn more about Elkhounds. It was there, on the sandy shores of the Pacific, that the Norwegian Elkhounds reached their potential for reach and drive.

Whelped in 1964, Ch. Vin Melca's Vickssen (Ch. Vin-Melca's Hi-Ho Silver x Ch. Vin-Melca's Rebel Rouser) was a Best in Show winner, Specialty Best in Show winner and top producer. He was the sire of three all-breed Best in Show winners, Ch. Vin-Melca's Vagabond, Ch. Vin-Melca's Valley Forge and Ch. Vin-Melca's Viscount. Valley Forge was in the Top Ten Hounds in 1972. In 1973, he was a Quaker Oats winner, Number One Hound in the U.S. and Number Five dog All-Breeds.

Ch. Vin-Melca's Victoria, a litter sister to Viscount, Vickssen's third B.I.S. son, was the dam of Ch. Vin-Melca's Buckpasser, Ch. Vin-Melca's Smuggler and Ch. Vin-Melca's Just Plain Jane, the foundation bitch for Korneliusen's Sirdal kennel. The Smuggler had 25 all breed bests in show to his credit. Not only was he number two hound, but he won a Group II placement at Westminster in 1984.

In 1968, Ch. Vin-Melca's Howdy Rowdy HA721555 (Ch. Windy Cove's Rowdy Ringo x Ch. Vin-Melca's Vikina) won the NEAA 3rd National Specialty under Olav Campbell. He had four other BIS wins and four SBIS wins. Howdy attained and maintained the all-time top producer record with 166 champions. He was the sire of Ch. Vin-Melca's Harlow of Maddox's Rebel Ridge kennel. She was the top producing bitch of all times with 25 champion get. The record was later topped by Ch. Vin-Melca's Last Call. Litter sisters were Ch. Vin-Melca's Happy

Hour and Ch. Vin-Melca's Saga av Red Hill, foundation bitch for Freeman and Betty Claus' Red Hill kennel.

Ch. Vin-Melca's Vagabond HA887693 (Ch. Vin-Melca's Vickssen x Ch. Vin-Melca's Vikina), half brother to Howdy Rowdy, was Top Dog All Breeds All Systems and Quaker Oats Winner in 1970. He was Group Winner at Westminster in 1970 and 1971. He had 24 Best in Show wins and sired 36 champion get. At age 14, Bond was in the Parade of Champions at the Garden, the oldest dog ever to appear in that event. He lived to be almost 18 years old.

Ch. Vin-Melca's Huck Finn HB358032 (Ch. Vin-Melca's Howdy Rowdy x Ch. Wandec's Sylva av Vin-Melca) won the 4th NEAA National Specialty in 1971. Another Vin-Melca champion won the 1974 5th National NEAA Specialty. It was Ch. Vin-Melca's Happy Hour HB-11178 (Ch. Vin-Melca's Howdy Rowdy x Ch. Branstock's Vika of Baba Yaga) who continued the spectacular domino effect by producing Ch. Vin-Melca's Night-cap HB652761 (Ch. Vin-Melca's Vagabond x Ch. Vin-Melca's Happy Hour). Nightcap became a top producer with seven champions.

Ch. Vin-Melca's Nimbus (Ch. Vin-Melca's Nordic Storm x Ch. Vin-Melca's Marlinda) was whelped in 1974. Nimbus won 63 all-breed bests in show. Twice he was best hound at Westminster, 1977 and 1979. In the Quaker Oats competition, he was Number Two all-breed and, twice, he was top hound. Nimbus was the top winning Norwegian Elkhound of all time before Ch. Vin-Melca's Calista and was among the top 10 sires for Elkhounds. He is still the top winning male Elkhound of all time.

Ch. Vin-Melca's Last Call HC692265 (Ch. Vin-Melca's Namesake x Ch. Vin-Melca's Bottoms Up). Gilda, as she was called, won her first specialty best in show from the puppy class. She had 14 all-breed bests in show to her credit in addition to 10 specialty bests and was the top winning Elkhound bitch of her time. Gilda is the top-producing bitch of all time, dam to 27 champion get.

Ch. Vin-Melca's Before Dawn HC905924 (Ch. Vin-Melca's Namesake x Ch. Vin-Melca's Morning Star II) won the Norwegian Elkhound Association of California Specialty show from the 6 - 9 puppy class. She went on to win three consecutive all-breed bests in show from the 6 - 9 puppy class. Dawn was in the Top Ten.

RUGGEN
CH. TRYSILL KNUT AV TALLO
GRO AV TALLO
LONELAND ODD
TOM
OLA AV GRA
SWED. CH. LOVA II AV GRA
CH. KOLTORPET'S PAFF (03-20-50)
TOM
FALL AV GRA
SWED. CH. LOVA II AV GRA
SKALL MUCKI
SWED. CH. DRAM AV GRA
NETTA II AV GRA
SWED. CH. LOVA II AV GRA

CH. VIN-MELCA'S REBEL ROUSER (06-25-58)

LUSTRE LYN
ARDMERE LUDOLPH OF THE HOLLOW
BINNA OF THE HOLLOW
CH. CARRO OF ARDMERE
GUY FAWKES
VAAGSO OF ARDMERE
GURLI OF OUSEFLEET
LOKA (09-28-52)
CH. MARTIN OF THE HOLLOW
CH. ROLF OF LINDVANGEN
CH. KARI OF HALFRED
KIRSTEN OF NORDKYN
CH. THOR OF LINDVANGEN
HULDA OF LINDVANGEN
CH. KARI OF HALFRED

Pedigree: Ch. Vin-Melca's Rebel Rouser.

Ch. Vin-Melca's Rebel Rouser.

Ch. Vin-Melca's Vikina.

Ch. Vin-Melca's Valley Forge.

Ch. Vin-Melca's Vickssen.

Ch. Vin-Melca's Howdy Rowdy.

Ch. Vin-Melca's Vagabond.

Ch. Vin-Melca's Happy Hour.

Ch. Vin-Melca's Nimbus.

Ch. Vin-Melca's Last Call.

Ch. Vin-Melca's Marketta.

Ch. Vin-Melca's Calista HD459195 (Ch. Vin-Melca's Mandate x Ch. Vin-Melca's Bottoms Up) has produced 10 champion get, including four group winners and a BIS winner. She won 66 all breed bests in show and was top hound at Westminster in 1989 and 1990. Sarah is the top winning Elkhound of all times as well as Top Winning Hound of All Time-Science Diet. She was Quaker Oats winner in 1989 and 1990, Number three All Breeds in 1989 and Number Two All Breeds in 1990. Sarah finished her career in whelp, winning 12 groups and seven bests in show out of the 12 shows in which she was shown while in whelp.

Ch. Vin-Melca's Bombardier HD569700 (Ch. Vin-Melca's Barnstormer x Ch. Vin-Melca's Before Dawn), with 39 bests in show, was in the Top Ten all systems for two years. Bombardier won top hound Quaker Oats in 1992.

Ch. Vin-Melca's Marketta HM354474/02 (Ch. Vin-Melca's Bombardier x Ch. Vin-Melca's Calista) has a place among the stars. Marketta's sire and dam were both Quaker Oats winners, making Marketta the first get of winning parents to win the award. Marketta was the 1993 Quaker Oats winner, Westminster group winner in 1994 and 1995 and second All-Time bitch only to her dam.

· Patricia Vincent Craige's determination to breed the best yet Elkhound continued throughout her years of successful breeding and showing. She always kept in mind the strengths as well as the needs of the Elkhounds in her breeding program, whether it was to improve the head, control size or give leg length. She was not afraid to linebreed to maintain correct structure as with Rebel Rouser. Nor was she afraid to run the extra mile before and after putting in a full day of teaching junior high youngsters. All this and a three-, sometimes four-, show weekend.

The priorities instilled early in her life provided the stepping stones to success. Vin-Melca, as close to producing the most perfect Elkhound the world has ever seen, has been present in many pedigrees since the 1960s and will provide the basis for perfection for many years to come.

WINDY COVE KENNEL

A family with three boys needs a dog—one that will run and play in the snow and not mind the cold wind that blows much of the winter as it does in Spokane, Washington. That is the way Joe and Marie Peterson figured it in 1953 when they got their first Norwegian Elkhound. They did not think much about a kennel name because they really had not thought much about starting a kennel. In 1955, however, they acquired a dog and a bitch from reputable breeders and the bug bit.

When you have a dog and a bitch, often times a litter is in the offing. And when you have a litter of puppies and are enthused about Norwegian Elkhounds, it seems most appropriate to add a kennel name to the registration papers to identify your puppies to the rest of the world. What better name to choose than Windy, to signify the cold, windy winters, and Cove to name the quiet shelter the dogs seek in their efforts to hide from the wind. And so Windy Cove it has been for 40 years.

The real foundation stock for Windy Cove was a puppy dog out of Mrs. Linda Scott's Greenwood Kennel in Edmonds, Washington—Ch. Windy's Tusko of Greenwood CD (Ch. Trond's Son of Greenwood x Ch. Lady Kazana of Greenwood—and a puppy bitch out of Boatman's Baadkarl Kennels in Iowa—Ch. Baadkarls Tona of Windy Cove (Norwegian Import Ch. Tortasen's Bjonn II x Ch. Kristen of Bofe). Tusko and Tona proved compatible, producing three litters of puppies. Nine of the puppies became champions and can be traced in many pedigrees on the west coast.

Familiar names from the first Tusko/Tona litter are Ch. Windy Coves Sweda and Ch. Windy Coves Silver Son, who not only finished their championships at an early age but accumulated impressive show records.

The second Tusko/Tona litter produced four champions out of five puppies. They were Rugged Rokk, Rowdy Ringo, Ruff N Reddy and Ruska. Rowdy Ringo, a best in show dog, produced Ch. Vin Melca's Howdy Rowdy, one of the top show dogs and sires in Elkhound history.

The third and last Tusko/Tona litter produced three champions out of four puppies. Ch. Windy Coves Sweda became a Top Producing Dam, 10 champions out of 42 puppies. Four of the 10 champions were from a breeding with Am. Can. Ch. Crafdal Trygvie Vikingsson. The other six were from breedings with Ch. Windy Cove Wendy's Silver Sun, a grandson of Sweda.

Although Spokane had been the Peterson's Windy Cove for 10 years, they moved lock, stock and kennel to Atascadero, California, in 1965. Atascadero was similar to Norway only

Ch. Windy Coves Sweda.   *Ch. Windy Coves Rowdy Ringo.*

Ch. Windy Cove Wendy's Silver Sun.   *Ch. Windy Cove Tass av Oftenasen.*

Ch. Windy Cove Mona av Oftenasen.

— 43 —

Ch. Windy Cove Gunnar of Norway.

Ch. Windy Cove Jr. Bicentennial.

Ch. Windy Cove Tara's Nimbusson.

NEAA 1984 National Specialty. Bicen's Cut Krystal, Indian Maiden and Chief Cochise.

Ch. Windy Cove Rider's Carney.

Tortasen's Bjonn O'Windy Cove.

when you closed your eyes and imagined that there was snow on the hills that you and the Elkhounds raced up and down, chasing wildlife and, in the process, keeping trim. It did not take long, however, for the dogs and the family to acclimate to the warmer temperatures. Windy Cove continues to thrive in Atascadero.

The Petersons imported several Elkhounds from Norway to offer new blood into an already successful breeding program. Ch. Windy Cove Tass av Oftenasen was brought in from the Oftenasen Kennel in Norway in 1966 and his litter sister, Ch. Windy Cove Mona av Oftenasen, joined him in 1968. Norwegian judge Olav Campbell proclaimed Mona to be Winners Bitch, Best of Winners and Best of Opposite Sex at the NEAA 3rd National Specialty in Springfield, Massachusetts, in 1968.

Windy Cove Riiser Guy was imported in 1968. Other imports include Windy Cove Surprise of Vardetoppens (b. 1972), Ch. Windy Cove Ruffen (b. 1974), Ch. Tortasen's Ola of Windy Cove (b. 1978), Ch. Windy Cove Gunnar of Norway (b. 1979), Windy Cove Silva of Norway (b. 1979), Ch. Rasin Kiva (b. 1984), and the latest, Tortasen's Bjonn O'Windy Cove (b. 1993). In 1978, the Petersons spent two weeks in Norway visiting, learning, attending shows and searching for Elkhounds that would complement their breeding program. The imports have been an asset and can be found in many pedigrees of Elkhounds across the continent.

Ch. Windy Cove Jr. Bicentennial is one of the more than 200 champions produced by Windy Cove Kennel. His specialty wins at Minnesota and Puget Sound under Norwegian judges attest to the significance of the impressive list of wins at specialties, regional specialties and all-breed shows.

Always striving to combine their successes with the successes of other breeders, the Petersons bred a Tass daughter—Tara—to Ch. Vin Melca's Nimbus. From that breeding they reaped an only puppy, a super puppy they labeled Superson. He sired 39 champions and is today the foundation for many well-known kennels. He did, indeed, live up to his predicted reputation.

The 1984 NEAA National Specialty was indeed special for Windy Cove. Ch. Windy Cove Chief Cochise was acclaimed Best In Specialty and his litter sister, Ch. Windy Cove Indian Maiden, was named Best Opposite Sex. Brood bitch first place went to their dam, Ch. Windy Cove Bicen's Cut Krystal.

Other special Elkhounds carrying the Windy Cove prefix are Ch. Windy Cove Mona's Cadero Jr., Ch. Windy Cove Super Charger, Ch. Windy Cove Gunnar's Easy Rider, Ch. Windy Cove Snowdrift Iceberg, Ch. Windy Cove Carney's Dakota, Ch. Windy Cove Star Dust Dancer, Ch. Windy Cove Indian Maiden, Ch. Windy Cove Rider's Carney, Ch. Windy Cove N Norelka Snow Bird, Ch. Windy Cove Carney's White Dove, Ch. Windy Cove Chase a Wild Bird, Ch. Windy Cove Sun Bonnet Sue and the list goes on.

Many things have changed since the decision was made to call their kennel Windy Cove. The hard work, the search for new blood, and the handling/showing of their own dogs that has been the way of life for 40 years. All this can be explained in a silver-gray bundle of love called a Norwegian Elkhound.

CANADA: KARIN Perm Reg'd.

Canada with its beautifully rugged terrain and abundance of game is a natural habitat for the Elkhound. Kennel names synonymous with Canada are Elvlund, Glitnir, Hurtzlheim, Houndhaven, Karin, Melreva, Millarsville, Stormfjell, Torr, Vakker-Lund, Vigeland and Vikinghund, to name a few.

The name Barbara Innes is synonymous with Norwegian Elkhound. She founded her kennel, Karin Perm. Reg'd., in 1955, taking the KAR from husband Karl and the IN from Innes. The foundation stock for Karin was Ch. Tall Grass Kara and Ch. Elmwood Bootes.

Imports from Great Britain include Ch. Lillabo Senta, Witch of the Holm, Ch. Namik's Toreador and Lillabo Heidi.

Imports from the United States include Am. Can. Ch. Crafdal Tryg N' Thor's Rock and Am. Can. Ch. Vin-Melca's Marksman. Karin, with its carefully planned program of breeding, has produced more than 40 champions.

Karin Elkhounds have done their share of winning in the show rings of Canada and the United States. Significant wins included the following: Am. Can. Ch. Crafdal Tryg N' Thor's Rock won the first Canadian National Specialty held in Toronto, Ontario. The first Canadian-bred dog ever to win the NEAA National Specialty from the classes was Am. Can. Ch. Karin's Yogi Bear, owned by Gary Proudfoot and bred and handled by Barbara Innes. It was the 1982 specialty held in Boston.

Karin Kennel was well represented at the 1984 NEAA specialty in California. First place in the 12-18-months bitch class

Karin's Big Beaver.

Am. Can. Ch. Karin's Rolph.

Ch. Karin's Elka.

Am. Can. Ch. Karin's Yogi Bear.

Ch. Karin's Calamity Jayne.

Ch. Karin's Sir Alexander McKenzie CDX.   *Am. Can. Ch. Karin's Rolph.*

Ch. Llychlyn Callan.

Ch. Ravenstone Silver Gerda.

was won by Ch. Karin's Calamity Jayne (Am. Can. Ch. Karin's Yogi Bear x Ch. Karin's Heavencanwait).

Ch. Karin's Sir Alexander McKenzie CDX was the second top hound in obedience in 1987. He is owned by Stephen and Gail Klinck. Other outstanding dogs produced by Karin are Ch. Karin's Amoz, Ch. Karin's Anka, Ch. Karin's Drummer, Karin's Big Beaver, Ch. Karin's Misty Thor, Ch. Karin's Witch of the Holm, Ch. Karin's Big Benny, Ch. Karin's Heavencanwait, Ch. Karin's Mala, Ch. Karin's Silver Shadow, Ch. Karin's Calamity Jayne, Ch. Karin's Miss Spitfire, Ch. Karin's Skoa, Ch. Karin's Second Chance and Ch. Karin's Niels.

Ch. Karin's Rolph and his progeny compiled commendable show records in the United States as well as in Canada.

ENGLAND: LLYCHLYN KENNELS

The *elghund* made its way to Great Britain long before it was introduced in America. Many devoted breeders charted the progress of the Elkhound through the early years. Kennel names such as Aalesund, Fourwents, Friochan, Holm, Jarlsberg and Of The Hollow provided a sound basis for the next era. There continue to be many well-established kennels producing quality Elkhounds in Great Britain: Borellan, Eskamere, Kistrand, Lillabo, Mageroy, Malator, Mindas, Myrdal, Norsled, Peyvre, Ravenstone, Rogersome, Rothenborg, Torden, Tortawe and Vandavell, to name a few.

Although Marion Foster became involved with the breed many years after its arrival there, she did preserve a little of the Elkhound's heritage by calling her kennel *Llychlyn,* the old Welsh word for Viking.

Borellan Iona, Ch. Llychlyn Callan and Ch. Ravenstone Silver Gerda were the foundation stock for her breeding program that began in 1972. Borellan Iona was bred by Joan Block out of Mageroy Gaupa's Grei and Ch. Borellan Trene. Iona was then bred to Joan Block's Ch. Borellan Kaymaur Thor, a breeding that produced Ch. Llychlyn Callan. He was the sire of 10 champions, as well as being awarded 18 challenge certificates and two hound groups. Ch. Ravenstone Silver Gerda, bred by Margaret Harper, produced two litters out of Callan.

The first litter from Gerda and Callan produced three outstanding Elkhounds. Ch. Llychlyn Meredid was dam of American Ch. Kristina Karandor. Two other champions from the breeding were American Ch. Llychlyn Idris and Llychlyn Irina who was awarded Junior Warrant and reserve challenge certificate. She was the dam of the Canadian Champion Whittimere Amund. An Irish Green Star and Reserve Green Star winner from the litter was Llychlyn Sorena. Ch. Llychlyn Idris was exported to Marlene Oliver of Peer Gynt Kennels in the United States.

The second Gerda/Callan litter produced Ch. Llychlyn Morgan who became the top- winning male Elkhound of all time in Great Britain. He has to his credit 35 challenge certificates at championship shows, Hound Group and Reserve Hound Group, B.O.B. at Crufts, B.O.B. and B.I.S. at British Elkhound Club shows and Elkhound Association of Scotland shows.

Though not shown widely, Ch. Llychlyn Talfryn won eight challenge certificates and was a winner of a champion show hound group.

Ch. Llychlyn Gwythr, out of Ch. Llychlyn Callan x Ch. Ravenstone Silver Gerda, and Ch. Llychlyn Moriah were two more Elkhounds who brought acclaim to Llychlyn Kennel.

Ch. Llychlyn Llywelyn.

Ch. Llychlyn Meredid.

Ch. Llychlyn Irina.

Ch. Llychlyn Idris.

Ch. Llychlyn Talfryn.

Ch. Llychlyn Gwythr.

Ch. Llychlyn Moriah.

NORWAY: TORTASEN KENNELS

The Gray Elkhound is the national dog of Norway. A visitor to Norway would expect to see many Elkhounds. Quite the contrary. There are few large breeding kennels. Many of the people in Norway who breed Elkhounds live on farms. The dogs are bred when the farmer is in need of a hunting dog or a dog to help with the chores. The dog earns his keep and is a valued asset to his owner.

Tortasen's Kennel which has been active for more than 40 years is located in the midsection of Norway. Dogs produced by Tortasen's are evident in the pedigrees of Norwegian Elkhounds in some of the prominent kennels of the United States.

Nestled in a valley, hidden at times by a layer of snow that seemingly lasts forever, stands a modern dairy farm. It is located in Norway's midsection, Jorstad, Snasa, Trondelag, Norway. There has been a dairy farm there for several hundred years—as long as Jakob Petter Holsing can remember —replete with a huge red barn filled with milk cows. Holsing can remember the coming and going of many harsh Arctic winters, 78 to be exact.

As is traditional, most Scandinavian people ski and many of the men become avid sportsmen. In earlier years, they hunted to provide the family with meat during the long winter months. Dogs were necessary to help track and scent the elk in the forests, keeping the huge animals at bay while the hunters moved in for the kill. The Holsing family was no different. There were always dogs at the farm. But, to quote Holsing: "In 1948, I bought Nussi as a puppy. She was my first Gray Elkhound. In 1950, I bred Nussi to Ch. Steig of Jarlsberg. So in this way I became a breeder."

Holsing considers Ch. Moa to be his foundation stock. Her name can be traced back to most of the Elkhounds his kennel has produced. His current breedings are great-great-great grandsons and granddaughters of Ch. Moa.

Holsing established Tortasen's Kennel with Ch. Moa 14915 (Ch. Steig of Jarlsberg x Nussi) as its foundation bitch. Excellent quality Elkhounds began to appear in the United States, England and Australia, bearing the Tortasen name. Bred to Ch. Bamse, Ch. Moa produced International Champion Tortasen's Bjonn II, Ch. Tortasen's Garm, Tortasen's Moman and American Ch. Viking, C.D., to name a few. Ch. Bamse was a son of

Ch. Finn av Skromtefjell 869 A

Ch. Grei av Kirkemo 460 C

Nora av Kirkemo 12308

Ch. Steig of Jarlsberg 891 G

Ch. Mirkel of the Hollow KCSB 909 NN

Ch. Anna of the Hollow 1390 D

Shian of the Hollow KCSB 1500 AA

Ch. Moa 1491 Z

(Elgstolens) Buster 135 D

Brisk av Jarlsberg 398 L

Nussi 3997 T

Ch. Anna of the Hollow 1390 D

Buster 553 M

Snarra 2162 R

Stella 371 L

Pedigree: Ch. Moa.

Holsing (L) with Ch. Moa and Perponche.

Ch. Moa at age 10.

Ch. Tortasen's Bjonn II.

Ch. Tortasen's Ane.

Ch. Rebekka.

Holsing with eight-week-old puppies.

Jakob Olav Holsing.

A visit with Jakob Petter Holsing.

Ch. Glennas Skrub. Ch. Viking and Bjonn II were exported to the United States where they made a major contribution to the breed in leading kennels in America.

Ch. Tortasen's Bamse Brakar went to Australia and another dog was sent to England. Other familiar names in American pedigrees include American Ch. Tortasen's Ola and American Ch. Roy of Pitch Road, grandsons of Ch. Moa. Tortasen's Kaisa (Buster x Ch. Moa) appears in many pedigrees.

Holsing's grandson, Jakob Olav Holsing, helps care for the Elkhounds. One of the puppies in the litter shown with Holsing now lives in America. The dam of the litter is Alberte.

Holsing was authorized as a judge in Norway in 1954. He judged many shows in Norway and Sweden and, in 1984, judged the 10th NEAA National Specialty in Anaheim, California. His country home is filled with mementos from his travels and he enjoys reminiscing over the scrapbooks of pictures from the specialty.

On June 6, 1989, a great-great-great-grandson of Ch. Moa was whelped. He is Ch. Tortasen's Jakko, as close to the ideal as can be imagined. After 43 years, the quality continues to emerge. Although Holsing has curtailed most judging assignments, he enjoys the dogs, ably assisted by his son, Olav A. Holsing and his grandson, Jakob Olav Holsing.

SUMMARY

The Norwegian Elkhound continues to thrive in and out of his native Scandinavia. Many kennels in addition to the ones spotlighted are producing quality dogs that excel in the conformation ring, in the obedience ring, as hunting dogs and in hunting trials, and as devoted companions.

Pedigrees reflect a sharing of the gene pool among breeders in many countries. Just as kennels in the United States are not as identifiable by specific marks as they once were, Elkhounds from other countries are not as stamped with particular features as they once were. As long as the melding of pedigrees fosters strength of desired breed characteristics, the future of the breed is headed in the right direction.

CHAPTER THREE

NORWEGIAN ELKHOUND STANDARDS

An architect is an artist who draws a very detailed pattern for a building, including specifications for size, wiring, plumbing, down to the most minute detail. The pattern is called a blueprint. All buildings erected according to the blueprint will appear identical. Because of the time and expense involved in drafting a blueprint, the pattern is used repeatedly. The architect may alter it to correct a problem in design, but the basic structure remains the same.

Breeders of purebred dogs are somewhat like architects. They use a blueprint of sorts called a breed standard. The breed standard for Norwegian Elkhounds includes specifications for size, color, tail set, down to the finest detail in describing the ideal Norwegian Elkhound. Breeders, like architects, use the standard as their basic pattern. They choose stud dogs and brood bitches as the building blocks to produce the ideal model. Hypothetically, all puppies produced according to this plan will appear to be identical. The breeder may alter the breeding plan to correct an undesirable trait, but the basic standard for the breed remains the same.

Standards are drawn up and agreed on by groups of knowledgeable breeders of Elkhounds. The purpose of a standard is to ensure that all purebred Norwegian Elkhounds exhibit similar breed characteristics. Regardless of how rigid the standard, how minutely detailed, there will be as many interpretations of it as there are stars in the universe. To the untrained eye the Elkhounds will all look alike, just as the architect's buildings will be similar. But to the knowledgeable breeder, each animal is unique.

The original standard for the Norwegian (Gray) Elkhound was written in Norway in 1879. After the Elkhound became popular

Ch. Kamgaard Klear Skies Ahead.

in the United States, a group of fanciers applied to the AKC to be able to show their Elkhounds in the Miscellaneous Class, a dog-show class for breeds not officially eligible to show in regular conformation classes. As part of its game plan for acceptance by the AKC, the group of Elkhound devotees wrote a standard similar to the Norwegian standard and submitted it to the AKC for approval. It was accepted by the AKC in 1923. It has been revised periodically, the latest revision occurring in 1988.

The Elkhounds of old had a different look about them. Although many of them were of a rangier hunting type, heavier bodies, larger heads and darker coats were prevalent. They seem to have changed with the times. The revisions in the standard had nothing to do with the subtleties of change. Usually, the only changes in a standard, once it is accepted, are to clarify an ambiguous meaning. The 1988 revision was made to adapt the format of the standard to the AKC's format for all breed standards. A statement concerning ears was added to the standard: *When relaxed or showing affection, the ears go back, and the dog should not be penalized for doing this during the judge's examination.* The AKC breed video of the Norwegian Elkhound was revised in 1992.

OFFICIAL AKC NORWEGIAN ELKHOUND STANDARD

The official standard of the Norwegian Elkhound as approved by the AKC on December 13, 1988, follows:

General Appearance. The Norwegian Elkhound is a hardy, gray hunting dog. In appearance, a typical northern dog of medium size and substance, square in profile, close coupled and balanced in proportions. The head is broad with prick ears, and the tail is tightly curled and carried over the back. The distinctive gray coat is dense and smooth lying. As a hunter, the Norwegian Elkhound has the courage, agility and stamina to hold moose and other big game at bay by barking and dodging attack, and the endurance to track for long hours in all weather over rough and varied terrain.

Size, Proportion, Substance. Height at the withers for dogs is 20 1/2 inches, for bitches 19 1/2 inches. Weight for dogs about 55 pounds, for bitches about 48 pounds.

Square in profile and close coupled. Distance from brisket to ground appears to be half the height at the withers. Distance from forechest to rump equals the height at the withers.

Bone is substantial, without being coarse.

Head. Head broad at the ears, wedge-shaped, strong and dry (without loose skin).

Expression keen, alert, indicating a dog with great courage. Eyes very dark brown, medium in size, oval not protruding. Ears set high, firm and erect, yet very mobile. Comparatively small; slightly taller than their width at the base with pointed (not rounded) tips. When the dog is alert, the orifices turn forward and the outer edges are vertical. When relaxed or showing affection, the ears go back, and the dog should not be penalized for doing this during the judge's examination.

Viewed from the side, the forehead and back of the skull are only slightly arched; the stop not large, yet clearly defined. The muzzle is thickest at the base and, seen from above or from the side, tapers evenly without being pointed. The bridge of the nose is straight, parallel to and about the same length as the skull. Lips are tightly closed and teeth meet in a scissors bite.

Neck, Topline, Body. Neck of medium length, muscular, well set up with a slight arch and with no loose skin on the throat.

Topline. The back is straight and strong from its high point at the withers to the root of the tail. The body is short and close-coupled with the rib cage accounting for most of its length. Chest deep and moderately broad; brisket level with points of elbows; and ribs well sprung. Loin short and wide with very little tuck-up. Tail set high, tightly curled, and carried over the centerline of the back. It is thickly and closely haired, without brush, natural and untrimmed.

Forequarters. Shoulders sloping with elbows closely set on. Legs well under body and medium in length; substantial, but not coarse, in bone. Seen from the front, the legs appear straight and parallel. Single dew claws are normally present.

Feet. Paws comparatively small, slightly oval with tightly closed toes and thick pads. Pasterns are strong and only slightly bent. Feet turn neither in nor out.

Hindquarters. Moderate angulation at stifle and hock. Thighs are broad and well muscled. Seen from behind, legs are straight, strong and without dew claws. Feet as in front.

Coat. Thick, hard, weather resisting and smooth lying; made up of soft, dense, woolly undercoat and coarse, straight covering hairs. Short and even on head, ears, and front of legs; longest on back of neck, buttocks and underside of tail. The coat is not altered by trimming, clipping or artificial treatment. Trimming of whiskers is optional. In the show ring, presentation in a natural, unaltered condition is essential.

Color. Gray, medium preferred, variations in shade determined by the length of black tips and quantity of guard hairs. Undercoat is clear light silver as are legs, stomach, buttocks, and underside of tail. The gray body color is darkest on the saddle, lighter on the chest, mane and distinctive harness mark (a band of longer guard hairs from shoulder to elbow). The muzzle, ears and tail tip are black. The black of the muzzle shades to lighter gray over the forehead and skull.

Yellow or brown shading, white patches, indistinct or irregular markings, "sooty" coloring on the lower legs and light circles around the eyes are undesirable. Any overall color other than gray as described above, such as red, brown, solid black, white or other solid color, disqualifies.

Gait. Normal for an active dog constructed for agility and endurance. At a trot the stride is even and effortless; the back

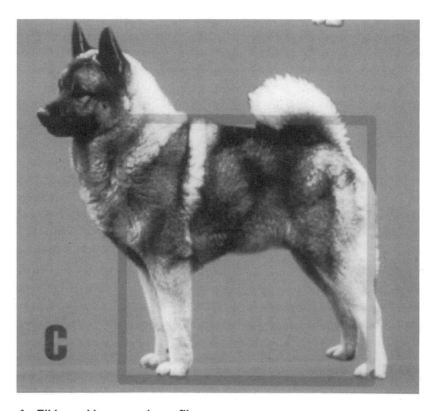

An Elkhound is square in profile.

remains level. As the speed of the trot increases, front and rear legs converge equally in straight lines toward a center line beneath the body, so that the pads appear to follow in the same tracks (single track). Front and rear quarters are well balanced in angulation and muscular development.

Temperament. In temperament, the Norwegian Elkhound is bold and energetic, an effective guardian yet normally friendly, with great dignity and independence of character.

Summary. The Norwegian Elkhound is a square and athletic member of the northern dog family. His unique coloring, weather resistant coat and stable disposition make him an ideal multipurpose dog at work or at play.

Disqualification. An overall color other than gray.

INTERPRETATION OF THE STANDARD

The Norwegian Elkhound Association of America offers several documents that summarize each point of the standard, suggesting what to look for when evaluating a Norwegian Elkhound and what to avoid. The pamphlets are available on request from NEAA as part of the organization's continuing education program. (See Bibliography.)

BREED TYPE

Breed type, literally, would mean an exact likeness of the perfect Elkhound according to the accepted standard. Since the standard uses inconclusive words, such as substantial, medium, comparatively and slightly in describing the Elkhound, there is ample opportunity for breeder interpretation. Therefore, all Elkhounds do not look alike.

Plotting the infinite number of gene combinations is mind-boggling. It would be easier to sort out and classify the grains in a bucket of sand. As a result, breeders plot their strategies on paper pedigrees and take what they get. This is not to say that experienced and conscientious breeders cannot exercise a certain amount of control in their breeding programs. For example, one breeder may produce heavier-boned, darker-colored, longer-legged dogs with larger eyes, ears and feet than another breeder produces. Both can be well within the standard. However, when one or more of the breed characteristics are out of balance, the dog becomes undesirable for showing or breeding.

PROPORTION

A given dog may be *square in profile and balanced in proportion* according to the standard, but if he stands more than an inch above or below the suggested height at the withers, he is either too tall or too short on leg. The Elkhound does not have a size disqualification; however, breeders adhere as closely as possible to the ideal height stated in the standard. Elkhounds that exceed or fall below the size limits are objectionable specimens for showing or breeding purposes.

An Elkhound may appear well proportioned and be within the size limitations. However, a hands-on examination of his skeletal structure could reveal that he is not short coupled; instead, he is either long-backed or long in loin.

In an attempt to breed dogs that are square in profile, breed-

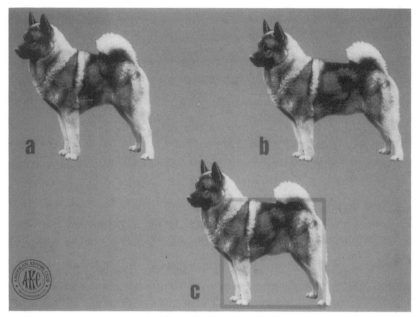

A: Too short; B: Too long; C: Just right.

ers sometimes produce dogs with straight shoulders. When the dog is standing still, he appears well proportioned. However, his reach is restricted, causing him to take shorter, mincing steps. In the same way, a too-straight or too-long stifle causes improper drive in the rear even though the Elkhound appears well proportioned.

The length of neck is functional in the overall balance of the dog. Without the proper neck length he loses an extent of maneuverability when he is keeping a moose at bay. He is not as adept at nipping at and avoiding the hooves of the moose if he has too short a neck. Strength of neck aids him as he jumps from boulder to boulder, jumps across streams and ditches and when a situation calls for a sudden burst of speed. The Elkhound must have a neck of medium length, well set up with a slight arch. He may appear to be square in profile and well proportioned but if his head seems to be set on his shoulders he is out of balance and loses his aristocratic bearing.

GAIT

Soundness is a result of the proper relationship of all the parts working together in harmony, much like the effortless movement of a spinning gyroscope. If soundness exists, there is no reason why the dog will not gait properly.

The normal gait for an Elkhound is a smooth, effortless trot. The back feet seemingly step into the print of the front feet as the front feet reach forward. A dog side-winds when the back feet must step aside to avoid colliding with the front feet as happens when the dog is not well balanced. As the dog increases his speed, the feet tend to move toward a center line beneath him which is referred to as single-tracking. Elkhounds that move close in the rear at a slower pace are not single tracking; they are moving close because they are not properly balanced. Elkhounds are capable of moving at great speed, but it is not necessary for them to do so in a conformation ring situation.

There are times when an Elkhound must be swift in the hunt. Agility is just as important as speed. A properly conditioned dog, square in profile and balanced in proportion, can move effortlessly and has the agility and stamina to work for hours over rocky terrain in pursuit of his prey.

NORWEGIAN STANDARD

The standards for the Norwegian Elkhound in the United States, England and Canada are based on the original Norwegian standard. The following is an English translation, not an exact literal translation, of the Norwegian standard for the Norwegian (Gray) Elkhound, redrafted and adopted in 1950 in Norway.

General Description. The Grey Elghund is a typical Northern dog with compact short body, squarely built, and with good carriage. Dense, thick, but not bristling coat, prick ears. The tail should be carried curled over the back. The Elghund should have a bold and energetic temperament.

Head. Wedge-shaped, relatively broad at ears. The forehead and back of skull slightly arched, no great stop. The muzzle thickest at base (not pinched), tapering evenly when seen from above or from side, without being pointed. No loose skin. Lips to be tight.

Ears. Set high, firm and erect and relatively small. Higher than their width at base. Tips pointed. Very mobile.

Eyes. Not protruding, brown, preferably dark.

Neck. Powerful, compact and short. Broad deep chest, well-sprung ribs, back straight from withers to base of tail, powerful loins, and stomach very little drawn up.

Legs. Forelegs sound and dry and strong. Elbows closely set on. Hind legs sound, dry and strong, slightly but definitely angulated at stifle and hock, straight when seen from behind. No dew claws.

Feet. Comparatively small, slightly oblong with tightly closed, forward-pointed toes.

Tail. Strong, high set, relatively short, densely haired, but without brush. Tightly curled, preferably carried over centerline of back.

Coat. Thick, rich, rough (meaning not soft), without curl. On head and front of legs short and smooth, longest on neck, buttocks and back of foreleg, and under side of tail. The coat is made up of longer, coarse, straight guard hairs, and a soft woolly undercoat.

Color. Darkish or lighter gray. Lighter on chest, belly and legs, underside of tail, and around anus, and harness markings. The gray color is made up by the guard hairs having more or less long black tips, while the underwool is pure light gray. Ears and the front part of the muzzle should be dark (dark mask). Coloring of yellow and brown, irregular distribution of color, soot coloring on legs, light spectacles around eyes, and white markings are not desired.

Height at withers. Ideal height for dogs 52 cm (20 1/2 in.), and bitches 49 cm (19 in.).

Disqualification. Short (stump) tail, pronounced variation from gray color. Yellow eyes.

BRITISH ELKHOUND SOCIETY

Many Norwegian Elkhounds were imported by fanciers in England who formed the British Elkhound Society in 1923. Under the auspices of the newly formed club, breeders formulated a standard for the Norwegian Elkhound using the Norwegian standard as the basis. It is referred to as the *Standard of Points of the Elkhound,* and, like the standards of other countries, has undergone several revisions.

General Appearance. The Elkhound is a hardy sporting dog of Nordic type of a bold and virile nature and has good scenting power. It has a compact and proportionately short body, a coat thick and abundant not bristling, and prick ears; tail tightly curled over back. Its disposition should be friendly and intelligent, with great energy and independence of character, and without any sign of undue nervousness.

Head and Skull. Broad between the ears; the forehead and back of the head are slightly arched with a clearly marked but not large stop. Muzzle moderately long, broader at the base and gradually tapering—whether seen from above or from the side but not pointed; bridge of the nose straight, jaw strong with lips tightly closed.

Eyes. Not prominent, in colour brown and as dark as possible, giving a frank, fearless and friendly expression.

Ears. Set high, firm and upstanding, height slightly greater than their width at the base, pointed and very mobile.

Neck. Of medium length, firm, muscular and well set up.

Forequarters. Legs firm, straight and powerful with good bone; elbows closely set on.

Body. Short in couplings, back wide and straight from neck to stern; chest, wide and deep with well-rounded ribs; loins, muscular; stomach, very little drawn up.

Hindquarters. Legs straight at the hock and when viewed from behind. There should be no dew claws on the hind legs.

Feet. Compact, oval in shape and not turned outwards; toes, slightly closed; toe nails, firm and strong.

Tail. Set high, tightly curled over the back but not carried on either side; hair, thick and close.

Coat. Thick, abundant, coarse and weather resisting; short on the head and on the front of the legs; longest on the chest, neck, buttocks and behind the forelegs and on the underside of the tail. It is composed of a longish and coarse top coat, dark at the tips with a light-coloured, soft and woolly undercoat. About the neck and front part of the chest the longer coat forms a sort of ruff, which with the pricked ears, the energetic eyes and the curled tail gives the animal its unique and alert appearance.

Colour. Grey, of various shades with black tips to the long outer coat; lighter on the chest, stomach, legs and the underside of the tail. Any distinctive variation from the grey colour is most undesirable and too dark or too light colouring ought to be avoided. Pronounced markings on legs and feet are also not desirable.

Weight and size. For dogs, the height at the shoulder is about 20 1/2 inches, and for bitches, about 18 1/2 inches. Weight approximately 50 lbs. and 43 lbs. respectively.

CANADIAN KENNEL CLUB

The Canadian Kennel Club is the umbrella agency for pure-bred dogs in Canada. The Norwegian Elkhound Club of Canada functions in the same way as the NEAA in the United States. The official Canadian Norwegian Elkhound standard is as follows:

General Appearance. The Norwegian Elkhound is a typical northern dog, of medium size, with a compact, proportionately short body, with a thick and rich, but not bristling, grey coat, with prick ears, and with a tail that is curled and carried over the back.

Temperament. His temperament is bold and energetic.

Size. Dogs, about 20 1/2 in. (52 cm) at the shoulder; bitches, about 19 1/2 in. (50 cm).

Coat and Colour. Coat thick, rich and hard, but rather smooth lying. On head and front of legs, short and even; longest on neck and chest, on buttocks, on hindside of forelegs and on underside of tail. It is made of longer and harder covering hairs, dark at the tips, and of a light, soft, woolly undercoat. Colour grey, with black tips to the long covering hairs; somewhat lighter on chest, stomach, legs, underside of tail, and around anus. The colour may be lighter or darker, with a slight shading towards yellow; but a pronounced variation from the grey colour disqualifies. Too dark or too light individuals should be avoided; also, yellow markings or uneven colouring. There should be no pronounced white markings.

Head. "Dry" (without any loose skin), broad at the ears; the forehead and back of the head only slightly arched; the stop not large, yet clearly defined. The *muzzle* is of medium length, thickest at the base and seen from above or from the side tapers evenly without being pointed. The bridge of the nose is straight; the lips are tightly closed. *Eyes* not protruding, brown in colour, preferably dark, lively, with fearless energetic expression. *Ears* set high, firm and erect, are higher than they are wide at the base, pointed (not rounded) and very mobile. When the dog is listening, the orifices are turned forward.

Neck. Of medium length, "dry" (without any loose skin), strong, and well set up.

Forequarters. Legs firm, straight, and strong; elbows closely set on.

Body. Powerful, *compact,* and short, with broad deep chest, well-sprung ribs, straight back, well-developed loins, and stomach very little drawn up.

Hindquarters. Hind legs with little angulation at knees and hocks. Seen from behind, they are straight. Feet comparatively small, somewhat oblong, with tightly closed toes, not turned out. There should be no dewclaws on hind legs.

Tail. Set high, short, thickly and closely haired, but without brush; tightly curled, not carried too much to one side.

Disqualification. Pronounced variation from grey colour.

SUMMARY

Even though the United States, England and Canada have written their own standards for the Norwegian Elkhound, they have based them on the original Norwegian standard for the Gray Elkhound. Often using ambiguous wording, the standards in these countries depict the identifiable breed characteristics, inadvertently allowing room for breeder interpretation. Nevertheless, breeders and exhibitors are able to show their dogs competitively in other countries. As a result, it is not unusual for a Norwegian Elkhound to hold championship titles from Norway, Ireland, Sweden, England, Canada, the United States and other countries. Examples of international champions are Irish and American Champion Crafdal Thor Mhor, Norwegian and American Champion Tortasens Bjonn II and American and Canadian Champion Trygvie Vikingsson.

CHAPTER FOUR
STRUCTURE AND FUNCTION

The original standards were efforts based on experience and dreams. In retrospect, the standard for a particular breed of pure-bred dog was a written description of the best dogs available at the time of the writing—or of the dogs owned by the framers of the standard—or of dogs lingering in the memories of the framers. The writers were more than likely avid sportsmen, experts at spinning yarns about the big one that got away. As the years passed by, dogs changed and standards were revised—subtle changes, barely noticed by even the most discerning eye, but changes, nevertheless.

Experienced breeders perceive a mental picture of the ideal Norwegian Elkhound and interpret the standard to fit the proto-types they are producing. Because of the ambiguity of phrases within standards, the Norwegian Elkhound standard included, other equally discerning breeders may produce dogs that are slightly different renditions of the same standard. As long as the breed characteristics are preserved and attention is given to soundness and function, who is to say every Norwegian Elkhound must fit into an exact mold?

A WORKING DOG

The Norwegian Elkhound is a hardy, gray hunting dog, bred for function not fashion. The first impression of an Elkhound is one of stamina, athletic prowess and intelligence—an image of strength and beauty. In his native Scandinavia he earns his keep as a working dog. He is a multipurpose dog, found primarily on farms, serving as a hunter, guardian and companion.

An Elkhound hunts by scent although his keen eyesight cannot be ignored as a contributing factor in finding a moose or bear

— 71 —

Author's husband, Paul, tracking elg *in Norway, August 1994.*

in a dense forest. His job is to keep his prey at bay by circling it, barking at it and jumping out of the way of its dangerous hooves, antlers or, in the case of a bear, powerful paws and jaws. To his prey, the Elkhound is a nuisance, an incessant insect, too quick to be swatted.

Although the Elkhound is not used for hunting in America as much as he was during earlier times in Scandinavia, his hunting instincts and physical adaptations are intact and are to be taken into consideration in his appraisal. Leg length is of great concern: Short-legged as well as long-legged Elkhounds should be avoided because neither would possess the agility to maneuver on rocky terrain, let alone outmaneuver their prey. Other faults that would interfere with the capability to hunt all day are obesity and atypical movement.

SIZE

To function in an athletic capacity, the Elkhound should be within one inch of the suggested height. Dogs that are too small have difficulty hunting in rugged terrain, especially in deep snow. On the other hand, dogs that are too large may pose a threat to an already nervous moose, adding to the difficulty of keeping it at bay.

WEIGHT

Elkhounds tend to carry more weight than is desirable. Only a dog in lean, hard condition would be capable of a long hunt. Ideal weight for dogs is between 50 and 55 pounds and for bitches, between 45 and 48 pounds. A well-conditioned dog or bitch with good bone may reach the upper limits of height and weight but still appear lean.

Legs appear too long.

PROPORTION

The overall appearance of an Elkhound is one of a square profile. A diagram showing correct proportion is helpful in discerning correct squareness as opposed to squareness achieved by disproportionate parts. For instance, a short rib cage and long coupling or a deep body with short legs will give appearances of squareness but are incorrect.

HEAD

A typical Elkhound head is wedge-shaped and broad at the ears. The dog's head is larger and more masculine than the bitch's, but that is not to say the bitch has a narrow wedge-shaped head. An Elkhound's head continues to broaden until he is two, sometimes three, years of age.

The head and muzzle appear to lie in parallel planes when viewed from the side. The muzzle, which is medium in length and tapers to a blunt nose, should portray strength. A Roman nose is undesirable. The strength of head and muzzle are not necessary in hunting big game because the Elkhound keeps the

Head and muzzle lie in parallel planes.

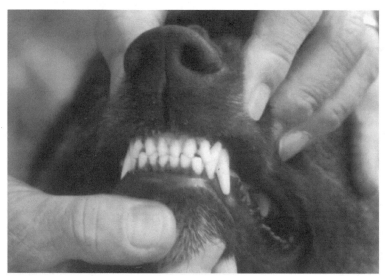

A correct scissors bite.

prey at bay, making no effort to catch and hold. The portrayal of strength is, however, paramount to the overall demeanor of the Elkhound.

The underjaw denotes strength, which is further enhanced with a scissors bite. A scissors bite results when the outer side of the lower incisors touches the inner side of the upper incisors. Overshot, undershot and even bites are incorrect. When the front teeth or incisors of the upper jaw overlap and do not touch the front teeth of the lower jaw when the mouth is closed, the dog's bite is said to be overshot. On the other hand, if the front teeth or incisors of the lower jaw overlap or project beyond the front teeth of the upper jaw when the mouth is closed, the dog's bite is said to be undershot. If the upper incisors meet the lower incisors without any overlapping, the dog has an even bite. A Norwegian Elkhound should not have any missing teeth. Full dentition is desirable.

The Norwegian Elkhound portrays his innate intelligence and courage by having a keen alert expression. He uses his dark, oval eyes to establish eye contact with the game he is working.

Correctly set eyes are not as prone to injury from working in rugged terrain and wooded areas as protruding eyes would be. Eye faults include light-colored, round or bulging eyes.

EARS

An Elkhound's ears, being comparatively small, are set high and are firm and erect. He uses his ears constantly, almost as a

Ears set high, firm and erect. Correct eyes.

means of communicating. He turns them forward when he is alert, causing the outer edges to be vertical, adding to the general character of his head. In this manner of communicating, he may momentarily lay his ears back. But this should not be confused with weak ears, ears that aren't prick, ears that are too large or ears that flare at the outer base, all of which are undesirable.

Elkhound breeders are aware that ears are, indeed, slightly large for even the broadest interpretation of the standard.

Ears are functional whether the Elkhound is being used as a hunter, guardian or companion. They are highly mobile, allowing the dog to detect sound from any direction. The combination of keen eyesight, hearing and scenting add to his ability to function effectively in diverse situations.

The overall expression of a Norwegian Elkhound is enhanced by black ears, a black muzzle and black mascara markings that run from the corners of the eyes to the outer corners of the base of the ears. There are several faults that detract from proper expression: light circles around the area of the eyes, referred to as spectacles; loose skin or wrinkles on the head; a pinched or foxy look; and ears that are too low set, too high set or that are set so that the tips tend to touch.

NECK

The appearance of an Elkhound is greatly enhanced by the way he carries himself. If he has a well-set and arched neck, he conveys an aura of superiority. If he has a short neck without an arch or if he has a swan neck, he loses the overall appearance of balance and his air of being something special. Another common problem occurring around the neck is a tendency toward loose skin in the throat area. Several theories have been tendered in defense of throatiness, excess skin or waddle. Allegedly, the Elkhound's owner kept him too fat as a puppy and he never grew into his skin. Or, his littermates used to pull him around by the skin on his throat and stretched it. Quite simply, the problem is in the genes and needs to be treated as such.

When hunting over rough terrain, jumping precariously from rock to rock and keeping big game at bay, the Elkhound's neck tends to be a balancing factor. The dog spends a lot of time balancing on his hind legs and bobbing up and down like a puppet on a string. A short neck interferes with his balance. Occasionally the ruff, made up of the longer hair around the top and sides of the neck, is so profuse that it gives the illusion of a short neck. Having straight shoulders of less than the desired degree of shoulder layback also shortens the appearance of the neck.

TOPLINE

The topline of an Elkhound is straight and strong, sloping slightly from the high point at the withers to the root of the tail that is set on high. Long, soft or sway back Elkhounds tend to look rectangular rather than square.

The loin should be wide and well muscled which can only come from proper conditioning. A short-coupled dog will have no more than a three-inch coupling, about the width of four fingers fit snugly between the rib cage and the loin. An Elkhound with a short rib cage and a long coupling may appear square in profile but the dog is incorrect.

CHEST

Ideally the Elkhound has a deep, moderately broad chest. If the chest drops below the elbow, it is incorrect. There again, he may have a square profile but his legs are too short to make him proportionately correct. The distance from the brisket to the ground should be approximately half the height at the withers. The reverse can be said for a shallow-chested Elkhound. A too broad or too narrow chest interferes with lateral agility, causing wasted motion.

TAIL

The crowning glory for a good specimen is a high, center-set, tightly curled tail, covered with an abundance of close, thick hair. The underside of the tail is always silver-white, not the white as in a white blaze, but the silver-white of the undercoat. The upper side of the tail has black-tipped guard hairs and looks much the same as the overall coat. About midway down the upper side of the tail is a black diamond shape where the curvature of the tail causes the tips of the guard hair to lie together. The tip of the tail also appears black. Usually, a tightly curled tail will have a definite hook at the tip that can be relaxed but springs back when the tail is up. Just as an Elkhound communicates with his ears, even the most serious one will give a slight flicker of his tail when acknowledging the presence of a human or other animal.

The tail is purposefully curled tightly over the back out of the way. In a small way, it helps with balance. The Norwegian standard declares a stump tail to be a disqualification for this

Correct tail.

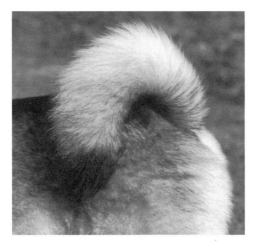

Incorrect tail.

reason. Tails with a side curl or a loose curl have the tendency to flag or stand up or out when the dog moves. Not only could the tail snag on a low hanging branch but an overly zealous prey such as a wildcat or bobcat could use the tail as a convenient handle.

An Elkhound's tail detracts from an otherwise correct specimen if it is low set, loosely curled, carried down, lies to the side or has excessive brush. Extremely long silver-gray hair on the tail is considered excessive brush. It stands up instead of lying with the curvature of the tail. The temptation is to trim the brush to blend in with the rest of the tail hair. However, scissoring is frowned upon. A nest is formed in the coat on the back of the Elkhound where his tail rests, a telltale sign of a correct, tightly curled tail.

FOREQUARTERS

An Elkhound's shoulders have a 45-degree to 55-degree angle slope and his legs are set well under him if he is to have lateral agility. The shoulder blades should be flat and close together at the withers. It is difficult to detect straight shoulders when a dog is standing still because of the profuseness of coat but it becomes apparent when he moves. He will not have the reach of a dog with properly sloping shoulders and his movement may appear stiff.

His legs should be straight and parallel with elbows closely set. Problems of the front are straight shoulders, out at the elbows, loaded shoulders, too narrow or too wide a front and knuckling over, thus interfering with agility and stamina.

FEET

An Elkhound's feet play an important role when he is on the hunt. They should be comparatively small and oval-shaped. Ideally, the pads are thick and the toes are tightly closed. If a dog is seldom on a surface that keeps his nails ground down, his nails must be trimmed periodically to keep his feet from splaying. The nails are black. An occasional white nail is present if the puppy was born with a white marking on his paw. However, neither moose nor judges pay any attention to it.

An Elkhound's feet are often ignored even though their importance is stressed. Especially undesirable are cat or hare feet,

Proper feet.

flat feet, thin pads and splayed feet. Tough pads are needed on tough terrain. It is easier for the Elkhound to manipulate his footing if his feet are correctly formed.

HINDQUARTERS

Conditioning is important in developing well-muscled thighs. The thighs should have moderate angulation and be broad without being too wide. The rear legs appear straight when they are viewed from the rear. Common problems are too straight stifles,

Legs appear straight and parallel.

cow-hocks and sickle-hocks. Sickle-hocks are bent hocks, making it appear that the dog is walking on his heels rather than on his feet. An overangulated stifle causes the dog to thrust his rear feet and legs well behind his body. Some judges mistake this for correct movement and reward the dog with a win. Correct angulation can be determined by dropping an imaginary line from the point of the rump to the hocks at the point where they are set perpendicular to the ground. Hindquarters must be strong, acting as springboards for the jumping and bouncing the Elkhound engages in during the hunt.

Correct bend of stifle.

COAT

The Elkhound's coat is unique in several ways. He has an outercoat of black-tipped guard hairs that feel hard without being coarse. The guard hairs lie flat as if protecting the silver-white woolly undercoat that is soft and dense. A wavy coat is undesirable.

A shedding Elkhound.

The outercoat serves as an all-weather coat, protecting the undercoat and skin from the elements. An Elkhound whose outercoat is open would stand a good chance of suffering from the freezing rain in his native Scandinavia as well as in the cold, mountainous areas of the United States. Likewise, the coat insulates him from the heat, although he should not be subjected to a day in the hot sun without shelter. The harsh outercoat also repels burrs and tangles.

When an Elkhound sheds, the woolly undercoat must be removed by combing and brushing. If left ungroomed, the dog looks like an old mattress that is losing its stuffing. The clumps of wool hang in the outercoat. Grooming yields pile after pile of wool that, by the way, is of excellent quality for spinning. The undercoat can become matted, especially during a shedding period. The Elkhound tends to shed twice a year but should be brushed routinely to keep the coat free from loose guard hairs and tufts of woolly undercoat. Lack of undercoat is a fault.

Diet affects coat condition. Continual shedding, a dull, brittle coat and/or a sparse undercoat often signal dietary deficiencies. A veterinarian can be consulted to help determine the cause of coat problems. It is not unheard of for a lack of undercoat to be a genetic factor. If such is the case, much consideration should be given to eliminate that particular Elkhound from the breeding program.

COLOR

A distinguishing characteristic of the Elkhound is his gray color. His muzzle, ears and the tip of his tail are black and his undercoat, legs, belly, buttocks and the underside of his tail are silver-white. The rest of his coat will have variations of a medium gray depending on the profuseness of the guard hairs and the length of the black tips of the guard hairs.

The coat is darkest on the saddle and lighter on the chest, mane and harness mark, which is a band of longer guard hairs from the Elkhound's shoulders to his elbows. The black of his muzzle shades into gray as it spreads to his face and head.

Even the finest Norwegian Elkhound may sport a small white star on his chest; however, a white blaze of any size is discouraged. The elimination of white markings should be given careful consideration in every breeding program. Other white patches, shadings of brown or yellow, sooty-looking legs or other irregular markings should be totally avoided. And, of course, any overall color other than gray as it has been described is a disqualification and must not be tolerated. The shading patterns of Elkhound coats do not vary as much as the shading itself. It is not unusual to see extremely dark or extremely light specimens in a show ring. Since color is controlled by genetic makeup, dogs from the same line tend to have the same degree of shading. The ideal color is gray with black ears, muzzle and tail tip, blending with the silver-white of the legs, rump, belly and the exposed undertail.

GAIT

If an Elkhound is proportioned correctly and properly conditioned, he will gait correctly. His particular balance of design enables him to bounce, spin, turn and jump on a dime. It is not unusual to see an Elkhound jump four or five feet in the air from

Correct Elkhound bitch.

a standing position. The thrust of the rear is so great that an Elkhound can leave a trail of dust much like a speeding car on takeoff. In the house, he delights in leaving area rugs askew. This is another reason mats under the jumps in the obedience ring must be secured.

As he moves into his usual effortless trot, the Elkhound will single track, converging his front and rear legs toward a straight line centered beneath his body. Obvious problems in gait are moving too wide or too close, crossing over in the front and moving the front legs in a mix-master fashion instead of in a straight line.

An engineer designing a prototype of a mechanical Elkhound would have no problem building a model with all the prescribed angles and size proportions. He would, however, have difficulty simulating the movement expected in the show ring. More than likely, the engineer would compromise with a slightly longer body and wider angles in the leg assemblies.

TEMPERAMENT

The key descriptors of Elkhound temperament are bold, energetic and friendly, a necessary combination for him to be effective as a hunter, a guardian or a companion. His independence and dignity should not be mistaken for downright aloofness.

Although Elkhounds are possessive, they should not show overaggression. They can be taught to respond to voice control and to walk on lead. Overly aggressive as well as shy Elkhounds are undesirable and should be avoided for breeding purposes. Since the breed characteristics of the Norwegian Elkhound are prepotent, there are many outstanding specimens available, making it unnecessary to tolerate the occasional undesirable ones. The dog with a true Elkhound disposition will not be intimidated by large prey, gunfire or noise.

SUMMARY

The approved standard for the Norwegian Elkhound allows room for breeder interpretation. However, breeders would do well to use the standard as a guide in planning their breeding programs instead of using it as a crutch to justify what they have produced. The key to producing quality Elkhounds is to breed quality to quality. A dog is only as good as his genetic makeup.

CHAPTER FIVE
BREEDING WITH A PURPOSE

Too many times breeders get calls from people who want to buy a female so they can let her have puppies. They want their children to witness the miracle of birth. Another prospective buyer may want a female so he can earn some extra cash selling puppies. Yet another caller may want a big male for a guard dog and to use as a stud. The reasons go on and on. Reputable breeders will not sell a puppy unless the buyer has an acceptable reason for wanting a Norwegian Elkhound. Many breeders deny a request for a puppy after they interview a prospective buyer.

The market for selling Elkhounds in not extensive. In fact, there are more reasons not to breed than there are to breed. Perhaps the principal justification for having a litter is to improve the Norwegian Elkhound as it exists in today's world—or at least, to maintain the breed in its present state of well-being.

PRODUCING QUALITY PUPPIES

In 1938, Miss Julia Rands, a very wise Norwegian Elkhound fancier in England, wrote an essay entitled, "Scandinavian Invasion." Her insight is as relevant today as it was then when she ended her essay with the following charge to breeders: "And lastly, dear modern breeders, do realise what a responsibility lies in your hands: the making or marring of this charming and ancient breed. Do not think only of selfish, fleeting triumphs in the show ring but of the beauty and character of the breed as a whole, and the joy it may bring to future generations."

Words of wisdom must be sought and heeded, for as surely as there are male and female, there will be breedings. And breedings there must be for any species to survive. After years of hard

CERTIFIED PEDIGREE

Name of Dog __KANDAHAR OF RAVENSBROOK__   Sex __MALE__   Reg. No. __HB52103__

Breed __NORWEGIAN ELKHOUND__   Color __BLACK AND SILVER__

Date Whelped __AUGUST 21 1974__   Breeder __BRUCE L PETERSMEYER__

			15 CH CRAFDAL TRYGLIK TRYLL HA439331 8-67
		7 CRAFDAL TRYGLIKK TRYLLIEF HB17051 1-70	
			16 CH CRAFDAL TRYGLIK TRYTTA CDX HA653366 5-68
	3 CH CRAFDAL TROLL TURI THOR KIEF HB264089 4-72		
			17 CH CRAFDAL TRYGLIK BLITZEN HA666468 7-67
		8 CRAFDAL TRYG N THORS KYA HA968653 1-70	
			18 CH CRAFDAL LILLARD KVINNA HA712577 9-66
1 TRYGUIE STORM AV WINDY ACRE HB647148 6-73			
			19 CRAFDAL TRYGLIK TIMBA HA783752 8-68
		9 CH CRAFDAL TRYGLIK TALL TIMBER HB94218 12-70	
			20 CRAFDAL TRYGS TALLI HA687713 8-68
	4 TIMBER'S LIEFLET HB457806 6-72		
			21 PRINCE ERIC AV RANGAARD HA144550 3-67
		10 PRINCESS KIRSTEN OF FIE-DELL HA933663 6-70	
			22 CH CRAFDAL TRYGLIK KIRSTEN HA578977 3-67
			23 CH FANEVAKT AV RUNEFJELL H329055 5-60
		11 CH FANEBJORGS BJORN AV BJDRKSYN HA260583 8-62 CD	
			24 BJORG AV BJORKSYN HA243233 6-62
	5 ODIN'S SIN HB278172 5-70		
			25 CH BAADKARLS BOLT THUNDER HA124549 9-63
		12 NOR-ELKS KRISTY ANNA HA932510 2-69	
			26 NOR-ELK MISTY DAWN HA327494 9-53
2 ELSA VALKYRIE HB698889 12-74			
			27 MR GUNNAR AV NORTHGATE HA12985 4-63
		13 GUNNAR'S THUNDER HA724740 1-68	
			28 GIDGET AV NORTH GATE HA272262 4-63
	6 KIRSTEN'S ANGEL HB41798 5-70		
			29 OSCAR ALFRED H667991 6-59
		14 SPARKLES HA697192 5-66	
			30 ELFREDA FREYJA H840624 6-59

The Seal of The American Kennel Club affixed hereto certifies that this pedigree has been compiled from official Stud Book records.

Date Issued __6-13-75 SH__

Pedigree.

work, success and failure, an experienced breeder will produce many excellent quality puppies. With few exceptions, however, success is not always immediate or imminent.

Paramount to successful breeding is the good fortune to acquire quality breeding stock. It may take several years and a tidy investment to secure stock with the compatible genetic basis for producing the aspired combination of Norwegian Elkhound traits. Breeding an outstanding dam to an outstanding dog does not assure outstanding offspring. However, the same dam bred to a different dog, or the same dog bred to a different dam, may be the right blend. Therefore, it will take several breedings to achieve the expected outcome. In the meantime, there will have been a considerable outlay of money, time and patience.

It is not always necessary for breeders to own their own stud dogs. They may breed their bitches to dogs owned by other persons. The same in-depth study of the genetic background of the *at-stud* dog must be exercised before taking a bitch to him for breeding. The owner of the dog must be contacted in advance to ensure that the stud dog's services will be available when the bitch comes into estrous—season or heat.

Scrupulous breeders will require a pedigree, picture and hip

Bitch ready to whelp.

x-ray before agreeing to a breeding. Many Norwegian Elkhound breeders rely on The Orthopedic Foundation of Animals (OFA) to read and grade x-rays to determine if their dogs are dysplastic. Breeders will require a health certificate from a licensed veterinarian, ascertaining that the dog and bitch are clear of brucellosis and other communicable conditions.

A legal contract between the owners of the stud dog and the bitch should be signed to offset problems relating to puppy registration and to a repeat breeding, or no repeat breeding, in the event the bitch did not conceive. The amount of the stud fee is stipulated in the contract.

Often a bitch is leased for the purpose of breeding. All the details of the arrangement should be specified in a legally binding contract to be signed by the leasee and the owner of the bitch. The same precautions are taken as with the stud dog.

An average litter.

EXCERPTING PUPPIES

A breeder must be willing and have the stamina to cull puppies with obvious defects at birth. A veterinarian can help in this situation. As disconcerting as it is, in severe instances, it must be carried out. Examples are puppies with physical deformities including dwarfism, internal abnormalities and mismarkings. Dwarfism is not always obvious the first few weeks but mismarked puppies are noticeable immediately. They are quite possibly not purebred or, in the case of a reddish-brown puppy, may be mutations.

Internal abnormalities such as heart and intestinal deformities manifest within a short period. Congenital eye disorders involving cataracts often result in blindness. Puppies are occasionally born blind. But even total blindness of a puppy cannot be detected for several weeks because puppies do not open their eyes before at least nine days.

Expert surgical procedures performed by a veterinary specialist can correct a limited number of congenital disorders and the dogs can lead normal lives. However, it is misleading to believe the surgically corrected dog can then be used in a breeding program. The underlying fault lies within the genetic makeup of the dog. It is imperative that breeders act scrupulously in their attempts to eliminate dogs that possess the ill-contributing genes from their breeding stock.

USING A GROWTH CHART

A puppy growth chart is an essential evaluative tool used by breeders in the puppy selection process. A chart should be set up to follow growth progress of the litter. Birth weights, as well as daily and weekly weights, can be entered on the chart. Seeing a litter every day helps in the evaluation process. However, a good evaluation may be made at five weeks and again at eight weeks by an experienced breeder.

Factors other than weight enter into the evaluation of a litter. As the puppies open their eyes and begin to toddle around, personality traits can be noted. Aggressive puppies tend to play and amble around the litter box while shy ones stay to themselves. Physical attributes begin to manifest in the individual puppies. Low tail sets are obvious although tails do not begin to curl until a little later. As teeth are cut, extreme overshot or undershot bites can be detected; however, the degree of overshot or undershot changes as the bones in the head and muzzle develop. Therefore, unless the bite is extreme, it should not be used as a determinant when puppies are but a few weeks of age.

EVALUATING PUPPIES

At eight weeks, if there is a puppy the breeder definitely does

PUPPY GROWTH CHART

Dam: **Qheni**   Sire: **Topp**

Whelping Date **8/23/91**

PUPPY	Birth Wght.	3 da.	7 da.	10 da.	14 da.	17 da.	3 wk.	4 wk.	5 wk.	6 wk.	7 wk.	8 wk.	10 wk.
A	1 lb 2 oz	1 lb 6 oz	2 lb 2 oz	2 lb 6 oz	3 lb —	3 lb 4 oz	4 lb 7 oz	4 lb 8 oz	7 lb —	9 lb 4 oz			
B	1 lb 2 oz	1 lb 2 oz	1 lb 8 oz	1 lb 12 oz	2 lb 4 oz	2 lb 8 oz	2 lb 12 oz	3 lb 13 oz	5 lb 4 oz	6 lb 12 oz			
C	1 lb 2 oz	1 lb 4 oz	2 lb —	2 lb 4 oz	2 lb 15 oz	3 lb 3 oz	4 lb 3 oz	5 lb 4 oz	6 lb 6 oz	8 lb —			
D													
E													
F													
G													
H													

Growth chart.

— 92 —

not want to keep, he may sell it as a pet. Buying an eight-week-old puppy as show quality is as unsound as buying a size six dress with the intentions of going on a diet to lose 25 pounds. It may or it may not happen.

A breeder can determine which puppies can be sold and which ones are to be kept for further evaluation when the puppies are three months old. Front and rear movement can be evaluated and, although some puppies go through a stage of the uglies with everything seemingly falling apart, an experienced breeder can tell at six months which puppies are show quality. By 9 or 10 months, a breeder will know for certain which puppies to keep.

It is easier for a puppy to adjust to a new home at six to nine months of age. The older he gets, the longer the transition takes. The breeder knows that puppies continue to change for as long as a year to a year and a half for bitches and a year and a half to two and a half or even three years for a male.

TRAFFICKING IN DOGS

Unfortunately, trafficking in dogs does occur. People who buy or sell dogs as a means of making their livelihoods are not con-

Breeding for the wrong reasons.

sidered breeders of repute. It is wise not to do business with them. It is unfortunate when the pedigree of a pet store puppy reflects names of dogs of reputable breeders. Although breeders exercise caution when selling puppies, an occasional puppy gets into the wrong home and is used as a producer for dog traffickers.

Some pet stores appear to operate well within the margins of cleanliness and take proper care of the pets they attempt to sell. Even in these cases, the trauma puppies are subjected to is severe enough to discredit all such stores.

To begin with, puppies are taken from their dams at four or five weeks, much too early to be weaned totally. Usually they have not been immunized. A great percentage of them do not survive the ordeal. A great percentage of the remainder are often sickly and have lasting effects from their trauma. Seizures, stomach problems and diarrhea are but a few examples of lingering health problems suffered by unfortunate trafficked puppies.

SELLING PUPPIES FOR PETS

Persons wanting to buy a Norwegian Elkhound puppy will benefit from contacting NEAA for a list of breeders in their area. Actually there should not be that much difference in appearance between a pet-quality Elkhound and a show-quality puppy. Breeders label puppies pet quality if they are improperly balanced to the extent that they are out of proportion. The puppy's color may be too light a gray or it may be too black. Eyes may be bulged or of a light color. The puppy may not have a scissors bite. Overshot, undershot or even bites are genetically acquired. Missing canines would not be noticeable until the puppy is several months older.

In addition, the puppy may be cow-hocked, sickle-hocked, move too closely in the rear or cross over in the front. The problems would keep a breeder from showing the Elkhound in conformation or from using the specimen in a breeding program. Although the puppy may be considered as pet quality by the breeder, it can be a perfectly beautiful Norwegian Elkhound for an owner not interested in breeding or showing.

COMMON PROBLEMS

Not all undesirable traits are evident at the time of whelp. It is the invisible that haunts breeders. Even after a breeder has researched and studied for a planned breeding, occasional problems arise.

Temperament is of major concern. It can be the ruination of the most perfect puppy. Causes are not necessarily genetic. Lack of socialization can turn an otherwise satisfactory puppy into a basket case. Whether genetic or acquired, Elkhounds with temperament problems should never be bred or shown. And it is an unwise breeder, indeed, who would sell one to an unsuspecting buyer. A typical Elkhound is bold, energetic and friendly.

Another invisible problem is hip dysplasia. It, too, can be genetic or acquired. Only the most severe cases are obvious in a young puppy. A veterinarian can give an opinion after an examination and x-rays. Dysplastic Elkhounds should not be bred or sold. Mild cases of dysplasia often go undetected and many afflicted dogs live long happy lives.

Weak or floppy ears are not obvious until a puppy reaches four or five months of age. It is not a widespread problem in Elkhounds but it does occur. The ears are to be held erect and should be of good leather, meaning they are not paper-thin so that they flap with the wind when the dog moves.

In other words, atypical characteristics can occur, either congenital or acquired, that are not obvious at the age puppies are usually sold to pet owners. Therefore, breeders cannot be faulted for selling a puppy that develops a problem in later months. However, a discerning breeder would appreciate being informed of the problem so that the problem can be addressed in future breedings if it is of genetic origin.

BUYING A SHOW DOG

Show dogs are born not sculptured. It is not apparent to the novice whether a Norwegian Elkhound puppy is show quality until the puppy is at least six months old. Breeders, on the other hand, can make educated guesses and be correct most of the time but even the most promising puppy can fall apart as he matures.

The novice who wants a show prospect should work with a reputable breeder in selecting a puppy. Knowledgeable Elkhound people always work with a breeder when they are in a position to purchase a show prospect. It is to the advantage of the breeder to attempt to provide quality Elkhounds to people who purchase Elkhounds with the intent to show. No breeders want poor quality Elkhounds shown with their names listed as breeders.

BUYING FOR BREEDING

All reputable breeders had to start someplace. Someone took the time to sell them quality Elkhounds. Someone took the time to tell them the rudiments of breeding quality Elkhounds. It stands to reason that those same reputable breeders owe it to novices to impart some of that knowledge. The future of the breed lies with the breeders.

Basically, buying Norwegian Elkhounds for breeding purposes is much the same as buying for show purposes. The high quality must be present. Breeders may use a particular bitch for breeding that they would not use for showing but they are in a position to know basically what genes the bitch possesses and what she produces when bred to a dog with which they are equally familiar.

However, to buy an Elkhound of lesser quality just because someone says the dog will be a good producer is not wise. Those are decisions and practices that should well be left with the experienced, reputable breeder.

A study and knowledge of the pedigrees of prospective breeding stock is necessary. Most pedigrees go back three to five generations. Pedigrees will indicate the extent certain dogs are used on both sides, sire and dam. Well-known, top-winning Norwegian Elkhounds in a pedigree do not guarantee quality offspring. Neither do unheard of Elkhounds.

STRINGS ATTACHED

Often breeders will attach stipulations to the contract when selling a puppy. The contract may state that the puppy must be neutered at a certain age in the case of a pet. AKC has included options for breeders to indicate on the registration papers, including one that would preclude breeding.

The contract may state that the breeder will choose the sire or dam to be used for breedings in the case of a quality Elkhound. The breeder may want first pick of each litter. The breeder may stipulate that the breeder's name will appear as co-owner on the registration papers of the breedings or of progeny from the breedings. Whatever the stipulations, buyers must read the contract carefully and be in full agreement and understanding before the contract is signed and the Elkhound paid for; otherwise, misunderstandings and loss of friendships may result. Often, the dog is the greatest loser in the deal.

SUMMARY

There are several valid reasons for breeding Norwegian Elkhounds and even more reasons for not breeding Elkhounds. The principal purpose is to improve the quality as it exists at the present or, at least, to maintain the breed at its present level of quality. Scrupulous, long-time breeders study and strive to produce puppies close to the ideal as they interpret the standard. At the same time, they are discriminate in selling only to people who provide good homes for the Elkhounds and those who have the potential and desire to become discerning breeders.

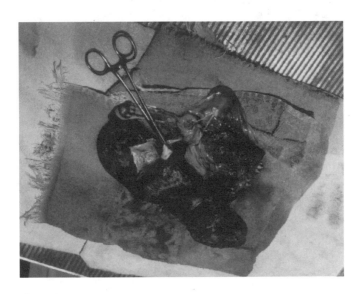

A newborn puppy.

Nursing newborn puppies.

CHAPTER SIX
RAISING A LITTER OF PUPPIES

Many excellent books are available on breeding and whelping puppies. Most breeders can recommend at least one they use as a reference. It is a good practice to buy a reliable text, read and study it for background information and then refer to it when the time comes for breeding and whelping. It is also wise to alert a veterinarian in case a problem arises during whelping.

Maybe it just seems like it, but many bitches whelp during the night—sometimes taking all night. Puppies may arrive at 20-minute intervals or 45 minutes to an hour may elapse. Most Norwegian Elkhound bitches have a will-do-it-myself attitude but it pays to check on one in whelp quite often and to write down on the Growth Chart the arrival time of each puppy.

AFTER WHELPING

After the last puppy has been whelped, the bitch should have a clean-out or pop shot. Arrangements must be made ahead of time with the veterinarian to have the necessary dosage available. It must be administered under the veterinarian's supervision. The purpose of the shot is to cause contractions of the uterus to expel any remaining afterbirth, clots, or as occasionally happens, another puppy. It also tends to bring the bitch's milk down. The bitch can be taken outside to relieve herself, have a drink of water and a treat—ice cream, or whatever she likes—and then settle down in a clean whelping box with her new family.

Puppies that do not have the hang of nursing should be held close to the mother and gently encouraged to nurse. There is always one that seems unsure and crawls about, voicing his objection to the birthing process. Elkhound bitches usually are good mothers and should be left alone to care for their puppies. However, if they find that the human in attendance will assume much of the responsibility, they will lie back and take advantage of the situation.

GROWTH CHART

As each puppy is whelped and the mother is through cleaning him, he can be gently rubbed dry with a soft terry cloth and returned to his mother. He should be weighed and the information, including birth time, order of birth, sex, weight, other identifying information such as white markings, and any coloring applied for identification purposes, placed on the Growth Chart. The weight should be taken and recorded each day for the first three weeks, every seventh day for the next three weeks, and then every two weeks until the puppies are 12 weeks of age. It should be checked once a month after that.

A baby's scale is ideal for weighing puppies. A cloth liner can be used to keep the squirming puppies from slipping off. Caution should be taken to prevent a puppy from falling off the scale or table.

Weighing a puppy.

Other bits of information can be recorded on the Growth Chart: eyes opened, stood on all fours and barked are examples. This data provides a comparison between littermates as well as between litters. It gives a warning signal if one puppy is not gaining weight, crawling or developing normally.

The mother should be taken to the veterinarian for a checkup as soon as it is feasible. If the veterinarian does not take a vaginal smear slide to check for infection, the breeder should request one. Elkhounds are notorious for developing vaginal infections after whelping. If the culture shows the presence of bacteria, administration of medication can begin immediately.

Ordinarily the mother will lose much of her coat, beginning with the hair on her belly. The breeder should keep it cleared to prevent the puppies from ingesting it. After a few days, the mother will settle into a routine of eating, exercising and caring for her brood. Cranky puppies will be a signal to check the mother for a possible problem: an infection, not enough milk or a problem with her milk.

COLOR AT BIRTH

Norwegian Elkhound puppies are solid black at birth. Their coats are smooth and feel mouse-like. The only other color is the white that commonly appears on the toes and a chest blaze. The coats open up and turn silver almost overnight. The puppies resemble little bears with their black ears plastered to their heads, their blunt noses and their black legs. As they grow, the distinguishing Norwegian Elkhound markings begin to appear. By the time the puppies are three months old, they look like miniature Elkhounds. Their ears are up, although flop ears are common up to six months, especially when teething occurs. Occasionally, a puppy is a year old before his ears are strong. The breeder will be concerned about weak ears if the ears have not shown any signs of coming up by six to nine months. Quite often an ear will come up and then flop. More than likely both ears will become erect within a short time. Once the ear cartilage has a horizontal crease from being flopped, it usually does not stand erect.

By three months, the puppy's legs have turned silver-white and any white on his feet has blended in. His tail has curled over his back and will tighten in the next few weeks if it is going to be a tightly curled, center-set tail. The hair on the tail will

Three-week-old puppy.

become more profuse so that by four or five months it is fully coated. There is nothing more striking than a well-proportioned puppy in full puppy coat between the ages of 6 and 10 months.

Although the bitch carrying an average-sized litter may resemble a stuffed sausage, she will not have gained more than two or three pounds, assuming, of course, that she was not overfed. The size of her newborns depends on certain variables. The puppies are seldom less than four ounces or more than 18 ounces: usually the larger the number in the litter, the less the weight of each. For example, in a litter of eight, puppies will average 12 to 14 ounces. They will weigh four to eight ounces in a very large litter and up to 18 ounces in a litter of one or two. Although litters range from one puppy to 14 puppies, the average tends to be seven or eight. An occasional litter of 17 has been recorded. Regardless of the size of the litter, the puppies tend to weigh close to the ideal when they reach 12 weeks.

After the first day, the puppies will begin to gain weight and average a pound a week, weighing about eight pounds at six weeks, 16 pounds at three months and 30 pounds at six months. There is usually one puppy in each litter that is a little ahead or a little behind the rest in growth and development. But by the time he reaches adulthood, he usually weighs within the acceptable limits set forth in the standard.

AT SIX WEEKS

Puppies can be offered supplemental formula at about four weeks. Baby formula, goat's milk or milk replacer is acceptable. When the puppies begin to get the idea of eating, the formula may be mixed with baby cereal—the rice blend or mixed blend—into a thin gruel. It can be thickened and the amount increased as the puppies take to it. Pureed puppy food can be gradually substituted for the baby cereal so that by six weeks they are eating well enough to survive without their mother's milk. Most puppies will lick the bowl clean and then one will curl up in the bowl for a nap while the others take turns eating the cereal off each other. It happens in even the most well-bred families.

The formula/cereal puree can be gradually replaced by soaked and mashed puppy food and, as soon as the puppies can eat and digest it, a commercial puppy food should become their mainstay. Chances are the mother will have weaned her brood at five weeks. If she has not done it on her own, the

Eating cereal.

breeder should start the weaning process at six weeks by gradually increasing the time the mother is kept away from her puppies.

Veterinarians have their own theories as to when puppies should receive their first worming, immunizations, heart worm control or other treatment. A breeder always works closely with a veterinarian in administering a prescribed immunization/ health-care program. Proper health care of a litter of puppies is extremely expensive.

Six-week-old puppies like to play, eat, cuddle and sleep. It is important to talk to them, hold them and expose them to the sounds of the household. Puppies need the security of their litter as they are entering into the life of the household. It is better to wait until they are eight weeks old, at least, before they are placed in a new home.

Breeders who are looking for pick of the litter are reluctant to let a puppy go before they have made a definite evaluation. Puppies of a litter resulting from a researched and planned breeding are often so similar that subtle differences are not evident until the puppies mature. Puppies are still too wobbly to determine definitely which has the best movement. Growth spurts can cause even the finest puppy to appear awkward. It is not unusual for the most discerning of breeders to let the best one get away.

HOUSEBREAKING

Norwegian Elkhounds make excellent house dogs. An Elkhound can be trained to household rules and life styles and become a contributing member of the household. The secret to success lies in introducing those rules to the puppy at a very early age.

Many litters of puppies are raised on newspaper or newsprint in their whelping boxes. They are used to relieving themselves on the paper. One of the easiest ways to house-break a puppy is to use newspaper on the floor of the kitchen or other area where the puppy can be confined. Spread enough paper that the puppy will almost assuredly hit the paper when he urinates. Praise him outlandishly each time you see him accomplish this feat on the paper.

Gradually decrease the amount of paper, moving it closer to the door the puppy uses to go outside. In the meantime, let the puppy outside the first thing in the morning and immediately af-

Ch. Kamgaard Kountry Kinsman at 8 weeks.

ter he is fed. Let him out at set intervals during the day and before bed time. As he gets older and walks on leash, take him for walks, praising him each time he relieves himself. Watch for telltale signs that the puppy needs to go out. He may run to the door, whine or act restlessly. A great percentage of his accidents will be the owner's fault for not remembering to let the puppy out.

Use a command word when you send him outside to go, such as go wet, go potty or anything else just as ridiculous. You will not sound any sillier than a parent trying to toilet train a child and the results will be just as gratifying. Just as you praise the puppy each time he relieves himself when and where he is supposed to, you mildly scold him when he has an accident and put him in the area he is supposed to use. Many puppies look forward to a small biscuit when they have gone out and relieved themselves as expected. Although a puppy will have an occasional accident, especially when the owner forgets to let him out, many puppies are housebroken by the time they are 10 or 12 weeks old.

TOYS

A puppy, like a child, should be given toys to play with. There are federal regulations governing the manufacturing of children's toys—nontoxic, nonflammable, chokeproof. The same laws should hold true for pet toys. Unfortunately they do not. All too often a dog will chew off and swallow squeakers and other parts of an unfit toy. The multitude of objects that have been found in dogs' stomachs/intestines is astounding: buttons, squeakers, nylon stockings, plastic toys, bones, rawhide, furry toys, staples from cardboard cartons used for puppy beds, to name a few.

Commercially sterilized bones available at pet supply stores are usually safe. If the dog is able to crack the bone and chew off slivers, the bone should be discarded. Dogs enjoy supervised play with balls, Frisbees and other toys. Care must be exercised during play to teach the difference between play and aggression. Overagressiveness must not be tolerated. Just as important as supervised play is to have a large exercise area for running, digging and playing. Elkhounds are notorious for digging for moles or running halfway up a tree after squirrels. When they are tired, they like to jump onto the top of their flat-roofed house and spread out for a nap. The house should be placed in a shaded area.

SOCIALIZATION

A puppy needs to become a member of the household from the very beginning. He will get used to the vacuum cleaner, dishwasher, washer and lawnmower. He will soon learn which noise is the telephone and which is the doorbell. Some puppies will respond to sounds by barking and racing back and forth. The owner must decide whether he wants the puppy to bark at the telephone or the doorbell. The first time the dog responds by barking, the owner must respond by saying, "No!" if he prefers that the puppy does not bark in response to the sound.

Puppies enjoy company. Let children and adults pick the puppy up, play with him and pet him. Correct the puppy for jumping or chewing by saying, "No!" Puppies have a tendency to get rougher than a small child can manage. Children should be supervised when playing with a puppy. Unfortunately, the puppy gets blamed when there is a mishap.

Unless the puppy is in a secured area, he must be on a leash. Puppies that are raised with other animals—cats, dogs, goats, cows—usually accept them. However, letting a puppy run loose where other animals are loose is inviting trouble. Many breeders refuse to place a puppy in a home unless it is

Sirdal's Victoria's Morn at 12 weeks.

understood that the puppy will never be allowed to run loose except in his own secured enclosure.

A puppy should get used to riding in a car. There are times when he will be taken to the veterinarian for immunizations, grooming and checkups. If he is taught to ride in a crate in the car, the trips become pleasurable rather than frightful ordeals for him. The crate is for his safety in case of an accident, a sudden stop or a door or window left open inadvertently. No dog should ever be left in a closed car. The heat builds quickly and kills the dog almost immediately.

SUMMARY

Norwegian Elkhound bitches generally whelp naturally without complications. However, it is recommended that the veterinarian who usually treats the bitch be alerted when the bitch goes into labor. The veterinarian should be contacted immediately if a problem arises. The bitch should be administered a clean-out shot after whelping to remove possible afterbirth. She should be checked for infection within a few days of whelping.

Keeping a Growth Chart provides a comparison between litters as well as a quick reference and will be an invaluable reference for future litters.

Puppies need to be cuddled and talked to during their early stage of growth and development. They enjoy supervised play with dog-safe toys. Patience and understanding are essential to successful housebreaking. Socialization is as important to a puppy as nutrition, for both provide the nourishment that will help the puppy grow into a companion willing to lay down his life for his master.

CHAPTER SEVEN
SHOWING IN CONFORMATION

All breeds of dogs that are recognized by the AKC are classified into seven groups based on similarities in breed type and the breed's function. The seven groups of breeds are Sporting, Hound, Working, Terrier, Toy Breeds, Non-Sporting and Herding. The Norwegian Elkhound is a member of the Hound Group. There are 25 hound breeds in the group, including two varieties of Beagles and three varieties of Dachshunds.

In Norway, the Norwegian Elkhound is called *Elghund.* Translated into English, *Elghund* becomes Moose Dog. *Elg* is the Norwegian word for moose or elk. *Hund* is the Norwegian word for dog. When the Elkhound was introduced in England, the name was erroneously translated to *Elkhound.* The misnomer followed it to the United States and Canada. As a result of the error, the Elkhound was placed in the hound group. There have been several attempts by groups of Elkhound fanciers to rectify the mistake but to no avail. There was some discussion of forming a group for Northern Dogs but the impetus was not strong enough for recognition by AKC. Therefore, the Norwegian Elkhound, in his splendid coat of silver, literally, *runs with the hounds.*

CHAMPIONSHIP TITLE
Of the various reasons for showing an Elkhound in a conformation show, the obvious one is for the Elkhound to earn an AKC conformation championship title. The championship title designates a purebred dog that mirrors all the desirable traits of his breed according to the accepted breed standard. Breeders like to finish as many champions as possible from their kennels.

BLUE RIBBONS
Another reason for showing an Elkhound in conformation is

to win a blue ribbon. Blue ribbons are used for several—though not necessarily valid—reasons. First of all, a novice is impressed by a blue ribbon, thinking it means the dog must be good because he won. Therefore, sellers of dogs dangle blue ribbons to peddle puppies.

On a higher level of contrivance, blue-ribbon wins are used in advertising. Catchy phrases—such as never out of the blue, from a family of blue ribbon winners and generations of blue ribbon winners—make impressive advertising material; and, perhaps, the stratagem is to use blue ribbons to adorn an exhibitor's kennel area at a dog show.

CHOOSING A DOG TO SHOW

Every purebred Norwegian Elkhound is not necessarily conformation dog-show material. Although displaying a legacy of ideal breed traits is foremost, there are certain other prerequisite characteristics a dog must possess. Breed type is important; a square profile is important. But of utmost importance for a dog destined to a show career is for him to have a good attitude. Otherwise he should be left at home.

There are Elkhounds who tolerate being shown but lack enthusiasm for the sport. Then there are those who refuse to tolerate any of the noise, people, dogs and scents that are a part of every show. After several unsuccessful attempts at showing these Elkhounds, the owners should keep them at home and let them earn their keep as devoted companions. Too often an unhappy dog is pushed to the point where he will rebel by growling or snapping, in addition to making his handler look inept. There are many really beautiful purebred dogs living quality lives at home and, in the process, adding quality to the lives of their owners.

MATCHES

Matches are mini dog shows. They are held to give owners an opportunity to acquaint puppies and young dogs to the world of dog shows. Novice handlers as well as their dogs gain valuable experience. It is socialization on a grand scale. There are ribbons for the first four place winners—pink, brown, light green and gray—but no championship points are awarded. The blue, red, yellow and white ribbons are reserved for point shows.

Judges at matches are usually dog people aspiring to become AKC-approved judges. They follow the same judging procedure as in a point show. Matches provide excellent opportunities to familiarize dogs with simulated show conditions, as well as provide novice exhibitors with handling experience.

There are three types of matches: fun matches, B matches and A matches. However, the type should be of little consequence to the exhibitor. Fun matches are held for fun, to make money or to accommodate owners with young dogs that need socialization. B and A matches are held by clubs in an effort to meet AKC requirements. Clubs must hold successful matches to become AKC member clubs, to become show-giving clubs and to remain show-giving clubs.

TYPES OF SHOWS

Just as there are different types of matches there are different types of shows, benched and unbenched. The rules are different for each type. For instance, every dog that is 12 months and older, upon being entered in a benched show at which admission is charge, must be on his bench throughout the hours advertised as being show hours. Exceptions are when the dog is being groomed, shown or for an allowable hour before he is to be shown in breed or group competition. He may not be taken from the show building until the conclusion of the show.

Each dog entered in a benched show is assigned a space in the benching area. The bench itself is a raised platform designed much like a stall. All entries of one breed—Norwegian Elkhounds for example—are benched in a series of stalls in the same area. The dogs are fastened in their stalls by means of a special benching collar and chain. Exhibitors are not expected to bench dogs under 12 months of age. There are few benched shows being held in the United States because of the inconveniences incurred by exhibitors.

Unbenched shows are more popular. Many are held across the country each weekend. Exhibitors may arrive with their dogs at any time prior to their scheduled judging time and may leave at any time thereafter. The shows are held in fairground buildings, convention centers, gymnasiums, parking lots, football fields, race tracks or any other area approved by AKC as suitable for meeting the needs of the dogs, exhibitors and spectators.

SPECIALTIES

Unlike all-breed shows, Norwegian Elkhound specialties are

NEAA Specialty winner.

shows for Elkhounds only. NEAA holds an independent specialty every two years, hosted by a regional Elkhound club that holds a show the same week at the same location. Specialties are often held in hotel ballrooms or on the grounds of a hotel. Judges from Great Britain, Norway, or other Scandinavian countries are invited to pass opinion on the Elkhounds entered in national specialties.

In addition, regional clubs may hold Elkhound specialties in conjunction with an all-breed show. These shows are referred to as having a supported entry. In either case, the shows are considered point shows with the awarding of blue, red, yellow and white ribbons. It is considered a high honor to be proclaimed Best Elkhound in Specialty.

UNENTERED DOGS

There are no classes for puppies under six months of age at a point-giving show. In fact, many show-giving clubs often publish a notice on the premium list and on the show grounds stating that unentered dogs may not be brought onto the premises. It is not in the best interest of a puppy under six months of age to be taken into a dog-show situation. Even if he has had all the suggested immunizations, he will be unnecessarily subjected to a variety of viral infections, skin disorders and parasites, internal and external. Although Elkhound puppies are notably immune to illnesses, there is no reason to risk contact with an infected dog.

REGULAR CLASSES

The regular classes offered at an AKC show are Puppy, Twelve-to-Eighteen-Months specialty classes, Novice, Bred-by-Exhibitor, American-Bred, Open and Winners. Best of Breed provides additional competition. Winners Dog and Winners Bitch compete with the Best of Breed entries. If classes for veterans—seven years and over—are offered, the first place veterans compete in the Best of Breed circle.

PUPPY CLASS

The Puppy Class is for Elkhound puppies between six and twelve months that are not champions. Exact calculation is necessary when determining age, inclusive of the first day of the show. Even though some exhibitors enter puppies for the experience of showing, many win points from the puppy classes. The puppies are in full puppy coat, have their ears erect and possess the disarming aura that only a puppy can have.

Norwegian Elkhound specialties can offer a Twelve-To-Eighteen-Months Class. Again, strict age calculation is adhered to inclusive of the first day of the show. An advantage to showing in this class is that Elkhounds in this age bracket are in between being puppies and adults—much like adolescents. They appear very leggy and have not developed in the chest. They are able to compete with other Elkhounds on the same level of development and do not look as awkward as they sometimes do when compared to a more mature dog.

NOVICE CLASS

An Elkhound of any age may be entered in Novice. Wins

rather than age stipulations determine eligibility. If the Elkhound has won three first places in Novice, a first place in Bred-by-Exhibitor, American-Bred or Open classes, he may not be entered in the Novice Class. The number of entries in Novice at Norwegian Elkhound specialty shows far exceeds the number entered in the Novice Class at regular all-breed shows. One reason is that there are usually more Elkhounds entered in a specialty. Exhibitors often have more than one dog entered; therefore, they enter each dog in a different class so that they can show their own dogs.

BRED-BY-EXHIBITOR CLASS

The Bred-by-Exhibitor Class is the showcase for breeders of Norwegian Elkhounds but there are eligibility requirements. Elkhounds must be at least six months of age, not champions, and owned or co-owned by the person or spouse of the person who is one of the breeders of record. Dogs individually registered in the AKC Stud Book but whelped in Canada are also eligible.

When an Elkhound is entered in the Bred-by Class, he must be shown by the breeder or a member of the immediate family. To win points from this class is a tribute to the breeder.

AMERICAN-BRED CLASS

The American-Bred Class is for Elkhounds at least six months of age that are not champions and that were whelped in the United States. Few Elkhounds are entered in American-Bred at a regular all-breed show. However, the classes are larger at Elkhound specialties. The advantage of entering this class is that the classes are usually small, thus allowing a better opportunity for a blue ribbon and a chance to go to the winners circle.

OPEN CLASS

Any Elkhound at least six months of age can enter the Open Class. Elkhounds that have been imported from foreign countries and registered with AKC are required to show in the Open Class regardless of age. The Open Class is usually the largest class, even at an all-breed show. More often than not the winners are chosen from the Open Class. Whether this is coincidental or whether the better Elkhounds are entered in Open is hard to say. It depends on the individual show and entry.

WINNERS CLASS

The Winners Class is divided by sex. The undefeated winners of each of the classes compete with each other for the championship points. Therefore, there is a Winners Dog and a Winners Bitch, providing there were dog and bitch entries and that ribbons were not withheld for lack of merit or other reasons.

First place winners of each of the classes enter the ring and line up in the reverse order in which they were judged, unless the judge stipulates differently. The winner of this class is given a purple ribbon and is awarded championship points. The second place winner who was defeated in his regular class by the winner enters the ring so that the judge may choose a Reserve Winner. The Reserve Winner receives a blue and white ribbon but no championship points.

BEST OF BREED

The Winners Dog and Winners Bitch, in addition to all entered Elkhounds who have earned a championship title, compete for Best of Breed. If Veteran Classes were offered, the winners of those classes also compete for Best of Breed. After the judge chooses the Best of Breed winner, he declares either the Winners Dog or the Winners Bitch as Best of Winners. It is possible for the Best of Winners to also be Best of Breed. Last of all, the judge chooses a Best of Opposite Sex to Best of Breed. It is possible to choose the Winners Dog or Bitch as Best of Opposite.

CHAMPIONSHIP POINTS

Championship points are calculated on the number of dogs entered for points in dogs and the number of bitches entered for points in bitches. Best of Winners receives the higher number if there is a difference. Points vary by geographic location. The AKC has divided the United States into 12 geographic divisions, calculating points on a ratio of the number of Norwegian Elkhounds being registered.

NON-REGULAR CLASSES

Non-regular classes are judged the same way regular classes are judged. The difference is that no championship points are awarded. The only first place non-regular class winners eligible to compete in Best of Breed competition are the first place Veteran dog and Veteran bitch. Other non-regular classes include

Best of Breed.

Brace, Team, Stud Dog and Brood Bitch. They do not compete in Best of Breed competition. However, they compete at the breed level for Best Brace, Stud Dog, etc. The winner then competes at the group level. Group winners compete for Best Brace, etc., in Show.

Brace and Team classes may be offered at all-breed shows as well as specialties. Stud Dog and Brood Bitch classes are held at specialties. Specialties also offer Sweepstakes, Futurities and Veteran Sweepstakes. All of these classes are treated as non-regular classes.

ENTRY FORMS

Premium lists are available from show superintendents for all scheduled dog shows. The premium list is accompanied by entry forms for the show being announced. The premium list gives the location of the show, the show date, entry fee and closing date for entering the show. The judging panel for all breeds and classes is included. If any trophies are being offered for Elkhounds, the donations and donors are listed.

Each entry form must be completely and correctly filled out. Breed refers to Norwegian Elkhound. That information is followed by the sex of the Elkhound being entered. The name of the show class is next, followed by specific information on the Elkhound. The dog's full registered name, AKC number, date of birth and place of birth, namely USA, Canada or Foreign, must be noted.

All the necessary information can be found on the dog's registration certificate. The name of the breeder of the dog, the dog's sire and dam and the actual owners are to be included on the entry form. The address and telephone number should be printed at the bottom along with the entrant's signature. A check for the appropriate fee is to accompany the form.

The form and check must be mailed in time to reach the superintendent before the closing date. Occasionally, a show has a limited entry. Unless the entry reaches the superintendent before the limit is reached, the form will be returned. Many superintendents offer entry services and accept FAX entries.

ACCESSORIES FOR SHOWING

Many exhibitors have special accessories for preparing their Elkhounds for the show ring even though Norwegian Elkhounds are to be shown in their natural state. A good bath and brushing are all that is necessary for grooming a dog for the show. Trimming whiskers is optional. More and more exhibitors are leaving the whiskers on, although Elkhounds entered in the Best of Breed competition usually have their whiskers trimmed.

A special collar and lead are needed for showing in conformation. Many veteran exhibitors use a properly fitted choke collar and nylon lead. Heavy leather or chain collars are inappropriate as are heavy leather leads. The Elkhound may not enter the ring with tags or other identification on his collar. For that matter, exhibitors should not wear obvious identification either.

It is necessary to have a crate in which to keep an Elkhound during the day of the show. It is well to teach an Elkhound to stay in a crate. Crates are useful at home, for traveling and for crating at a dog show. An Elkhound requires a crate large enough to allow him to stand comfortably and to be able to turn around. All shows provide a grooming area where exhibitors can set their dogs' crates and other belongings while waiting for the time for their dogs to be judged.

Sometimes exhibitors use bait when showing their dogs. Although it is not necessary to *bait* an Elkhound to get expression during showing, many exhibitors use bits of liver or other tidbits. The exhibitor should carry the bait in a pocket for convenience during actual judging and not let it interfere with the judge's examination of the dog.

TRAVELING TO THE SHOW

A crate is necessary for traveling to shows. Elkhounds are safer and more comfortable while crated. Problems arise when exhibitors leave dogs crated in cars during hot weather. It takes only a few minutes for a dog to become overheated. It is better to plan to carry the dog's crate into the show building or to a shady area while waiting for the scheduled judging.

If the show is too far from home to travel back and forth in time for judging, staying in a motel overnight is advantageous. Motel managers insist that dogs are crated rather than loose in motel rooms. Again, the crate is convenient for the safety of the dog and it prevents him from damaging motel furnishings by chewing or soiling. Show sites and motels that will accept dogs are becoming increasingly difficult to find because of the carelessness of many exhibitors.

Dogs can travel for several hours without being exercised but they should not be expected to go much longer before being

Elkhound in a crate.

taken out of their crates to relieve themselves. The courteous thing to do when a dog defecates in a public place is to pick up the feces and dispose of it. Shows provide exercise pens as a convenience for exhibitors to exercise their dogs. They are generally marked for dogs or for bitches. Implements for picking up the refuse are usually available but most exhibitors carry their own *pooper-scoopers*.

JUDGING SCHEDULES

It is the responsibility of the exhibitor to be present at ringside with his Elkhound before the scheduled time of judging. A ring steward works at each ring to aid the judge by giving out identification armbands and calling exhibitors into the ring for judging. The steward is not required to page an exhibitor when his turn comes nor is the judge required to wait for an exhibitor.

Seasoned exhibitors find it helpful to observe the ring procedure of the judge before showing to the judge. They watch his procedural pattern and the way he goes over each dog.

Getting expression.

When it is time for judging, the ring steward calls each class. After the judge has checked the armbands of the class against the listing in his judge's book, he will ask the exhibitors in the class to gait their dogs around the ring. Then he will examine the first dog in line.

When a judge examines an Elkhound, he begins by looking at the overall type. Next, he looks at the head and the teeth/bite. Often a judge will ask the exhibitor to show him the Elkhound's teeth/bite. Elkhounds can easily be trained to stand patiently for the examination, allowing the exhibitor to open the dog's mouth so that the judge can see the dog's teeth.

The judge will check the Elkhound's coat for undercoat and hardness. Many judges lift the Elkhound's tail, which is not really necessary but they think it is the correct thing to do. Either the Elkhound's tail is tightly curled or it is not. A tightly curled tail will leave a telltale nest where it rests against the dog's back.

After the initial examination, the judge will want to see the Elkhound give expression. An Elkhound will usually respond by pricking his ears while waiting for the coveted tidbit. Often the exhibitor will throw the bait in front of the dog to encourage the dog to prick his ears. The standard states that the Elkhound only has to prick his ears one time for the judge. A happy, well-adjusted Elkhound keeps his ears up most of the time in the show ring.

Finally the judge will ask the exhibitor to move the dog in a specified pattern. If the exhibitor has been watching, he knows what the judge wants him to do. At any rate, the judge expects the exhibitor to be able to follow directions.

COURTESIES

The exhibitor should thank the judge for his opinion regardless of the placement he receives. If the exhibitor disagrees with the judge, he must remember that he paid for an opinion. If he feels that the judge did an inadequate job, he need not enter under him again. *Badmouthing* judges seems to be a favorite pastime for some people. However, it tends to discredit the "mouther" more than the "mouthee."

Judges work on a tight schedule, allowing two to three minutes to judge each dog. They do not have time to chat. Other than a courteous response to a judge's directions, there is no time for conversation. Most judges will take time to answer questions during a pause in their schedules.

It is proper protocol for the other exhibitors to congratulate the handler of the winner of their class. Novice exhibitors should stay and watch the rest of the Elkhound judging and group judging. Watching the judging of other breeds will further their knowledge of exhibiting and judging.

Trophy cards are given at the same time ribbons are awarded. If the exhibitor would like to have a picture of his Elkhound's win with the judge, the ring steward will call the photographer. The Best of Breed Norwegian Elkhound is eligible to show in the Hound Group. Norwegian Elkhounds have done well in conformation shows in the United States. They often place in the Hound Group and it is not unusual for them to win Best in Show.

AFTER-SHOW PRECAUTIONS

All dogs are required to be properly immunized before they are brought to a dog show. However, there will be dogs there who are carriers of every disease, bacteria, virus and parasite imaginable. Exhibitors can lessen their chances of carrying problems into their homes, possibly transmitting an unwanted parasite or virus to other pets at home, by following a few simple rules of hygiene. By taking off their shoes before entering the house and immediately washing their hands with soap, exhibitors can eliminate some of the potential problems. Maintaining a clean and sanitary environment for dogs at home and providing proper diet and exercise will aid in the control of other health problems.

SUMMARY

There are show-giving kennel clubs located in many areas of the United States, making it possible for those who want to exhibit their Elkhounds to enter shows on a regular basis. Showing a dog can become an expensive hobby, depending on the depth of involvement. It can be a satisfying and worthwhile adventure as long as it remains a sport and is enjoyed by both the dog and his handler.

CHAPTER EIGHT
TRAINING A NORWEGIAN ELKHOUND

Norwegian Elkhounds are independent by nature. They are also highly intelligent. The combination of the two traits results in a breed of dog that will rule the roost if not trained at an early age. Dressed in their beautiful silver-gray coats, they portray a stylish arrogance that often humbles the owner who had every intention of training his Elkhound. But trained they must be if they are to be enjoyed as happy manageable members of the family.

TRAINING A PUPPY

The concept of early puppy training is not new. Many training clubs offer a kindergarten approach to training. Although training begins as early as two months of age, it is more like organized play during which time a puppy establishes a bond with his master and learns a few basic commands. Puppy training can become the basis for a more rigid obedience training program when the puppy is six months old.

A Norwegian Elkhound puppy is typical of puppies of many other breeds. He likes to chew, especially expensive shoes and furniture. His needle-like teeth cling to shoelaces, pant legs and anything else that catches his attention as he interacts with his surroundings. He likes to play in his water bowl, then leave a trail of wet paw prints on the once-clean floor. Only the irresistible charm of being a puppy keeps him from being sentenced to the great outdoors to grow up untrained.

Early training includes teaching the puppy to walk on lead, play with toys, walk through doors, walk up and down steps and recognize the basic commands of sit, stand, down, come and stay. The puppy learns to walk in the heel position and to retrieve an object thrown for his benefit. As the puppy learns the

Three-month-old Norweigian Elkhound puppy.

basic commands, he learns to react to his trainer's tone of voice and body language. In time, he transfers the isolated skills he learns in training to his pattern of living with his family and his behavior becomes more acceptable.

COLLAR AND LEASH

Soft, round, leather, buckle collars or lightweight, metal, slip-on collars are appropriate for training. A slip-on collar should be put on the puppy with the free ring extending through the other ring on the top over the puppy's back and to his right. Heavy, metal chain collars, wide leather collars or spike collars are inappropriate at any time.

A puppy can be introduced to a collar when he is three or four weeks old to become accustomed to having it around his neck. A good time for him to wear a lightweight slip-on collar is while he is being socialized, but no training should take place at this early age. The collar must never be left on the puppy when he is put back in the whelping box or pen. It is too easy for the collar to become entangled on something, risking the possibility of choking the puppy. Becoming accustomed to wearing a collar is not to be confused with regular puppy training that begins when the puppy is eight weeks old.

A puppy should not be expected to tolerate wearing a collar and leash immediately. The owner should let him wear the collar and leash, allowing the leash to drag around until he ignores it. Only then should the owner pick up the leash to begin training. From the very beginning of training, the puppy should be taught to walk in heel position on the owner's left. The collar and leash should be worn by the puppy only during training periods. Otherwise, the puppy might accidentally entangle the collar and become injured, or worse yet, hanged.

Collars have a tendency to break the tips off the guard hair around the dog's neck. In addition, wide collars wear the coat down and cause the undercoat to mat if the collar is worn full

Correct position for a training collar.

Becoming accustomed to a collar and leash.

time. When the collar is removed, there is a telltale ring around the collar. Wearing the collar only for training purposes causes no problem with the coat.

STAND COMMAND

The first command to teach in puppy training is *Stand*. With a firm hold on the puppy, the owner, who is in a kneeling position, should put the puppy in a standing position. The owner uses his right hand to hold the collar below the puppy's neck and his left hand, palm down, to support the loin area below the puppy. A slight forward pressure on the collar and a firm verbal command—*Stand*—help the puppy understand what is expected of him.

If the owner's left palm faces upward, the puppy may get the feeling he is being grabbed rather than supported and will react accordingly. If the palm faces down, it makes it unlikely that an impatient owner will inadvertently hurt the puppy in the loin area.

Praise is important each time the exercise is practiced. A simple *Good Puppy* is all it takes. Most puppies will work to please their owners for nothing more than a word of praise, a pat on the head or a scratch behind the ears. Many puppies appreciate a well-timed tidbit. Some newer methods of obedience training use tidbits as rewards in the training process.

Teaching a puppy to stand.

Teaching a puppy to sit

Teaching a puppy to go down.
Step 1.

Teaching a puppy to go down.
Step 2.

One of the fringe benefits of this exercise is that the owner develops good muscle tone in his legs from doing deep knee bends. For those not interested in body beautiful, it is easier to kneel on one or both knees while teaching the stand. The puppy enjoys it more when his owner gets right down on his level.

TEACHING A PUPPY TO SIT

The *Sit* is taught from the *Stand* position. The owner tells the puppy to sit. At the same time, he lifts the collar from above the puppy with his right hand and simultaneously tucks the puppy's hind legs under the puppy with the left hand, putting him in a sitting position. It is important to tuck the puppy's legs under him instead of pushing down on his hindquarters, a practice that could injure his hips. Reinforcing the puppy with praise, *Good Dog,* each time he does the exercise helps him remember the training as a pleasant experience.

This exercise should follow the stand and can be accomplished by the owner from a kneeling position. The puppy will weigh between 15 and 20 pounds at this age. Even though the owner has the advantage of more brawn, the puppy outweighs him in exuberance. Patience prevails.

TEACHING A PUPPY TO LIE DOWN

It takes a bit longer to teach a puppy the down command because he does not always understand what it is his owner wants him to do. While the puppy is still in a sitting position, the owner, with his palms facing upward, gently lifts first one front paw and then the other, letting the puppy's paws rest on the owner's palms. At the same time he lets his left arm cross over the puppy's shoulders to gently help the puppy down with the left arm and elbow and tells the puppy, *Down!* As he lowers the puppy to the floor, he uses his palms for support rather than for grasping the puppy's paws. The owner must resist the inclination to grasp the puppy's paws, letting the puppy rest his paws on the owner's palms instead.

Teaching the down exercise takes a lot of praise and patience. Occasionally, the puppy becomes frightened and feels he is being punished by being told emphatically *Down!* That is why praise is important and necessary to encourage the puppy to remain in a down position.

Here again, the owner can accomplish more from a kneeling position. It is not uncommon when introducing the down to the puppy that owner and puppy both end up in a down position to the utter delight of the puppy.

TEACHING A PUPPY TO SIT FROM THE DOWN POSITION

As a matter of routine, the sit command follows the down position. The owner tells the puppy to sit. At the same instant, the owner lifts upward on the puppy's collar with his right hand. With his left hand, the owner holds the rear in position. Again, praise is in order for the puppy.

With a slight forward pull on the collar using the right hand and an emphatic stand command, the owner puts the puppy into the stand position. As before, there is a simultaneous lifting movement under the loin with the left hand, palm down.

The stand-sit-down-sit sequence of commands and exercises is used three or four times during each short session. The puppy soon learns the routine and is eager for the praise and attention he receives from his owner. Each session takes no longer than five minutes and can be repeated at intervals during the day. Each verbal command should be given only once for each lesson but it must be given emphatically. A repetitive *Sit-Sit-Sit* loses its meaning. In a few short weeks the puppy will be happily responding to the verbal commands of his owner without the accompanying tugs and lifts.

Occasionally, a puppy overreacts to praise and becomes hard to control. In such cases, a simple pat or quiet *Good Dog* will suffice. Dogs will do only what is expected of them. And expectations must be reinforced with love and firmness.

A well-trained puppy is a delightful member of the family. He enjoys romping without his collar and leash but walks and responds appropriately when walking on leash with his owner. He understands and responds to an ever-expanding vocabulary of words, signals, and body language. Most of all, he has bonded with his owner, devoting his life for a mere pat on the head.

OBEDIENCE SHOWS

Training a puppy to respond to a collar and leash gives him the basis for showing in matches and shows, whether conformation or obedience. Owners have often been successful in showing the same Norwegian Elkhound in conformation and obedience. Many of them use a different type of leash for obedience, a signal to the dog that he will be doing obedience exercises.

Elkhound owners are a proud lot. As they parade their well-trained charges down the street, heads turn, cars stop, little kids want to cuddle, big kids cross to the other side of the street, and the questions begin: "What did you breed to get him? Is he a husky? Will he bite? What's he good for? Where can I get one?" Most owners take the time to answer all questions, expounding on the virtues of owning an Elkhound—and, how easy they are to train!

Many owners of Norwegian Elkhounds take their dogs to obedience school for help in learning how to control their dogs. Now and then a dog responds so well to the training that the owner decides to continue working in obedience. It is not long before the owner and the Elkhound are ready for their first obedience trial.

To be successful in doing obedience work, it is necessary to have a happy well-adjusted Elkhound. Temperament is the single most important trait. Shy, skittish dogs are unsuitable. Another important factor is for the dog to have good hips if he is expected to do the required jumping for Open and Utility work. If there is a question about the status of a dog's hips, a veterinarian can arrange for an x-ray to determine whether the dog can withstand training involving jumping.

Norwegian Elkhounds can do well in obedience training. However, all owners are not successful in training their Elkhounds. The owner must understand his dog. If the Elkhound discovers that he can outsmart his owner by refusing to compromise, he will certainly do so. The formula for the successful training of an Elkhound in obedience is for the owner to know and understand his dog, to be firm without being harsh and to have the patience of Job.

Elkhounds can score consistently high at all levels of training. They learn the exercises quickly but seem to deliberately miss an exercise just to challenge their owners. For those who train their Elkhounds as a matter of control, a happy, willing worker is satisfaction enough. For those who train for high scores, it is a test of patience at every turn.

OBEDIENCE TITLES

There are six obedience titles available: Companion Dog (CD), Companion Dog Excellent (CDX), Utility Dog (UD), Tracking Dog (TD), Tracking Dog Excellent (TDX) and the newest title, Obedience Trial Champion (O.T.CH). A combination of titles is possible. For example, a dog with a UDT has earned his Utility Dog and Tracking Dog titles or a CDX-TD is a Companion Dog Excellent with a Tracking title. After a dog earns an obedience title, the title becomes part of his registered name. An example is Ch. Crafdal Tryglikk Takki CDX, a Norwegian Elkhound that earned his Companion Dog Excellent title.

COMPANION DOG

For an Elkhound to earn a CD he must be able to heel on and off lead. A typical Elkhound will look more like he is out for a Sunday stroll when being trained by a novice. For Elkhounds being trained by a seasoned trainer, an Elkhound can score perfectly on these exercises.

Other exercises include heeling fast and slow, Sit, Recall, Stay, Down, Stand for Examination, and the long sits and downs. The name of the obedience class for dogs working toward a CD title is called the Novice Class. There are Novice A and Novice B classes, depending on eligibility requirements as set forth in the AKC's Obedience Regulations.

COMPANION DOG EXCELLENT

The exercises for Open Classes or the Companion Dog Excellent title build upon the CD exercises. Dogs not quite ready for Open can be entered in a Graduate Novice, a non-regular class, if it is offered. Many owners like to keep their Elkhounds actively showing while they work on an advanced title. Therefore, there are divisions of classes for which dogs may qualify. In addition to Graduate Novice, dogs may enter in Open A or Open B, based on prior wins and the AKC regulations.

Additional exercises in working toward a CDX require the dog to retrieve the dumbbell thrown on the flat—floor or ground— retrieve the dumbbell thrown over the high jump and jump over the broad jump. The Recall has been advanced by requiring the dog to Drop on Recall at a signal from his owner. Three-minute-long sits and five-minute-long downs are done with the owner out of sight of the dog.

It is not unusual for an owner to return to the ring after a five-minute out of sight *Down* to be told that his dog failed the exercise. How can that be? He is still in the same *Down* position. And he looks so innocent! But while the owner was out of sight, his dog visited or crawled over to his neighbor or entertained the onlookers to while away the time. He knew he had better be back in position before his owner returned. This is an example of an Elkhound's innate intelligence.

UTILITY DOG

As with the CDX, the Utility Dog exercises are more complex. The dog is required to work by owner hand signals, do directed jumping over a high jump and a bar jump, and retrieve handler-scented articles from a collection of articles placed on the floor. The Utility Class may be divided into Utility A and Utility B in accordance with AKC regulations. Even though the UD requires concentration and many tedious hours of work, Norwegian Elkhounds can excel.

TRACKING DOG

Tracking a Norwegian Elkhound requires an understanding of how an Elkhound scents. When out hunting the Elkhound often keeps his head up to scent, using his sight as much as scenting. In a tracking test, he will follow the track with his head up or down but tends to lower it as he nears the leather glove that is used in tracking tests. It is not unusual for an Elkhound to earn his CDX-TD before he qualifies for a UD. The Tracking Dog Excellent (TDX) title is an extension of the TD. Ch. Crafdal Thor Mhor's Paulette UDT earned her tracking title in 1977 at age 10. She is one of only a few Elkhounds that have attained a championship and Utility Dog Tracker status.

One of the most rewarding experiences that comes from work-ing an Elkhound toward a TD or TDX is the bonding that takes place between the dog and his master. The nature of the train-ing allows a certain amount of freedom to the dog, giving him the opportunity to exhibit his intelligence and demonstrate his ability to understand what is expected of him. A mutual trust is formed between dog and master.

OBEDIENCE TRIAL CHAMPION

The Obedience Trial Championship was first offered July 1, 1977. Twenty-three days later, the first degree was conferred on Moreland's Golden Tonka UD, a Golden Retriever, owned and shown by Russell H. Klipple of Parkeford, Pennsylvania. To qualify for the O.T.CH title, a dog must earn 100 points by plac-ing first in Open B and Utility. Second places count for points also.

The first Norwegian Elkhound to attain O.T.CH was Ameri-

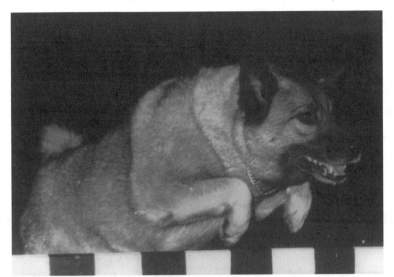

An Elkhound going over the Bar Jump.

An Elkhound going over the Broad Jump.

Paulette in tracking gear.

can/Canadian OTCH Camalot's Bella Tigra owned by Donald and Marilyn Rotier, of Minneapolis, Minnesota, shown by Don Rotier. American/Canadian OTCH Camalot's Trully Ayla, also owned, trained, and shown by Rotier, was the second Norwegian Elkhound O.T.CH. Tigra attained her title on November 23, 1980, at three years and nine months of age. Ayla finished her title on April 5, 1986, at age four years and 10 months. Both of Rotier's Elkhounds have numerous High in Trial wins to their credit.

Am. Can. OTCH Camalot's Bella Tigra.

Am. Can. OTCH Camalot's Trully Ayla.

TYPES OF SHOWS

There are obedience fun matches available to acquaint novice owners and dogs with a simulated show situation. Obedience training clubs, like kennel clubs, give AKC-sanctioned matches as part of their requirements to become and remain show-giving clubs.

Obedience shows may be held indoors or outdoors. Often they are held in conjunction with a conformation show. And just as often as not they are held in barns, ballrooms, parking lots and gymnasiums.

The Norwegian Elkhound Association of America includes an obedience trial at its national specialties. Classes are offered for each level of competition.

An Elkhound in Heel position.

QUALIFYING SCORE

In an obedience trial, the judge may use a score sheet for each dog and handler. As the dog completes an exercise, the judge writes down the score in the judge's book. At the end of the class, the judge computes the total score for each dog. The dogs and handlers are competing against a perfect score of 200; therefore, they are in competition with themselves. However, scoring high in trial is the aspiration of those handlers who devote considerable time and effort to training their Elkhounds.

A qualifying score of 170 points out of 200, including more than 50 percent of the available points in each exercise, is called a leg. Three legs are needed to earn each title. Each leg must be under a different judge. Non-regular classes such as Graduate Novice do not offer legs or titles; however, prizes are often awarded for first through fourth place in each class. Other prizes include the coveted Highest Scoring Dog and Highest Combined Score, the combined scores of Open B and Utility.

Unlike conformation shows, handlers are not allowed to use bait in the ring to encourage their dogs to do well. There is nothing more gratifying than to see a Norwegian Elkhound eagerly obeying each command given by his master, showing his true bold and energetic spirit.

EQUIPMENT

The only accessories needed for working in beginning obedience training are a training or slip collar and a six-foot lead. As the dog moves into training for the CD, the equipment needs are greater. A dumbbell the size comfortable for the Elkhound to hold is needed for retrieving. Broad jumps and high jumps are needed for the jumping exercises.

When the dog begins Utility training, a bar jump and a set of scent articles are added to his obedience paraphernalia. Tracking needs are minimal—a 20-foot to 40-foot lead, a tracking harness, and an old glove and the dog is in business. Starting flags and turn markers are used when training a dog for tracking but the markers are not used in a tracking test.

AGILITY

Many Elkhounds are earning titles in agility. Members of the Greater Milwaukee Norwegian Elkhound Association (GMNEA) are especially active as a group. The Elkhounds shown at team obedience practice are, left to right, TNT Christopher Robyns, Ch. Vikiro's Silverado, Ch. Vikiro's Bright Flame, Ch. Vikiro's Not A Pull Toy, Ch. Midnight Sun's Grin N Berrit, Ch. Midnight Sun's Heartlight, Ch. ThomThom's Joker's Wild, ThomThom Arctic Nite Sir Gus, and Ch. Travela's Ericka.

Team obedience practice.

Ch. Midnight Sun's Grin N Berrit, CD, CGC, Ag I, Ag II, AD.

The first Elkhound to earn an NCDA agility title was Ch. Midnight Sun's Grin N Berrit CD, CGC, AgI, AgII, AD. To add to her accolades, she was the first hound to earn an Agility II title, as well as being the only Elkhound to have both NCDA and USDAA agility titles.

ENTRY FORMS

The same procedure is used for entering obedience trials and conformation shows. The form must be filled out completely and correctly. It must be mailed with a check and received by the show superintendent before the closing date. If a dog is inadvertently entered in the wrong class, his score will not count toward a title.

JUDGING SCHEDULES

Although obedience judges follow the printed schedule as set by the show superintendent, they tend to be accommodating to handlers with conflicts. When there are two judges and a handler has dogs entered in more than one class, one of the judges will usually allow the handler to show out of turn. It is the responsibility of the handler, however, to apprise the judge of the situation.

SUMMARY

An untrained Norwegian Elkhound can be as intolerable as any undisciplined animal or human. But with tender loving care and a firm hand, he becomes a trustworthy guardian and a friend. He takes his place as a functioning member of the household, alerting the family to the ring of the telephone and the door bell, greeting visitors and ushering them to a chair and picking up crumbs that were mistakenly dropped on the floor. He gives a warning growl when he hears an unusual noise during the night. He is always there when his owner needs a sympathetic listener or a foot warmer on a cold night.

ELKHOUNDS IN OBEDIENCE
by Donald Rotier

Training a Norwegian Elkhound for competitive obedience work has many things in common with training the traditional competitive obedience breeds. This common ground lies in the need to train with a thoughtful approach, keeping the needs of the dog in the forefront. Training smarter is more important than training harder and, if the training is thoughtful, you should be able to minimize training errors. You are always in the process of teaching the dog something and training errors usually teach the wrong thing, often confuse and, most likely, lessen the dog's motivation.

While the Elkhound is not noted for being in the winning circle at obedience competitions, only a part of this is breed-related. Just as some very good Elkhounds do not have the spark to be candidates for top competition in the breed ring, some Elkhounds will exhibit a degree of independence that will make training for competitive obedience extremely difficult. My first Obedience Trial Champion, Tigra, was this type of dog, so even this trait can be overcome. Other individuals will show a willingness to please and the desire to learn. It is at this point that too many handlers fail to take advantage of this and set low standards in the belief that the Elkhound is just not capable of top obedience competition. The typical Norwegian Elkhound is indeed more independent than a Golden Retriever or Border Collie; however, setting low standards for the team becomes a self-fulfilling prophesy. A little more effort and a lot of care can build a true obedience competitor.

Getting a dog ready for a career in obedience competition is not a matter of simply getting the dog to follow your commands. This is not roll over and play dead trick dog training. While teaching the dog to perform certain exercises is necessary, the big picture is about a handler and a dog learning to operate as a precision team with the handler providing the knowledge and patience to create this team. It is about motivating the dog to the point where the dog wants to work and is concentrating on doing his best. It is about building the dog's confidence in each exercise to the point where the dog knows that he can do what is expected at all phases of an exercise. This is not a simple process and accomplishing these objectives will involve years of effort with any dog. With the typical Norwegian Elkhound, more effort will be needed on the subject of motivation than with more typical obedience breeds.

One essential ingredient in creating and maintaining a high level of motivation is minimizing the number of training errors you make during the teaching process. If you are just starting in the sport of obedience, it is important that you work with a good instructor. Finding one is not easy and not always possible. Go to obedience trials in your area and use the show catalog to find competitors from your area. After watching these individuals work their dogs, ask where they train. Usually, once people are finished competing for the day, they are happy to provide this information. Since you and your dog are both learning a new sport, and you are the only one in the team that can read, it becomes your job to do just that. Read several training books and, if feasible, go to training seminars. The techniques you learn will have to be adapted to the needs of your dog and to your capabilities as a trainer. Keep in mind that most people writing books and presenting seminars are working with dogs that are initially more motivated than your Elkhound. I say initially because you can build motivation through proper recognition of your dog's efforts.

Most of your classroom efforts will be spent in introducing new exercises and in evaluation of the results of your previous week's training efforts. At home the most important task you have is to plan your training sessions such that you are trying to solve one problem at a time and motivate the dog while solving the problem. In general when you begin to make progress on one problem another problem will surface. Try to solve big problems while only creating little ones and, above all, never correct conflicting errors. As an example, correcting a dog's lagging and then, shortly thereafter, correcting for forging can raise havoc with motivation.

Decide before training what problem you are trying to solve. If other problems show up, handle them later and, preferably, in a separate training session. At the start of your training, you will be putting most of the learning pressure on your dog through lead corrections or other physical actions. It is essential that the dog be praised as this pressure is applied. Later, as motivation builds, the dog will begin to put pressure on itself. The dog will be trying to do what it understands you want. This effort alone must be praised and the praise must be genuine. If you feel foolish telling a dog how wonderful it is and doing this in public, you will not be a successful dog trainer.

The foundation of all obedience work is the heeling done in the Novice classes. If your dog is a little slower in relating to this exercise than other dogs in your class, do not relax your standards to rush your entry into Novice competition. You will be building your skyscraper on a foundation of quicksand. Open and Utility classes depend on a dog that wants to work and the on-lead Novice work is the best place to build this motivation. If you are working with your dog as a team member and praising his efforts, boredom should not be a problem. If, however, you are bored, your dog will sense this. If you are having fun, or at least acting like it, your dog will also sense this.

As you get into the more advanced exercises, you may be tempted to make the excuse, "My dog knows this exercise but is just being stubborn." Most of the time you will be wrong! The Utility scent article exercise, for example, is extremely delicate for the green dog. Air motion across the article pack, ringside noises, distracting scents, too much scent, etc., can all present major problems to the new Utility dog. The dog needs 10 or 20 Utility legs before confidence is fully developed. If errors are made and you assume the dog is being stubborn, you can destroy the dog's confidence for months by the wrong correction techniques in training. The more complex an exercise, the more you must assume the dog needs guidance because, at this stage in training, the dog is probably trying.

When you take on the task of training your Norwegian Elkhound, remember that your most important training tool is located under your hat. You are the primary thinking member of this team. Do not let a lack of patience and planning detract from the progress of the team. Above all, do not accept the notion that an Elkhound cannot win in obedience competition.

CHAPTER NINE

THE ELKHOUND AS A HUNTING DOG

There was a time in the early history of Scandinavia when its rugged terrain abounded with herds of big game. Elg, a term used interchangeably for elk or moose, roamed the mountainous areas eking out a meager existence. Often times, their numbers became more than the sparsely vegetated land could support. So the herds ventured to the lower country in their never-ending quest for survival.

And then Nature would take things in her own hands to balance the fragile laws of the universe. History records at least one lamentable period in which the wolves ravaged the Norse country, killing for sustenance, and then for the thrill of killing.

Almost as though playing a game of musical chairs came the huge bears, parlaying with the elk, the wolves and man to see which one Nature would favor in her game of wits with the elements. And, thus, life struggled on as did the cold, rugged mountains in their heaving and lifting through the annals of time.

Following in the course of time, came the Norwegian Elkhound, first and foremost a hunter. A jack-of-all-trades down through the centuries, a guardian, a farm dog and companion, the Elkhound is still very much a hunter in Norway.

HUNTING IN NORWAY

Although the first game laws were enacted in 1818, the number of elk decreased at times to the point of near extinction. Causes for the decrease were ascribed to intensive hunting, poaching during the off-season, disease and wolves. Small herds of elk had survived the slaughter in the large forests of Norway and, with the decline in the wolf population, gradually made their way back to their old haunts where they multiplied until they flourished all over Scandinavia.

Waiting for the hunt.

The golden age of elk hunting came during the latter part of the 18th Century. Sportsmen from Germany, Austria and England frequented Norway to claim a share of her handsome elk— their antlers proclaimed to be some of the most spectacular in the world.

The Norwegian hunters came to rely on the Elkhound to help in their hunt for big game. Bears were hunted in the same way as the elk. The Elkhound's harsh outercoat shed the icy rains and sleet while his woolly undercoat kept him warm in subarctic temperatures. His small strong feet, protected by thick pads, let him scale the rocky terrain. He often jumped from boulder to boulder once on the trail of an elk. His keen eyes escaped the scratching branches that his harsh coat refused to entangle as he tracked for hours, sometimes on a hunt that lasted for days.

Full of energy and ready for adventure, the Elkhound pursued his prey. His uncanny sense of knowing when to bark and when not to bark allowed him to stalk an elk, leading the hunter in for the kill. His ability to bounce like a rubber ball enabled him to evade the threatening hooves and antlers of an enraged animal.

LOSHUND

There are two hunting methods used in Norway, loshund and bandhund. When there are great expanses of dense forest to be hunted, the loshund or loose dog, is used. He has the freedom to track unnoticed by the game; whereas, the crackling of twigs and other commotion caused by hunters tramping through the woods would serve to alert any big game.

The Elkhound can quietly follow the scent of his prey and lead the hunter to it. Once the Elkhound has approached the elk, he circles it, nipping and darting in and out to keep it preoccupied. The Elkhound's baying alerts the hunter who follows the sound of his dog, getting close enough to the elk to bring it down with a shot from his high-powered gun. The entire process takes hours of trekking for hunters and dogs.

If the Elkhound is being held on leash, a seasoned hunter can tell if he is getting the scent of an elk by the way the dog's hair rises on his back. The pull on the leash is more urgent once the scent is found.

Several hunters with dogs may work together. At the right moment, the hunter turns one dog loose. The dog works his way upwind toward the elk. He lets the elk see him and gradually works in closer. At this point, he begins to bay cautiously and in a somewhat rhythmic pattern. The Elkhound is intent on warning the hunter that he has located an elk and tries not to scare it.

A hunting party in Norway.

Elkhound with fallen elk.

Elkhound with his prize.

If the elk becomes angered, it will strike out at the dog with its powerful forefeet and swinging antlers. The Elkhound shows his agility and stamina by darting in and out, keeping the elk occupied with his antics while the hunter gets in position for a good shot.

Sometimes an elk takes flight, at which point a good hunting Elkhound stops baying and follows the elk to head the elk off and bring it to stand again. About the worse thing the Elkhound can do is to bay while chasing the elk. The elk will surely take to full flight, leaving the noisy Elkhound far behind with a disgruntled hunter.

BANDHUND

The bandhund or lurhund is used in open country. In this method of hunting, the Elkhound is kept on leash at all times. The hunter crisscrosses the territory he is hunting, always keeping upwind. He carefully monitors his Elkhound for signs that he has scented an elk. An alert hunter can tell if his Elkhound is following a trail or actual body scent. The Elkhound, using his keen nose, can get the body scent of an elk from a long way off.

When the hunter interprets the telltale signs of an elk downwind, he ties his Elkhound to a tree and stalks the elk upwind alone. If two hunters are working together, one holds the dog or dogs while the other stalks the elk. It would be too noisy for the hunter to use his dogs on leash in dense woods because of crackling twigs underfoot.

Elkhounds are able to find a wounded elk, one that has been hit by a truck on the highway or hit by a stray bullet. The elk doesn't have to be bleeding for the Elkhound to know it is wounded. After the Elkhound locates it, the hunter can get close enough to see if the elk is injured badly enough to be destroyed.

AN ELK HUNT

Many sportsmen use a combination of the two hunting methods, depending on the terrain. Some Elkhounds, however, work better on lead while others prefer the independence and freedom of working loose.

Wealthier Norwegian hunters often kept saeters, outlying farms where they could spend the hunting season and hunt to their hearts' content. Their farmhouses were conveniently located near areas frequented by elk. Diaries or logs kept by sportsmen during the early part of the 19th Century captured the excitement of the hunt using the Norwegian Elkhound.

An account of one particularly exciting hunt took place in the 1920s. The sportsman, Franz Rosenberg, lived in Norway and was familiar with the forests reputed to abound with prize elk. He had chosen to hunt in the Storaasen Forest with a friend who also knew the area intimately.

The two men with their Elkhounds—Flink and Var—crossed the Gauptjern River in an old steamer used to carry supplies as well as people. Rivers and fjords provided the transportation network for country folk and hunters. Even today, water transportation is indispensable in Norway. Upon reaching the other side of the Gauptjern, the men and dogs disembarked and walked toward the hills. Being in shape to walk, sometimes trudging through mud or over rocks, is a necessary part of hunting.

Sometimes native moccasins, komager, were lined with sennegrass—caren visicaria, a variety of sedge that grows around water. Stuffed in moccasins, it kept the feet warm and dry and allowed the wearer to walk on any kind of ground. It also eliminated the sucking sounds of heavy boots being pulled from the mire, a sound that alerted elk that humans were approaching.

As the men continued into the dense forest, their vision was obscured by a twilight cast much like the dimming of lights. It was impossible to move quietly because of the crackling debris on the forest floor. They had not gone far when suddenly a large, dark object loomed up a short distance in front of them. A glimpse through the binoculars proved it to be a female elk (cow). Cows and their young are spared the hunters' guns. But hunters know that where there is a cow, a bull elk will be close by.

Once the men reached the timberline, they were able to spot the bull hidden behind some bushes. The fickle wind had been playing tricks on them, but so far their scent had not reached the bull. He stood there, his magnificent shovel-shaped antlers like trees on a barren mountain. The Elk became suspicious. The sportsman got a bead on the likely spot behind the shoulder of the huge hulk and squeezed the trigger, certain the bull would fall. To his utter amazement, the bull wheeled and disappeared into the shadowy forest, vanished but for the permanent picture painted in his mind.

Recovering from the realization that he had missed his mark, the sportsman gave chase. Although he spotted the cow and calf, there was no sign of the bull, nor was there any sign of blood on the trail. He trailed it as far as the Gauptjern, and since it was getting late and a storm was collecting over the river, he decided to call off the hunt.

The next day, the men hired a man with a horse to bring down the meat from the previous day's hunt. They had killed three smaller bull elk. To dress or butcher an elk, the animal is first gutted and then its carcass is hung in a tree for safekeeping until it can be taken back to camp for use as meat.

Still determined to get another chance at yesterday's prize bull, the sportsman, accompanied by his friend and their Elkhounds, headed for the Storaas Ridge and the Gauptjern. Old Flink immediately caught the scent of elk, but nothing of consequence. Quite often, tame reindeer were in the area much to the consternation of the hunters and their dogs. However, as soon as the party reached the flats near the Gauptjern, Flink pulled hard on the leash heading toward a large, open bog. In the distance loomed an island-like grove of trees. The sportsman swept the area with his binoculars, zeroing in on a dark mass among the trees.

He immediately recognized the shovel-like antlers with 14 distinct tines on each. But there was no way to get a bead on it from his open position on the flats. His only hope was to go around the grove approaching from the other side. After slow careful maneuvering, he eased into the grove, relishing his opportunity to bag the elusive elk. The elk, big and wise with his years, sensing a threat of danger, thrashed away making it impossible for the sportsman to shoot. The bull eluded him a third time later on in the hunting season and the sportsman grudgingly admitted defeat.

The weather had turned wintry and the considerable amount of snow on the ground made walking difficult. On the last day of the season, the Elkhounds caught the scent of an elk. Its tracks left no doubt that it was a large animal. The hunting party followed the trail up and down the steep terrain and gradually into large bogs. The excited dogs led the hunters in and out of groves of trees, back and forth across swamps, turning and twisting to the extent that it was next to impossible to keep track of the ever-changing wind. Even in the fervor of the hunt, the determined dogs were silent.

When at last the bull was sighted, it was too far off to shoot. The elk seemed to know this and took its time walking into the safety of the forest. Since they were so familiar with the topography, the hunters decided to detour and intercept the elk on the opposite side of the plateau. Moccasins creaking in the snow, the hunters followed the persistent pulling of the dogs against their leashes. The sudden roar of the Gauptjern River was proof of their full circle of the plateau. Just as the sportsman reached a small gap between two rocks, they sighted the large, dark body of the bull elk, making his way toward a small grove of trees.

In one last furtive effort, the sportsman shot at the vital spot on its shoulder. The huge animal threw itself around and headed for the grove, safe once more until the games began again the next hunting season.

HUNTING TESTS

Hunting tests are held in Scandinavia for the Norwegian Elkhound, the Gray Dog (Grahund) and the Jamthund. All Norwegian Elkhounds in Norway must be good hunters to be considered for certificates of championship. To be awarded first prize in a test, an Elkhound must show an exceeding degree of desire for the hunt. He must show aptitude for running and searching for game with comparative ease in all terrain. At the same time, he must indicate an awareness of his master by checking back with him periodically.

The Elkhound should use a loud sharp bark at the correct time, approaching the elk calmly to keep it from moving away.

Elkhounds in Norway. Owned by Per Lovold.

He must have the fortitude to keep the elk at bay for at least an hour and a half, all the while dodging the dangerous hooves and antlers of the elk. If the elk decides to move away, the Elkhound must give chase without barking.

In a hunting test, leashed dogs must show much the same prowess. While some Elkhounds tend to do better on leash and some off leash, in actuality many Elkhounds are used both ways, depending on the circumstances of the hunt. However, during a hunting test, a leashed dog must be harnessed and is never let loose. He is judged on how quickly he can scent the elk and lead his master to it. He moves in complete silence across the terrain, carefully avoiding waterfalls and other obstacles that would be hazardous to his master.

If other game, cattle or tame reindeer are encountered on the hunt, the hunting Elkhound should ignore their presence or show no more than cursory interest in them. Above all, the Elkhound must not be unnerved when shots are fired.

When the Elkhound is on the scent trail he usually holds his head high. If he is following the scent of an elk and crosses the scent of a closer elk, he will sometimes leave the first scent to trail the closer one.

In addition to being used to hunt big game, the Elkhound is used to hunt forest birds and raccoons. Although he is instinctively a hunter, he is a trustworthy guardian of the reindeer herds for farmers. And, eager to please his master, he becomes utilitarian as a sled dog. Elkhounds, however, are not bred to pull heavy freight.

HUNTING IN THE UNITED STATES

While the Norwegian Elkhound has not received the acclaim in the United States as he has in Scandinavia, breeders and owners can attest to his versatility as a hunter. He hunts elk, bear and other big game, where game laws permit, much the same way as he does in Norway. The mountainous regions of the United States demand the same prowess as the terrain in Scandinavia. Every anatomical part of the Elkhound is a functional piece of the overall pattern of perfection. Therefore, the breed standard in the United States is basically the same as the Norwegian, Canadian and English standards.

The Elkhound is not limited to hunting big game. He is much sought after as a squirrel dog. His highly developed senses of scenting, seeing and hearing, combined with his innate intelli-

*Squirrel hunting
in Tennessee.*

gence, make treeing squirrels seem like child's play. Occasionally, an Elkhound will further astound his owner by actually climbing the tree in pursuit of a squirrel, raccoon or opossum.

Rabbits offer little challenge to the Elkhound. However, he has scant difficulty unraveling the crisscrossing trail of a rabbit. Just as he will switch scents of big game to trail the closer one, he will drop one rabbit's trail if another seems more convenient. And, just for fun, he will spend hours uprooting even the most industrious of moles.

Although the hunting methods of an Elkhound are similar whether hunting large or small game, his approach for bird hunting is different. His tightly curled tail makes pointing ludicrous.

Nevertheless, pheasant hunters in the cornfields of the Great Plains will attest to seeing him patiently standing, one front foot poised in the air, waiting for his master to take charge.

Without his gun-toting master, the Elkhound does a little bird hunting on his own. He charms them to their demise. In many instances, Elkhounds have been observed in the act of charming the birds. The Elkhound usually assumes a sitting position because of the lengthy ritual involved in charming. He thrusts his head back, typical of a wolf baying at the moon.

From deep within his throat he emits a tinkling, clear, high-pitched sound, like the breaking of fine crystal. The resulting sound is so unbelievably beautiful that even the most reluctant bird falls prey. The birds are so captivated that they circle closer and closer to the yodeling dog. Some experts believe that the bird is actually hypnotized by the sound. At any rate, the birds literally fall to the dog's feet in a stupor. While a hungry dog may partake of his dinner, most unfortunate birds are left for predators or are disposed of by the keeper of the kennel.

SUMMARY

The Norwegian Elkhound is truly a hunting dog. He employs many of the tactics of sight and scent hounds, yet has an inherent instinct to know when to bay and when to remain silent. Although game laws in many countries limit his use in hunting big game, the versatile Elkhound has retained his ageless ability and agility for the hunt—scenting, tracking and keeping enormous animals at bay in the most foreboding of terrain and weather.

HUNTING WITH GRAY ELKHOUNDS IN NORWAY
by Frank Christiansen

Author's note: Frank Christiansen is an avid hunter as well as a popular judge in Scandinavia. He lives in Malm, Norway, with his wife Hilda and sons, Bjorge and Torgeir. He is active in the kennel clubs of Scandinavia and recently helped constitute the standard for the Swedish White Elkhound.

The Norwegian Elkhound Club's Association is divided into 18 districts called Elkhound Clubs (EHC): Aust-Agder EHC, Telemark EHC, Vestfold EHC, Buskerud EHC, Oslo EHC, Follow and Oestfold EHC, Hadeland EHC, Hedmark EHC, Vest-Agder EHC, Vestoppland EHC, Hallingdal and Valdres EHC, Gudbrandsdal EHC, Oesterdal EHC, South-Troendelag EHC, North-Troendelag EHC, Nordland EHC, Troms EHC and Finnmark EHC.

In our district, Malm in North-Troendelag—about 150 km north of Trondheim—there have been many Elkhounds for a very long time. Although the Gray Elkhound is the most popular breed, the Norwegian Black Elkhound is prevalent in this region. Mostly the owners have their Elkhounds for hunting rather than for conformation shows. During the last five to six years more owners have taken them on elghund field trials and also to conformation shows. Puppies from parents that win both field trials and dog shows are very expensive. Even the top ranking show Elkhounds are expected to participate in field trials and elg hunting in Norway. If they cannot hunt, the dogs are considered worthless as far as breeding is concerned and, therefore, cannot become champions.

First, second and third prizes are offered in elghund field trials. To become a show champion, the dog must win three certificates at dog shows from three different judges. In addition, the dog must earn one first prize in a field trial. In order to become a hunting champion, the dog must achieve two first prizes on a field trial, one having been achieved on a two-day field trial and one first prize based on quality in a dog show.

Our two Norwegian Elkhound breeds—Gray and Black—are used primarily for hunting elg, a member of the moose family. In this respect, the name moose dog would perhaps seem more appropriate. The Gray Norwegian Elkhound is our national breed, and, therefore, the symbol of the Norsk Kennel Klub.

The hunting season for elg is between September 23 and October 31 with a one-week break the first of October. A few landowners get together to create a hunting district or area, vald, to which the local Wild Committee in each county decides a certain amount of animals to be shot. The Wild Committee or Big Game Committee decides both sex, age and number of elg to be shot on each vald. Beginning January 1, 1994, all hunting teams must have at least one approved dog on each area for tracking. This law was established to allow for the tracking of wounded animals.

The use of the Norwegian Elkhound as a Loshund

There are two ways to use Elkhounds for hunting elg, either as a loshund or as a bandhund. Both hunter and dog must be in good condition. It is necessary to do a lot of training—exercise and using the dog quite often in the forest before the hunting season begins.

In the Gudbrandsdael and the Osterdael there is a tradition to let the Elkhound try to find the elg on his own, either by open scent or by tracking it down. This is called free-ranging and the dog is called a loshund. When the dog has found the elg, he goes on barking and at the same time keeps the elg at bay for as long as necessary for the hunter to get in a position for the kill. The hunter must be careful so that the elg does not hear him as he creeps toward it. The decision to use a loshund is determined by the terrain. There are great expanses of dense forests in the valleys, daler, which are typical loshund districts.

The use of the Norwegian Elkhound as a Bandhund

The first field trial for the bandhund in the Malm district was arranged more than 40 years ago. It is traditional to use the Elkhound as a bandhund on field trials and hunting in this district. The terrain, mostly of sparse forests and mountains, is somewhat different from the big forest valleys. Here the Elkhound has to hunt by scent or tracking to locate the elg. It is important to know that the dog will instinctively use the wind when he tries to locate the elg, always leading the hunter up against the wind. By so doing, the dog can scent the elg without the elg being able to scent or hear the dog and the hunter. The harness mark on the Norwegian Elkhound is a symbol of the band used on the dog when leading the hunter.

Preparing for the hunt

One afternoon before the 25th of September, my hunting team will have a meeting to discuss and plan the elg hunting. We will decide where to go the first days and which dog is going to lead the team. The game license is collected at this time. Besides my dog, Torris, there is a gray bitch called Toya on the team. Both dogs are very friendly toward each other. After the elg is shot, they become aggressive toward one another when standing close to the elg.

Early the first morning, the hunters and the dogs are eager to get out in the forest. The hunting leader of the party makes the decision on which terrain and parcel the party will hunt and when the party is due to arrive back at the starting point each day. A hunting day lasts for at least eight hours, depending on the number of elg shot.

Out in the terrain, the dog leader—the hunter going with the bandhund—must be aware of the wind so the dog can start his tracking up against the wind. After having used the Gray Elkhound for many years, we have learned one thing for sure: Never mistrust your dog. However illogical it may seem for the hunter in the terrain, only the dog is the expert, knowing by his nose where the elg is moving. Younger dogs may, however, sometimes be distracted by other game, such as wood grouse, roe-deer or domestic animals. Once they have managed their first elg, they are no longer distracted by other game.

When the dog finds fresh elg tracks, he works intensely to locate the animal. He guides the hunter quite speedily and surely once he begins the tracking. The most important thing is that the dog must be absolutely quiet all the time. After the dog indicates that we are close to the elg, the silence is of utmost importance, otherwise the elg would become aware of our presence. The dogs have different ways to show the hunters that the elg is nearby. Some dogs do this by standing up on their hind feet. Others let their tails fall down from the curled position. Still others stand with their hackles up—this has nothing to do with bad temper. Although there was a time when hunters declared that a good hunting dog should be ill-tempered, this is not true today. Today, all Gray Elkhounds used for hunting and showing are good-natured and friendly; they are, therefore, easily handled both in the show ring and in hunting.

The dog's eagerness for the hunt must be strong enough to keep him working all day. And, he must not react to shots from the rifle. When the elg is located and the hunter is in position to shoot it, the Elkhound is quietly ordered to sit or to lie down. The dog must never stand in front of the hunter when the hunter is ready to shoot. This may be difficult for eager dogs to understand. They must be trained for this before the hunting season.

After the elg is killed, the dog is let free and rushes toward the prey. The normal reaction of a Gray Elkhound when it reaches the dead elg is to start pulling off the hairs of the elg. This is considered a normal reaction; it is of importance that the dog feels that the elg is his property. When the hunters slaughter or dress the animal, it is important to release the dogs close to the elg, letting them remain unleashed.

Sometimes the other hunters, guards, are shooting elg. These hunters are stationed in the terrain when the hunting team knows there is a fair possibility for the elg to pass. In such instances, it is important not to take the dog toward the place when a shot is heard. If you do so, the Elkhound will later stop his tracking route and only concentrate on the place he heard the shot. He will go there to find an elg, which he will guard from the other dogs. By tracking his first or original track, the dog will develop into a good tracker. Besides, there could be more elg that the dog leader may get an opportunity to shoot.

There are differences of opinion among elg hunters about which is the most exciting, sitting on guard or going with an Elkhound on lead. Those of us who have tried both ways are convinced of one thing—nothing is more interesting than going with your own bandhund. There is a feeling of closeness between a man and his dog deep in the big forests. Sometimes you both sense delight, other times adversity. In either case, you are two friends taking a rest and talking, and I am convinced an Elkhound understands everything that is said. There is no greater excitement than going into the Norwegian forests with a team of Gray hunters.

Crossing a red flower (RR) with a white flower (ww)

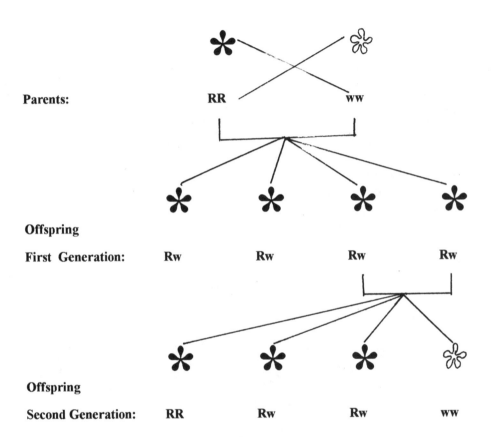

Parents: RR ww

Offspring

First Generation: Rw Rw Rw Rw

Offspring

Second Generation: RR Rw Rw ww

Basic Mendelian Theory using garden peas.

CHAPTER TEN
BASIC CONCEPTS OF GENETICS

When a gardener plants a packet of peas, he knows precisely, given proper care, what the seeds will produce. That has not always been the case. The work of a lone abbot in a monastery in Czechoslovakia—then called Brunn—opened the door to the secret manner in which plants and animals transmit their traits and characteristics, as well as those of their ancestors, to their progeny. That first revelation of the laws of inheritance constitutes the basis for the science of genetics.

MENDELISM

Gregor Johann Mendel, sequestered in his monastery, experimented for eight years crossing varieties of garden peas. His work was published in a little known botanical journal and consequently went unnoticed from 1866 until it was rediscovered in 1900. Three researchers working independently of one another verified the work done previously by Mendel. Mendel's original publication gained credibility and his "laws" became known as Mendelism.

Although work with garden peas seems detached from breeding purebred dogs, the regularities discovered by Mendel demonstrate that each individual is made up of a number of characters that can be inherited separately. These characters are unit characters found in contrasting pairs, for example, tall/short, smooth/wrinkled, red/white. Mendel referred to these units as dominant and recessive. He worked out a ratio of pure recessive, hybrid and pure dominant in the progeny of his controlled matings of plants. The same conclusions were reached in the controlled matings of animals. He theorized that traits or characters do not blend or dilute like dye in water but that these factors of heredity lay side by side like so many sets of different colored marbles.

Although truth lies in the simplicity of Mendelism, the science of genetics has expanded to the degree that through selective breeding man can predict and control outcomes in his canine breeding programs to a great extent. Norwegian Elkhounds are no different from dogs of other breeds when it comes to the study of genetics in establishing a breeding program.

GENES

As long as breeders know that the various traits of dogs are carried from one generation to the next as sets of unit characters and that the determining factors are carried in the sperm and the ovum that unite to form the zygote of the new organism, a more detailed study of the process of cell division— mitosis and meiosis—is unnecessary at this point. Many books have been written on genetics of purebred dogs and are excellent reference materials for breeders.

The whole purpose of breeding purebred Norwegian Elkhounds is to eliminate undesirable traits and, in the process, produce Elkhounds as close to the accepted standard as possible. Breeders of Norwegian Elkhounds must be aware that it is easy to bury an undesirable trait for several generations by breeding a pure recessive or pure dominant to cover up the unwanted characteristic but that the buried trait will surface eventually.

Fortunately, many of the traits breeders want to perpetuate are produced by dominant genes. A common example is breeding a dog with a correct bite to a bitch with an incorrect bite. If the dog is carrying a pure dominant for a correct bite, all the progeny will have correct bites. However, they will carry the trait for incorrect bites. If the progenies are later bred to Elkhounds carrying the trait for incorrect bites, even though their bites are correct, some of their progeny will have incorrect bites. Therefore, the undesirable trait for incorrect bites may remain hidden for a generation and then surface.

HEREDITARY FACTORS

It would be difficult to count the possible combinations of hereditary factors. Pairing a bushel basket of minuscule multicolored beads would be simpler in comparison. However, new technological advances make even the once impossible closer to reality. Even so, breeding out unwanted traits is difficult at best. Therefore, a scrupulous breeder spends much time on research

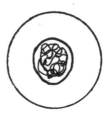

Parent Cell

1) The membrane of the
nucleus disappears.

2) The twin chromosomes
line up in the middle
of the cell.

3) The twin chromosomes
split apart and move to
opposite ends of the cell.

4) A nuclear membrane forms
around each group of chromosomes.

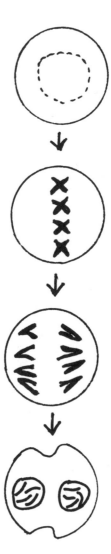

Process of Mitosis.

and planning to develop a workable breeding program. Research includes keeping records of known recessive traits carried by individual Norwegian Elkhounds. Some breeders keep a file on each Elkhound of which they have genetic knowledge. The information is taken into consideration when a breeding is planned.

Breeding becomes a genetic game of hide-and-seek. Invariably, an unwanted trait will surface in future generations, often spoiling an otherwise perfect dog. Breeding pure recessive or pure dominant to obscure a trait does just that—it hides the problem temporarily.

The ultimate success or failure of a breeding program hinges upon the selection of breeding stock. The laws of probability prevent a given breeding from producing puppies that carry 100 percent of the desired traits. However, stacking the deck insures more of the desired traits than random selection.

DETERMINING SEX

Although some breeders may believe they have a method by which they can influence the number of male and female puppies conceived in a given litter, the methods are, in substance, superstitions and old wives' tales.

One such suggestion is to breed the bitch early in her season to produce females and late to produce males. Another fallacious notion is that overfeeding the bitch in whelp produces females and underfeeding her produces males. Still others credit the man in the moon and other equally unfounded methods.

The fact is that the sex of puppies is determined at conception when the ovum and sperm unite to form the zygote. The ova all contain one X sex chromosome. Fifty percent of the sperm contain one X sex chromosome and the other 50 percent contain one Y sex chromosome.

If an ovum is fertilized by a sperm with an X sex chromosome, the resultant zygote will contain two Xs and the puppy will be female. If an ovum is fertilized by a sperm with a Y sex chromosome, the resultant zygote will contain an X and a Y and the puppy will be male.

For a breeder to be able to control the sex of puppies in a litter would not necessarily work for the betterment of the breed. Producing nothing but male puppies would not improve the males anymore than producing only females would improve the females. The resultant male or female puppies would not be any

Parent cell

1) The membrane of the nucleus disappears and twin chromosomes become visible.

2) Pairs of twin chromosomes line up in the middle of the cell.

3) The pairs of twin chromosomes move apart and go to opposite ends of the cell.

4) A nuclear membrane forms around each group of twin chromosomes.

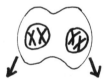

5) The cell divides into two new cells.

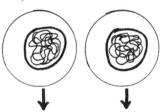

6) The membrane of tne nucleus disappears in each cell.

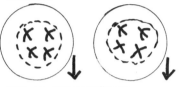

7) The twin chromosomes line up in the middle of the cells.

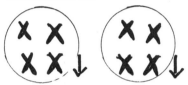

8) The twin chromosomes split apart and move to opposite ends of the cells.

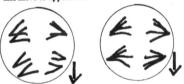

9) A nuclear membrane forms around each set of chromosomes.

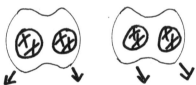

10) The cells divide into two new cells.

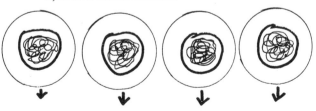

Process of Meiosis.

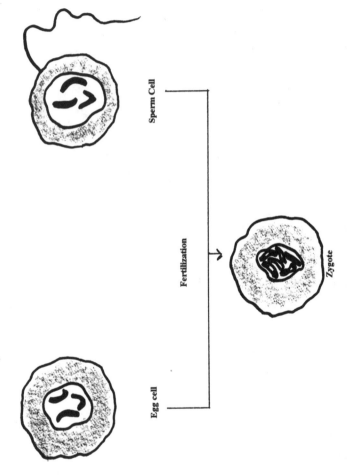

Sperm Cell

Egg cell

Fertilization

Zygote

The chromosomes in the egg and the sperm form pairs in the nucleus of the zygote. The zygote is the first cell of the offspring. It grows by mitosis and cell division.

Development of a Zygote.

better than the male or female puppies in a litter containing both sexes. Occasionally litters are of one sex, seldom a 50-50 ratio.

STERILITY
Once in a while Elkhounds are unable to reproduce. The causes are usually a result of sterility or impotence. A veterinarian should be consulted in either case to determine probable causes and related problems. A breeder must be knowledgeable enough to recognize sterility or impotence in his own dogs.

Sterility is a term applied to the failure of a dog or bitch to produce sperm or ova that will develop into living fetuses when properly united. Impotence, on the other hand, is the inability of the male to copulate. More often than not either condition can be corrected with proper management.

Bitches cannot be considered truly sterile if they conceive, whether or not the puppies go full term, live or die. Male sterility can be identified by examination of semen under a microscope to reveal whether spermatozoa are active or not. Even though sterility may be temporary, a male should be removed from stud service until his fertility is established.

HEREDITARY PROBLEMS
Specific studies involving Norwegian Elkhounds were made to determine the extent of congenital and inherited diseases. Generalized progressive retinal atrophy (PRA) and familial renal disease are the most profound.

Progressive retinal atrophy is due to a simple recessive trait. Norwegian Elkhounds have been found, through several research studies, to be affected by PRA. As the name implies, the condition results in the progressive deterioration of the retina. The disease is often not apparent until the dog is five to seven years old. It is characterized by a degeneration of the cells of the retina. First indication that a dog has PRA is a loss of night vision and the dog experiences difficulty in judging distance in darkened areas. Total blindness gradually occurs.

Puppies usually receive a complete physical checkup when they are taken to the veterinarian for their first shots at age six to eight weeks. An eye examination should be included. Certified veterinary ophthalmologists specialize in canine eye conditions and should be consulted if abnormal eye conditions are suspected. The Canine Eye Registry Foundation, Inc. (CERF) is an organization that collects and analyzes data on the inci-

Breeding a desirable trait (pure dominant) with a desirable trait (*buried* recessive)

Parents:
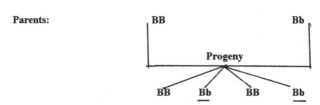
BB   Bb

Progeny

BB   Bb   BB   Bb

Two progeny now carry recessive (*buried*) genes.

Illustration: A buried recessive trait.

Breeding a desirable trait (*buried* recessive) with a desirable trait (*buried* recessive)

Parents:
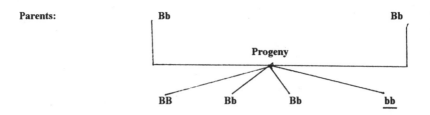
Bb   Bb

Progeny

BB   Bb   Bb   bb

One progeny now exhibits the *buried* recessive trait.

Illustration: Surfacing of a buried recessive trait.

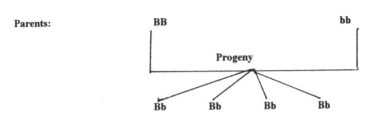

All progeny will carry one dominant and one recessive gene for the given trait.

Parents: BB   bb

Progeny

Bb   Bb   Bb   Bb

Breeding pure dominant to pure recessive.

dence of various inherited eye diseases in dogs. Certificates are issued to dogs determined clear of the problem.

Cataracts, opacity of the crystalline lens or the lens capsule, are carried by a recessive gene that may go undetected for years, only to emerge when a dog and bitch carrying the recessive gene are bred together. The trait may manifest itself in puppies totally blind at birth, partially blind or in a progressive state.

Not all cataracts are hereditary. It is virtually impossible to differentiate between hereditary and non-hereditary cataracts on the basis of the appearance of the lens. More information, such as breed predisposition and history of the condition within the dog's pedigree, is necessary for a conclusive analysis. Cataracts can develop in diabetic dogs and senile cataracts are common in old dogs.

Renal cortical hypoplasia is evident in Elkhounds. Often signs of hypoplasia, which is defective or incomplete development, are not evident until the puppy reaches a year of age. Uremia and, later, parathyroidism develop. Studies indicate the occurrence of maldevelopment of the kidneys in Elkhounds. Discerning breeders will check all puppies and eliminate those affected from their breeding programs.

Of the 23 pairs of chromosomes, one pair is called the sex chromosomes.

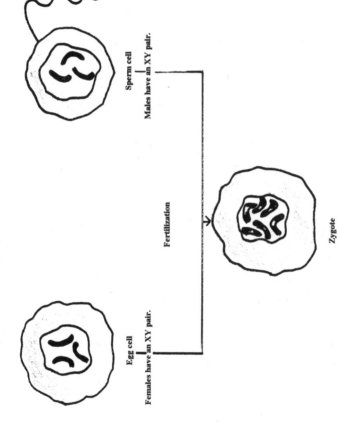

Sperm cell
Males have an XY pair.

Egg cell
Females have an XY pair.

Fertilization

Zygote

If an egg is fertilized by a sperm carrying an X chromosome, the puppy will be female.

If an egg is fertilized by a sperm carrying a Y chromosome, the puppy will be male.

Sex determinants.

HIP DYSPLASIA

Hip dysplasia is a deformity of the coxofemoral joints that form the ball and socket joints of the hips. The head of the femur, the thigh bone, fits into the cup-like acetabulum. Dysplasia occurs when the cup is too shallow to hold the head of the femur or when the ligaments are loose and the head begins to work free. Healthy hips occur when the pelvis is broad, the femur fits into the cup and the surrounding muscles and ligaments are strong and taut.

First signs of dysplasia occur during the period of rapid growth in puppies, usually between four and nine months. A puppy may walk with a limp, walk with a swaying gait or bunnyhop when he runs. He may have a hard time getting up from a lying position.

Outward signs of dysplasia range from no sign to severe hip lameness. Radiographic evidence shows degrees of shallowness of the socket and a flattening of the ball or femoral head. Degeneration of the joint may or may not occur.

Norwegian Elkhounds, like many breeds, have their share of hip dysplasia. While research indicates the condition is inherited, dysplasia can occur as a result of environmental factors, including hip injuries and excess weight in developing puppies and diets lacking in necessary nutrients.

Some Elkhounds show no clinical signs of the disease whatsoever and live perfectly normal lives even though there is x-ray evidence of dysplasia. Conscientious breeders do not use dogs or bitches for breeding purposes unless they have been x-rayed and declared clear of dysplasia. However, even parents with normal hips can produce dysplastic puppies.

The Orthopedic Foundation for Animals is headquartered in Columbia, Missouri. The foundation provides a consulting service for owners of purebred dogs. Many local veterinarians will take a hip x-ray according to OFA specifications. The x-ray may be submitted to OFA for evaluation at a nominal fee.

OFA has a panel of expert radiologists who review the x-ray and grade it according to conformation with the norm. If the hip conformation is normal for an Elkhound, the dog is assigned an OFA certification number. Dogs must be at least 24 months old when the x-ray is made in order for the dog to be certified free of dysplasia. A listing of Elkhounds that have OFA certification is available from NEAA. The list is updated in the AKC Awards publication on a quarterly basis. Most breeders willingly supply this information.

Other inherited conditions involving bones are slipping knee-cap (patellar dislocation) and popping hock or laxity of the hock joint. As with hip dysplasia, these conditions may be acquired through trauma. They do not occur with great frequency in the Elkhound breed.

SUBCUTANEOUS CYSTS

Subcutaneous cysts do occur in the Norwegian Elkhound, singularly or several at a time. They move freely under the skin and are not painful to the dog. Usually no treatment is necessary. A problem can occur, however, if the breeder or owner fails to differentiate the cysts from cancerous or precancerous lesions that usually extend into surrounding tissue. It may be necessary for the veterinarian to perform a biopsy to determine whether or not the cysts are cancerous. The cysts occur any place on the dog and vary in size.

HOT SPOTS

The cause of hot spots or moist dermatitis is not known for certain. It is a bacterial skin infection sometimes called pyotraumatic dermatitis. One way to eliminate hot spots is to eliminate external parasites that cause the Elkhound to itch. As the dog scratches he causes small lesions that harbor bacteria.

The Elkhound has a dense undercoat. When the coat becomes damp, it creates an environment conducive to bacterial infection. When a hot spot appears, it seems to spread rapidly in a short period of time. The area of the sore should be cleaned with a solution of one part hydrogen peroxide to 10 parts water. Surgical soap works well as a cleaning agent.

The area around the hot spot may be soothed by applying an antibiotic cream, ointment or lotions containing an anesthetic. Dogs should be prevented from licking or biting at their sores if at all possible.

Because the Elkhound has such a dense coat, it is difficult for the hot spot to heal. The tendency is to clip away the hair so that more air can get to the sore. The area should not be shaved. New hair growth is often darker than the existing hair and shows up as a distracting darker area in the coat.

SEBORRHEA

Seborrhea or flaky skin and dry coat are usually a result of inadequate nutrition. The condition can be corrected by diet.

Unsaturated fatty acids and oil soluble vitamins added to a balanced dog food aid in developing a lustrous coat. Although coat quality is affected by nutrition, heredity determines color, length, texture and susceptibility to certain types of skin and coat problems.

PERSONALITY DISORDERS

Aggression and shyness are inheritable disorders. Norwegian Elkhounds are naturally bold and energetic. Their disposition coupled with their independent nature can result in an Elkhound that is difficult to control if he is allowed to have his own way. However, an untrained Elkhound that is permitted to jump up on people and to roughhouse is not considered aggressive in terms of having an inherited behavior problem. Norwegian Elkhounds are highly trainable and can become acceptable members of a household.

Aggression is an uncontrollable urge to bite or overpower either humans or other dogs. In addition to being inheritable it can be the result of an environmental factor wherein the dog feels compelled to act aggressively for reasons known only to him.

Shyness is obvious in a very young puppy. A shy puppy is the loner of the litter. He stays to himself, often facing the corner of the whelping box. As he matures, he finds safety under or behind furniture. He is really unfit as a functioning member of the household. His shyness sometimes turns him into a fear-biter. Like aggression, shyness can also be acquired from environmental trauma. Neither aggression nor shyness should be tolerated and care must be taken to eliminate both traits from a breeding program.

MUTATION

Genetically speaking, a mutation is a heritable germinal variation of abrupt origin that is passed on to progeny of a given breeding. At times, it is only a minor variation but at other times it results in a trait that is quite dissimilar from the expected breed characteristics. A commonly used term for an unexpected trait is a *sport.*

In Norwegian Elkhounds, a mutation known by all breeders but seen by few is the red Elkhound. There is a striking difference between the red and the occasional brownish color that occurs genetically as a result of a combination of pairs of recessive genes relating to color. The rare instances in which the mutation occurs are seldom made known. Many breeders are reluctant to publicize genetic problems in their lines and simply destroy the evidence.

HEREDITARY TRAITS

In Elkhounds hereditary traits easily eliminated are light-colored or round eyes and teeth that are overshot, undershot or level. However, these same traits have a way of surfacing down the line unless they are carefully bred out. Even though many of the traits are carried by recessive genes, they can be recognized and eliminated.

Hypoglycemia occurs in Norwegian Elkhounds. It can be detected at an early age by a simple test made by the veterinarian. It is characterized by a concentration of glucose in the blood below the normal limit.

Because of their metabolism-efficient conversion of foods to fat and protein, Elkhounds have a tendency toward obesity. Their food intake should be controlled by feeding them a balanced dog food and by limiting the food intake to the needs of the individual dog. When intake is limited, the dog must have a vitamin supplement.

Norwegian Elkhounds need daily exercise. The proper weight of an active Elkhound is not as difficult to maintain as one that does little but lie around all day. Older dogs tend to gain weight because of a decrease in exercise. Kidney conditions such as chronic interstitial nephrites are aggravated by obesity in older dogs and are the usual cause of death in Elkhounds more than 13 years of age.

SUMMARY

Breeders can predict and control the outcomes in their breeding programs through selective breeding. Although Norwegian Elkhounds are known to be sound and relatively free from hereditary disease, the breed will stay that way only with cooperation among breeders and the diligent use of sound breeding practices. Conceding problems, not concealing them, is necessary to perpetuate purebred Elkhounds in the fullest sense of the term.

CHAPTER ELEVEN
BUYING AND CARING FOR A PUPPY

There is nothing like having a new baby in the house, even when the new baby is an exuberant bundle of joy charged with the speed of light, the curiosity of a cat, teeth like the needles in Grandma's pin cushion, a mind of its own, an expert puddlemaker and a manipulator of the heart that, in a nutshell, is a six-week-old Norwegian Elkhound. Having a new baby requires planning and changes in daily schedules. Equipment and supplies must be purchased. Someone must assume the parenting role—feeding, housebreaking, training and loving. Someone must pay the bills—food, equipment and doctor. Someone must take the time to nurture a new life to its fullest potential, administering dose after dose of tender loving care to temper a firm hand of authority.

BUYING A PUPPY

Buying a puppy should be a time-consuming, premeditated process. People in the market for an Elkhound should contact an Elkhound breeder. Breeders are a big help in matching puppies and owners and informing prospective owners of the pros and cons of pet ownership. The AKC, NEAA and regional Norwegian Elkhound clubs provide free referrals to breeders. Other reliable sources for information on locating breeders include local veterinarians and all-breed dog clubs.

If there is a local all-breed dog club, chances are there is a dog show given locally. Attending a dog show not only gives potential pet owners the opportunity to see many breeds of dogs, it affords an opportunity to talk with breeders and handlers about their dogs. It is a good time to find out something about the breed and the breeder before buying an Elkhound puppy.

The cute, cuddly, bear-like puppy does not always stay that

It's a boy!

way. He grows into an adult weighing between 45 and 55 pounds. He can pull any adult off balance if he has not been leash-trained and taught how to act around people. All this and more can be observed at an Elkhound kennel if a buyer is fortunate enough to be able to visit one.

QUALITY PUPPIES

A prospective buyer should be concerned as to whether the breeder produces quality dogs, dogs that exemplify breed type and dogs that are healthy. Talking with a breeder usually reveals whether the breeder is interested in the well-being of his puppies or whether he is interested in money. The breeder will always mention the puppy's pedigree because a conscientious breeder is proud of the dogs that appear in his pedigrees. A pedigree is the puppy's family tree, listing all ancestors for at least three generations. The AKC records department will provide additional generations on request for a minimum fee.

Other things a breeder will usually discuss with a potential buyer include the puppy's registration paper, a feeding guide and immunization record. The registration paper is a form indicating that the puppy may be registered with the AKC as a purebred Elkhound. A feeding guide is a summary of how much, how often and what the puppy has been eating. The immunization record is simply a listing of all shots the puppy has had, the dates of the shots and the due dates for booster shots.

Regardless of where a buyer finds a puppy for sale, he should never buy one that cowers when approached, one that trembles or is shy, or for that matter, one that is overly aggressive, growls or snarls. Sickly or diseased puppies should be avoided. Tell-tale signs include a runny nose, watery eyes or a fever.

There is no reason for a prospective owner to purchase a show-quality Elkhound unless he has a keen interest in showing or breeding. A pet-quality Elkhound that is healthy, exhibits breed characteristics and has good temperament becomes a part of the family as easily as a more expensive show prospect.

It is better to avoid commercial outlets or pet stores. They charge as much if not more for a purebred puppy than a breeder charges. The dogs are usually not of as good quality or in as good health as dogs purchased directly from a breeder. Commercial outlets or pet stores often purchase puppies at three to five weeks of age from indiscriminate breeders. As a result, many puppies die or develop health problems.

Having a Norwegian Elkhound as a pet is no different from having any other breed. Elkhounds are extremely hardy and demand little in the way of material requirements. Elkhounds are not particular about their living arrangements as long as they have plenty of fresh water, quality dog food, shelter and a cool place to sleep.

Eight-week-old puppy.

Who's there?

Couch potato!

SHELTER

Regardless of whether an Elkhound is destined to become a city dog, a country dog or a suburbanite, he must be kept in a fenced area. Ideally, an enclosed outside pen connected to the inside of the house by a dog door makes any Elkhound feel like he is living in Valhalla. If he is destined to become a yard dog, he must have shade, shelter and water. It goes without saying that his yard must be fenced. If he has the good fortune of becoming a house dog, he still must have a fenced exercise yard. Regardless of his quarters, he needs daily attention.

Whether the puppy stays inside or outside, he should stay where the temperature is comfortable. Although his coat is a good insulator against the elements, being exposed to the direct sun can cause heat stroke. Extreme cold, on the other hand, can cause frostbitten ears and feet.

The puppy should be free from insects in his surroundings. Excrement attracts flies and the resulting larvae. Mosquitoes are attracted to puddles. Other insects can cause discomfort and disease for pets. If possible the dog's surroundings should be cleanable with a chemical disinfectant made for that purpose.

BOY OR GIRL

People who purchase pets can opt for a boy or a girl. There is little difference in temperament between the two. Like all boys and girls, however, they do mature and start thinking a lot about the opposite sex. Females come into estrus—like a menstrual period—every six months. The period lasts about three weeks. During the middle of that period, the female can become pregnant if she is allowed to mate with a male. Pet owners have the option of spaying their charge if they do not plan to breed or show her. The ideal time to spay is eight months; however, it can be done at any age, at the advice of a veterinarian.

Male puppies become amorous as early as six months. They have the urge to breed at an early age and often succeed in siring a litter of pups as early as eight months. A dog that is permitted to breed indiscriminately is risking disease as well as spreading disease and infection. Male dogs, too, can be neutered if they are not going to be used in a breeding program or shown in conformation. Neutering dogs does not stigmatize the dog nor the owner other than showing that the owner is exercising his prerogative as a responsible pet owner.

Outgrowing a baby gate.

Learning to hunt.

EXERCISE

A puppy begins his regime of exercise the minute he is born. He finds his way to his dam's teats and begins sucking almost immediately. His front legs knead against his mother while his rear legs push to keep him at the dinner table. As he grows, his need for exercise increases, a necessary requirement to keep him in prime condition.

Overexercise can damage the fast-growing joints and bones of a puppy. It is not unusual for a puppy to drop in his tracks for a short nap and wake up ready to begin a new day a few minutes later. Puppies seem to have built-in sensors that routinely start and stop their mechanisms when they need refueling.

GROOMING

Grooming should become a part of the maintenance of a Norwegian Elkhound whether the dog has been acquired as a pet or as a show prospect. If done properly, there is actually little difference in grooming for home or for a show. Proper diet, exercise, daily brushing and clean quarters are the key factors for keeping an elkhound in a splendid coat. Eating a proper diet helps the dog produce a luxurious double coat. Exercise, coupled with diet, develops muscle tone and contributes to the general well-being of the dog. Brushing the dog's coat on a daily basis removes the dead hairs and brings a lustrous shine to its dark-tipped outercoat. Providing clean living quarters for the dog is a contributing factor to having a clean, odor-free dog. If pets or show dogs are provided all of the above, frequent bathing is unnecessary.

Grooming should start when the elkhound is a puppy. If the puppy is a show prospect, he can be groomed on a grooming table as part of his training for a show career. If the puppy is a pet, he can be groomed while standing on the floor, although it is often more convenient for the groomer to place the puppy on a table or bench. The puppy is usually easier to control if he is wearing a collar and leash. Grooming in the same area of the house or yard each day gives a fidgety puppy greater confidence.

To begin with, a light brushing of the puppy's coat with a soft pin brush is adequate. Next, brush the puppy's teeth with a soft toothbrush that has been dipped in water. Proper oral hygiene contributes to the puppy's general well-being, as well as preventing a buildup of plaque. Do not use human toothpaste because it may cause the puppy to gag or have an upset stomach. Tooth-paste for dogs is available.

At this same early age, the puppy's nails can be trimmed easily. A nail clipper designed for people can be used until the nails grow and harden; then it will be necessary to use a regular nail clipper designed for dogs. It is extremely important to clip the nails as part of the grooming process so the puppy will accept it as routine. Otherwise, later on, nail clipping could become a problem.

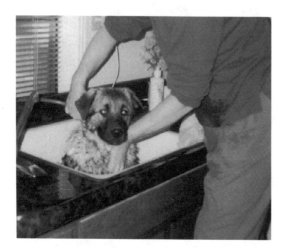

Saturday night bath.

Some dogs are cleaner than others and need fewer baths. Common sense must prevail in the decision to bathe or not to bathe. Keep in mind that bathing removes the natural oils from the dog's skin and coat. Bathe the puppy if he has an unpleas-ant odor—or is unclean—and needs a bath. As the puppy grows, he will stay cleaner and need fewer baths. Puppies that are bathed regularly often enjoy their baths to the extent that they will jump into the tub when you are ready to bathe them, and it is a wise precaution to keep the bathroom door closed if a hot bath is being run or an exuberant puppy may find himself in hot water.

Puppies should be rubbed with thick towels to remove excess water after their baths. Professional groomers use blow dryers, but because it is easy to burn a dog's skin don't use a dryer if you don't know the right way. Bathing a dog and then putting him outside in cold weather makes little sense, nor does it make sense to bathe a dog and put him back into a dirty kennel.

A good, quality dog shampoo should be used. Flea and tick shampoos are available when the dog has a flea or tick problem. When groomers and exhibitors bathe a dog for a show, they often use a shampoo formulated for gray or white dogs to highlight the gray and black contrast in the elkhound coat. It is extremely important to rinse all the shampoo from the dog's coat to keep the dog's skin from becoming irritated. The proper shampoo will enhance the color and texture of the coat and give it a sheen.

No scissoring of the coat is necessary. There is no longer a trend to remove whiskers from the muzzle of a show elkhound. The elkhound is meant to be shown in his natural state. Although a precious few elkhounds are used for hunting, it is thought that the elkhound uses its whiskers as feelers when he hunts in thick underbrush and rocky terrain. Quite often exhibitors will scissor their dogs' coats to hide faults. This practice is discouraged in the accepted standard for the Norwegian Elkhound and should be penalized by judges in the show ring.

An elkhound usually sheds twice a year. Daily brushing during a shed is extremely important. A dog comb is used to help remove the dead undercoat, but care must be taken not to pull and break the black-tipped outercoat. The groomer should be prepared with a large bag to collect the wool that the dog sheds. There will be enough wool for innovative persons to spin, knit or stuff pillows and toys to their hearts' content. One of the added problems caused by a shedding dog is vacuuming the carpet. The hair has a tendency to stick to the carpet. Sometimes it is helpful to sprinkle the carpet with a deodorant powder that is especially intended for carpets. This helps the vacuum cleaner pick up the stubborn hairs.

An elkhound's coat is his insignia. Brush it with loving care and always wear gray clothing.

EARS

Ears are seldom a problem and require little care unless a problem does occur. At that point, a veterinarian should be consulted. The ears, however, become irritated when the puppy gets soap, water or foreign objects in them. Earmites cause itching and the puppy will shake his head trying to get relief. Often excess wax is secreted and there is a buildup of wax in the puppy's ears, causing discomfort. If one of these conditions occurs, a veterinarian must be consulted. By keeping the puppy's ears clean and dry, the owner can eliminate most of the problems.

DIET

The extent of his exercise determines the amount of dog food a puppy requires. Commercial dog foods especially for puppies contain the vitamins and calcium he needs for optimal growth. Elkhounds are bred for an active life of hunting. Even though the puppy is fed a well-balanced food, he can become overweight and flabby without exercise. When an obese puppy walks, his skin seems to roll back and forth on his back like an oversized fur coat.

An Elkhound will obligingly eat anything available—dog treats, kid treats, people treats. He will be better off with two meals a day of a good dog food, one that is highly digestible and balanced in calories, protein, minerals and vitamins, if that is what he is offered. He should be fed at the same time each day and given the same amount of food each day. In fact, puppies like to have their own feed bowls. The amount of food to feed a puppy can be judged by the puppy's own response to his meals and to his general weight and condition.

Puppies need exercise.

WEIGHT

A puppy should be weighed at weekly intervals. A growth chart, or at least a record of his weight, should be maintained. His weight should be compared with the weight of other puppies of the same age. These comparisons can be found on a puppy growth chart for Norwegian Elkhounds. The puppy's weight can be controlled to equal the average growth weight for his age and structure on the growth chart.

As the puppy grows into adulthood, his puppy food can be switched to adult dog food. His two meals a day can be cut to one meal a day, depending on the amount of exercise he gets. Some Elkhounds, like some people, have difficulty maintaining a slim waistline. Others eat all they want and do not seem to gain a pound.

IMMUNIZATIONS

Rearing a puppy can be almost as costly as rearing a child. Both little ones need shots, checkups and vitamins, and occasionally they get sick or break a bone. One of the main differences between a puppy's veterinary bill and a child's pediatrics bill is that the pediatrician's fees are usually covered by an insurance plan.

Five-month-old puppy.

The veterinarian schedules a puppy for his shots and check-ups. He also advises the puppy's owner about using a heart worm preventive, vitamins, worming and even dental checkups. Veterinarians, like people doctors, are professional people. They must have a state license to practice medicine.

HOUSEBREAKING

Three requisites for successfully housebreaking a puppy are patience, praise and persistence—the three Ps of housebreaking. At times, it appears that the owner is the trainee instead of the trainer. The owner must remember to take the puppy outside often. When the puppy wakens from a nap, after he eats, at least once every half hour are all prime times. If the puppy begins sniffing the floor or walking in circles, it is a good sign that he is looking for a spot to relieve himself.

Puppy on a leash.

It is easier to get a puppy to relieve himself if he is loose in an enclosed area. However, he can be trained to go on leash if the owner is willing to spend a little more time and patience. A recoiling leash is an asset when the owner is trying to get the puppy to relieve himself while on leash. It allows the puppy to wander and find a spot. There are times when there is no enclosed area to exercise the puppy, for instance, when traveling, visiting or at a dog show. Then the puppy must relieve himself while on leash.

The puppy should be praised whenever he relieves himself at the right time. Praise can be in the form of kind words, a pat on the head, a tidbit or all three. Gentle scolding should be administered when the puppy has an accident. Harsh scolding or whipping is unnecessary and may cause more problems than it solves.

CRATING

Another aid in housebreaking is crating. A puppy can be put in a dog crate for a short period of time and then let outside to relieve himself. He can be put in the crate all night and let out in the morning for relief. Seldom will a dog soil his bed. However, if he is not let out in time, he has no other choice but to defecate in his crate and then all progress toward housetraining is lost.

PAPER TRAINING

If it is not convenient to take the puppy outside as often as is necessary, the owner can use newspaper on the floor. The puppy can be confined to the room in which the training is to take place. The entire floor must be covered with a thick coating of paper.

Each time the puppy soils the paper, the paper must be removed and replaced with fresh paper. In a day or so, a corner of the floor should be left bare of papers. The bare spot should be increased in size over a period of a week until there is just enough paper left on the floor for the puppy to use. It should be located near the exit door. In the meantime, the owner should keep taking the puppy out as often as possible. If and when the puppy has learned to control his bladder, the paper can be removed completely.

CHEWING

Many puppies go through a stage of chewing on furniture. Common sense would tell an owner of a new puppy not to let the puppy stay in a room where there is good furniture. An unsupervised puppy can turn a prized antique rocker into a pile of tinder in a short time. To find a beautiful piece of wood reduced to an unsightly, worthless piece of junk is devastating, to say nothing of what may happen to the puppy's gums, tongue and stomach.

During the chewing stage the puppy should be supplied with safe chewable toys. He should be crated when he is unsupervised, and scolded when he is caught in the act of chewing on furniture, shoes or other *objets d'art.*

Puppies find things to chew that owners have overlooked—lamp cords, objects accidentally dropped on the floor like buttons and pins, roach houses, mousetraps—to name a few. At the same time they have a knack for finding poisons, antifreeze and other potential death traps. Making a house puppy-safe is similar to making it child-safe.

SUMMARY

A Norwegian Elkhound will provide 13 to 15 years of devotion to a family that wants him and cares for him. He can bark when the door bell rings but he cannot be responsible for the person ringing it. He can get hair all over the floor but he cannot run the sweeper. He can tell you when he is hungry but he cannot fix his own dinner. He needs an owner who will be aware of and willing to satisfy his needs. In return for tender, loving care, he will be a good listener, an entertainer, a guardian and a friend.

The chewing stage.

CHAPTER TWELVE
NORWEGIAN ELKHOUND KENNELS
1970s - 1990s

Norwegian Elkhound kennels, like other purebred dog kennels, come and go. More than 300 owners of Elkhounds have bred at least one litter, registered the litter with a kennel prefix, and participated in some type of dog-related activity, using their kennel name, since 1923. Although many of the kennels no longer exist, a few continued their breeding programs and have made a significant contribution to the breed. The following are a few of the kennels that have been active at some point during the past 26-year period.

ARJESS: Ch. Arjess Sit'n On A Gold Mine HM340224/01 03-10-91. Male. Breeders: Roberta Jean Sladeck & Sandi Peterson. Ch. Polestar's That's Albert x Arjess Calamity Jane.

BOMARK. Ch. Bomark Top Gun HM345637/05 04/04/91. Male. Breeder: Jeanne Smolley (Mrs. Robert). Ch. Bomark Hi Ho Silver x Bomark Kinta.

BRISTLECONE. Ch. Bristlecone's I'm A Rebel Too HD 729929 01-29-89. Male. Breeder: Sharin Burson Graves. Ch. Bristlecone's Johnny Reb x Ch. Bristlecone's M and M.

CEEJAY. Ceejay's Take It To The Limit HM439069 10-31-92. Male. Breeder: Carla Catalano. Ch. Vindarne's Airwolf CD x Ch. Norelka's The Sky's The Limit.

CEEJAY. Ch. Norelka's The Sky's The Limit HD695863 11-01-88. Female. Owner: Carla Catalano. Breeders: Carter & Wood. Ch. Camalot's Rebel Yell x Windy Cove N Norelka Snowstar.

CHARILOR. Ch. Charilor Kimeg Sweet Lucinda HD796097 04-28-89. Female. Breeder: Charles W. Chamberlin. Owner: Lori Machacek. Gravind's Winter Knight x Charilor Sugar's Sweet Sasha.

CHARILOR. Ch. Charilor Sweet Magic HM348282/01 05-08-91. Female. Breeders: Bob & Lori Machacek, C. Chamberlin, Denise Farley. Ch. ThomThom's Gonna Fly Now CD x Ch. Charilor Kimeg Sweet Lucinda.

DUNHARROW. Ch. Dunharrow's Dust Buster HD288581 05-08-85. Male. Breeder: Judy Reichenbach-Silker. Ch. Somerri Kid Curry x Ch. Dunharrow's Dorrian.

EIDSVOLD. Ch. Eidsvold Vala's Solveig HD231616 01-22-85. Female. Breeder: Nancy Torbet. Ch. Vikiro Tara's Adventurer x K F Vala of Eidsvold.

EIKHUND. Ch. Eikhund's Week-end Warrior HC 667842 06-25-79. Male. Breeders: Robert W. & Linda J. Anderson. Ch. Graadtres Vamp's Center Snap x Ch. Graadtres Personal Foul.

GRASTEIN. Ch. Endrede av
Grastein HD413492 08-14-86.
Male. Breeders: Ginger Lawson,
Sandy Skidell & Marion Cason.
Ch. Vin-Melca's Call To Arms x
Ch. Grastein Go U Silva
Britches.

HAYFIELDS. Ch. Hayfields New
Animation HM438007/01 07-07-
92. Female. Breeder: Mary J.
New. Ch. Hojo's Mountain Hunter
x Ch. Hayfields Silver Katrina.

Ch. Hayfields New Locomotion
HM438007/02 07-07-92. Male.
Breeder: Mary J. New. Ch. Hojo's
Mountain Hunter x Ch. Hayfields
Silver Katrina.

HOMESTEAD: Ch. Homestead's
Bolt of Lightning HD673139 04-
26-88. Male. Breeders: William L.
Totten III & Maureen Lux. Ch.
Homestead's Lightning Bug x Ch.
Tarroma's Silver Sunshine.

JANBERTS. Ch. Janberts Circuit
Breaker HB836558 08-12-72.
Male. Breeders: Bert N. & Janice
C. Halsey. Ch. Vin-Melca's
Harbinger x Ch. Janbert's Freya.

HOMESTEAD. Ch. Norgrens Bugsy
Malone HC785851 03-15-80. Male.
Breeders: Sylvia Sizemore/Kelly
Sawyer. Owner: W. L. Totten III. Ch.
Norgrens Pith and Vinegar x Ch.
Oakwood's I'll Fly Away CD.

LISELDUN. Ch. Liseldun's Tristan
HM41565301 06-22-92. Male.
Breeder: Barbara D. Roby. Ch.
ThomThom Midgard Bjup Lars x
Ch. Satuit's Senny of Liseldun.

LINVICTA: Linvictas Preffered
Stock HM325538/03 11-15-90.
Male. Breeders: Ken & Judy
Strakbein. Ch. Linvictas Lethal
Weapon x Linvicta Pvt Blend of
Harka.

LONGSHIPS. Ch. Vikiro's Bright Flame HM344339/07 03-13-91. Female. HIC, CGC, TDI, TT, AG-I, AG-II, CKC/SKC CD, VCCX. Owner: Kari Olson. Breeders: R. & V. Lawton. Ch. KCK Felony's Grand Larceny x Ch. Vikiro Ruby's Ghostdancer.

MAELSTROM. Ch. Maelstrom's Monterey Jack HM414877/02 06-10-92. Male. Breeders: Mrs. John King & Mrs. Joe Peterson. Ch. ThomThom Midgard Bjup Lars x Ch. Windy Cove Carney's Winter Swan CD.

MIDNIGHT SUN. Ch. Midnight Sun's Grin N Berrit, CD, CGC, AD, Agl, Agll HD819625 02-22-90. Female. Breeders: Richard & Barbara Budny & Harry & Sandra Groleau. Ch. Vikiro Belle's Desperado x Ch. Midnight Sun I Am I Said.

MISTY TARA. Ch. Misty Tara
Trogankhya Kodiac HC564751 06-16-
78. Female. Breeders: Paul E. and
Nina P. Ross. Ch. Camelot Trogan x
Ch. Misty Tara Tryglikk Khya.

Ch. Misty Tara Mhawn av Diro
HC456966 09-09-72. Male.
Owner: Dr. Nina P. Ross.
Breeders: R. & D. Jones. Ch.
Misty Tara Khyrietuf Mho x Ch.
Midwest Sunshine's Nordic-
Dawn

NORD-VANN. Am. Mex. Ch. Nord-
Vann's Shana HD210739 02-22-85.
Female. Breeders: Jane Morris &
Cathy L. Simpson. Ch. Kamgaard
Kingfish x Ch. Shadowmist Ruffian
Nord-Vann.

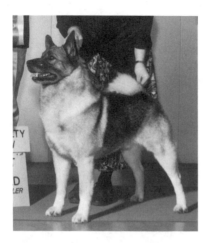

NORELKA. SBIS Ch. Norelka's Special Edition HD307250 10-05-85. Male. Breeders: Buzz & Kathy Carter and Valory Wood. Ch. Rikkana's Spinning Wheels x Windy Cove N Norelka Snowstar.

NORGREN. Am. Can. Ch. Norgrens Pasayten Warrior HM325523/03 11-28-90. Male. Breeder: Virginia Sawyer. Am. Can. Ch. Norgrens The Prides Inside x Ch. Windy Cove Wild West Jubilee.

NORMARK. SBIS Ch. Normark Moose's Legacy HD478923 01-12-87. Male. Breeders: Diane E. & Robert E. Coleman. Am. Can. Ch. Normark TNT Promise's Moose CD x Am. Can. Ch. Normark Tevia's Tiara.

NORTHMOOR. Ch. Vin-Melca's Desperado HD628727 03-14-88. Male. Owner: Dr. Michael J. Welch. Breeders: P.V. Craige/D. Schiller. Ch. Vin-Melca's Maverick x Ch. Vin-Melca's Life of the Party.

NORTHMOOR. Ch. Northmoors Prince of Polo HD413863 06-17-87. Male. Breeder: Dr. Michael J. Welch. BIS Ch. Vin-Melca's Call to Arms x Ch. Northmoor Khyries Sonia.

NORTHWIND: Am. Can. Ch. Northwind's Silverhawke HM339166/05 12-21-90. Male. Breeders: Cecilia Frye & Philip Thomas. Ch. Torden x BIS Am. Can. Ch. Northwind's Free Spirit.

NYNORSK.Can. Ch. Nynorsk Literary Innovation HM403128/01 01-23-91. Female. Breeders: Elizabeth & Randall Sykes. Am. Can. Ch. Normark Logo of Nynorsk x Can. Ch. Nynorsk Literary Air.

OSHIMA. Am. Can. Ch. Oshima's Windstorm HC 345524 10-03-76. Male. Breeders: Thomas M. & Betty R. Ricks. Ch. Vin-Melca's Chinook x Andy's Fancy Miss.

OSHIMA. Am. Can. Ch. Oshima's All That Love HD793354 10-08-89. Breeders: Thomas M. & Betty R. Ricks. Ch. Roundel's Turi of Nord-Vann x Ch. Tiro's All That Panache.

PAM-IDA. Ch. Pam-Ida's Greta Garbo HD615672 05-10-88. Female. Breeders: Patricia J. & Michael L. Bolyard. Ch. Vin-Melca's Social Acclaim x Pam-Ida's Firefly.

PEBBLEBROOK. Ch. Pebblebrook's Thunder HC680616 10-17-79. Male. Ch. Cricket's Tobey V HC680617 10-17-79. Female. Breeders: Pat & Fred Philipp. Ch. Nordsvaal's Mean Joe Green x Pebblebrook's Gray Princess.

PEER GYNT. Ch. Peer Gynt Going in Circles HM390330/03 12-27-91. Female. Breeder: Marlene M. Oliver. Ch. Rikkana's Full Circle x Ch. Peer Gynt's Trib To Teodor.

POLESTAR. Ch. Polestar's Free Flight HD630433 06-18-88. Female. Breeder: Janet C. Maier. Ch. Camalot's Rebel Yell x Ch. Polestar's Solar Flare.

QUIQUEN. Nynorsk Disturbing the Peace HM478701/01H 09-14-92. Female. Owner: J. Paul Woito. Breeders: Randall & Elizabeth Sykes. Can. Am. Ch. Normark Logo of Nynorsk x Can. Ch. Nynorsk Literay Air.

RAI-MAI. Ch. Rai-Mai's Brandy Alexander HD723989 03-28-89. Male. Breeders: Ronald R. & Sandra M. Peters. Ch. Karhu's O'Man Bojangles x Ch. Asgaard's Time To Remember.

REDHILL. Ch. Redhill's Champagne HC576863 02-16-78. Female. Owners: Freeman & Betty Claus. Breeder: Lana Hall. Ch. Saga's Shadow av Redhill x Ch. Rikkana's Look At Me Now.

RIVERWIND. Ch. Windy Cove Gold Medal CGC HD272984 06-26-85. Female. Owner: Elizabeth A. Parmer. Breeder: Mrs. Joe Peterson. Ch. Windy Cove Gunnar's Easy Rider x Ch. Windy Cove Bicen's Cut Krystal.

ROB-LYN. Ch. Rob-Lyn's Nordic Knight HD767290 08-27-89. Male. Breeders: Robert E. & Lynne E. Backer. Ch. Tantalum Tomten's Anders x Rob-Lyn's Silver Certificate.

ROUNDEL. Ch. Roundel Turi of Nord-Vann HD644550 06-16-88. Male. Breeder: Bonnie Turner. Ch. Roundel Valentino x Ch. Nord-Vann's Shana.

SANGRUD. Ch. Sangrud Toby's Brooke HD625747 06-28-88. Female. Breeder: Karen B. Elvin. Ch. Craika Sangrud Tomten's Toby x Ch. Sangrud's Windrow Tinker.

SATUIT. Ch. Satuit's Stately Sarabande HD086429 10-08-83. Female. Breeder: Janet P. Kaplan. Ch. Tekdal's Joe DiMaggio x Ch. Rivendell's Astria av Satuit.

SHARALO. Ch. Sharalos Sassy James Bond HD690422 01-28-89. Male. Breeders: Ray & Lois Mills. Can. Am. Ch. Sharalos Sassy Silver Ghost x Ch. Gidsy Smjor Av Stran.

SCANDIA. Ch. Scandia's Lexus HD905888 06-29-90. Female. Breeders: John & Georgia Shipley. Ch. Scandia's Budget Buster x Ch. Scandia's Porsche.

SIRDAL. SBIS Am. Can. Ch. Sirdals Haakon HD078943 05-08-83. Male. Breeders: Diana & Lee Korneliusen. Int. Ch. Vin-Melca's The Gray Raider x Ch. Vin-Melca's Just Plain Jane.

Ch. Sirdal's Mae West HD467125 10-06-86. Female. Breeders: Diana & Lee Korneliusen. Ch. Vin-Melca's The Wrangler x Ch. Vin-Melca's Just Plain Jane.

SOMERRI. Am. Can. Ch. Somerri Solv Penger HC002422 01-18-74. Female. Breeder: Laura Hall Lewis. Am. Can. Ch. Somerri Torsdags Barn x Am. Can. Ch. Somerri Frue Konfekt.

Ch. Somerri Kid Curry HD520461 04-04-78. Male. Breeder: Beatrice A. Hall. Am. Can. Ch. Somerri Fas Trekk x Ch. Somerri's Torvallen Freda.

STATTON. Ch. Statton's Jaded Watters UD, Can. CD HD092309 09-17-83. Male. Breeders: Cotton & Stan Silverman. Am. Can. Ch. Vikiro's Jenuine Jade x Ch. Satuit Sejaria av Statton.

Ch. Statton's Paws For Keljurno HM362970/04 06-06-91. Female. Breeders: Cotton & Stan Silverman. Ch. Sangrud Toby's Bingo x SBIS Ch. Statton's Silver Jurnda.

TANTALUM. Eidsvold Troika Av Tantalum HD828335 12-30-89. Male. Owner: Ruth Blackburn DVM. Breeder: Nancy Torbet. Ch. Tantalum Tomten Anders x Ch. Eidsvold Vala's Solveig.

TARROMA. Ch. Tarroma's Hooper HC874008 09-28-81. Male. Breeders: Rudy & Maureen Lux. Ch. Windy Cove Tara's Nimbusson x Ch. Windy Cove Ruffen's Romance.

TARROMA. Ch. Tarroma's Silver Sunshine HD037813 02-24-83. Female. Breeders: Rudy & Maureen Lux. Ch. Tarroma's Hooper x Ch. Rikkanas Looking Good.

THOMTHOM. SBIS Ch. ThomThom Midgard Bjup Lars HD005456 01-27-83. Male. Breeders: Chris & Gayle Thomas. SBIS Ch. ThomThom Acer Tab Jupitor x Ch. ThomThom PriSort Happy.

TIOKA. Tioka Haley's Comet HM351239/01 04-05-91. Female. Breeder: Lori Webster. Ch. Tiro's Smooth Sailing x Ch. Tiro's Satin Angel.

TIOKA. Ch. Tiro's Smooth Sailing HD588553 10-14-87. Male. Breeders: Lori Webster & Joan & Terri Brennan. Ch. Rikkana's With Love x Ch. Tiro's All That Glitter.

TIRO. Ch. Tiro's Love Triangle HD321511 06-04-85. Female. Breeders: Terri & Joan Brennan & Lori Webster. Ch. Rikkana's Spinning Wheels x Ch. Tiro's All That Glitter.

Ch. Tiro's Sound Track HD783356 06-14-89. Male. Breeders: Terri & Joan Brennan. Ch. Norelka's Special Edition x Ch. Tiro's Love Triangle.

T.N.K. Ch. TNK Kachina's Normark Charm HD767630 09-03-89. Female. Breeders: Tom & Nona Krena. SBIS Ch. Normark Moose's Legacy x Ch. Windy Cove TNK Kachina.

TRAVELAS. Ch. Travelas Dakota Bandit HD592613 02-03-88. Male. Breeders: David & Pat Gleaves & Diane Coleman. Am. Can. Ch. Normark Tevia's Topp x Ch. Normark's Keepsake.

TRAVELAS. Am. Can. Ch. Normark Tevia's Topp HD242308 10-26-84. Male. Owner: David Gleaves. Breeders: Diane & Robert Coleman. Ch. Windy Cove Chief Cochise x Ch. Norlund's Tevia.

TUNGSTEN. Ch. Windy Cove Carney's Concho HD794754 11-21-89. Male. Owner: Joe Wood. Breeder: Marie Peterson. Ch. Linval Eldorado Scamp x Ch. Windy Cove Riders Carney.

VALDEMAR. Ch. Valdemar's Critic's Choice HC754187 08-18-80. Male. Breeder: Nelson R. Huber. Ch. Rikkana's Brother Love x Ch. Strek's Liten Ulv.

VALIMAR. Ch. Valimar's Prairie Breeze HD778036 06-25-89. Female. Breeder: Katherine Ellis, DVM. Ch. Westwind American Storm x Ch. Royal Crown's Amaretto.

VIKREST. Ch. Vikrest Notorious Trouble HM836036/05 12-07-91. Male. Breeders: Patricia Viken & Leslie Forrest. Ch. Vikrest Firepower CD x Ch. Sunspot Vikrest Deep Trouble.

Ch. Vikrest Troublemaker HM386086 12-07-91. Female. Breeders: Leslie Forrest & Patricia Viken. Ch. Vikrest Firepower CD x Ch. Sunspot Vikrest Deep Woods.

VINLAND. Ch. Vinland's Dominoe By Gin HD643092 02-08-88. Male. Breeder: Molly Patterson. Ch. Vinland's Bulldogger x Ch. Vinland's Genuine Risk.

VIN-MELCA. SBIS Ch. Vin-Melca's Matinee Idol HC055126 11-13-73. Male. Owners: P.V. Craige & Peter Eckroat. Breeder: Robert Maddox. Ch. Vin-Melca's Vagabond x Ch. Vin-Melca's Harlo.

VIN-MELCA, Alaska. Ch. Vin-Melca's Party Chief HD882011 09-19-89. Male. Breeders: Patricia V. Craige & Dody Froehlich. Ch. Vin-Melca's Coat of Arms x Ch. Vin-Melca's Last Dance.

VOM BREE. Ch. Vom Bree Dance Hall Dollie HD863646 05-22-90. Female. Breeder: Dee Holloway. Ch. Windy Cove Vom Bree Autumn Snow x Ch. Windy Cove Cochise's War Dance CD.

WINDSHADOW. Riverwind Falcon's Au Tafeta HM387030/01 11-10-91. Female. Breeders: Elizabeth Parmer-Hall & Mrs. Joe Peterson. Ch. Windy Cove Kiva's Huntin' Falcon x Ch. Windy Cove Gold Medal.

Ch. Windy Cove Kiva's Huntin' Falcon HD584859 03-28-88. Male. Owner: LeeAnn Breading. Breeder: Mrs. Joe Peterson. Am. Nor. Ch. Rasin Kiva x Ch. Windy Cove N Norelka Snow Bird.

CHAPTER THIRTEEN
NORWEGIAN ELKHOUND ASSOCIATION
OF AMERICA
NATIONAL SPECIALTY WINNERS

The Norwegian Elkhound Association of America (NEAA) is the parent club for 12 regional breed clubs. It was recognized by the AKC in 1933. The first national specialty show was held in 1962. National specialties were held every three years until 1974. From that point forward, the specialties were held every two years.

National specialties are usually hosted by one of the 12 regional clubs. The location is changed with each specialty based on invitations from regional clubs, pending NEAA approval. The ultimate goal of a national specialty is to perpetuate the breed according to the accepted standard for the Norwegian Elkhound. It is an opportunity for fanciers to compare dogs from every part of the country, to see how closely breeders are adhering to the standard in their breeding programs and for all in attendance to delight in the sea of gray coats.

Each year, NEAA members are given the opportunity to nominate judges for the specialty. A slate is made up and mailed to all members for a vote. As of the 1994 specialty, all judges have been from England, Holland, Norway and/or Scotland. NEAA does not bestow a Reward of Merit (ROM) as many other parent clubs do. However, the national specialty judge has the option of presenting Awards of Merit to several dogs and bitches after he has chosen best in specialty.

The First National Specialty was held April 7/8, 1962, in conjunction with the International Club of Chicago. The judge was Herr Johnny Aarflot from Norway. There were 73 entries. Breeder of the Best In Specialty (BIS) dog, **Ch. Gladjac Royal Oslo**, was Armine St. Germaine. The owner was Susan D. Phillips.

The Second National Specialty was held January 16/17, 1965, in conjunction with the Golden Gate Kennel Club of San Francisco. Miss Gerd Berbom from Norway was the judge of an entry of 122 Norwegian Elkhounds. She chose **Arctic Storm of Pomfret**, whose breeder was Susan D. Phillips, as BIS. The owner was Doris Gustafson.

BIS winner of the Third National Specialty was **Ch. Vin-Melca's Howdy Rowdy**. The show was held May 11, 1968, in conjunction with the Springfield Kennel Club of West Springfield, Massachusetts. Judge Olav Campbell from Norway drew an entry of 132 dogs. Fred and Lois Turner were the breeders of the winner and John and Patricia V. Craige were the owners.

The president of NEAA at the time of the Fourth National Specialty, which was held in Minneapolis, Minnesota, October 23, 1971, was Mr. Warren D. Clark. Show chairman was Mrs. Sharon Henschel and chief ring steward was Mr. John Prentiss. The show, dedicated to the memory of Robert Crafts, was hosted by the Norwegian Elkhound Association of Minnesota. Judge Herr Johnny Aarflot returned by popular demand to judge an entry of 150, more than double his 1962 entry. He chose breeder/owner Patricia V. Craige's **Vin-Melca's Huck Finn** as his BIS.

Olaf Roig, the Secretary General of the Norsk Kennel Club, judged all dog classes and all intersex competition at the Fifth National Specialty held April 26/27, 1974, in Anaheim, California. Oivind Asp, also from Oslo, Norway, judged all bitches except those in intersex. Dr. Robert Indeglia was NEAA president, Mrs. Betty Claus, show chairman, and John Prentiss, chief ring steward. The show was hosted by the Norwegian Elkhound Association of Southern California. BIS was won by breeder/owner Patricia V. Craige's **Ch. Vin-Melca's Happy Hour** over an entry of 243. The show was dedicated to A. Wells and Catherine Peck.

As has been the custom of NEAA, the national specialty moved from the West Coast to the East for its Sixth Specialty Show. The Norwegian Elkhound Club of Potomac Valley hosted the show in Washington, D.C. It was held September 24/25, 1976. From over 203 entries, Norwegian Judge Dr. Jesper Hallingby adroitly chose **Loki of Stormy Lea**, bred by Brian and Lynn Riley, and owned by E. A. Hillman, as BIS. Show chairman was William A. Hoops Jr., with Robert Wunderlin, chief ring steward. NEAA president was Thomas Braly. The show was dedicated to the memory of Susan D. Phillips.

Ch. Gladjac Royal Oslo.

Arctic Storm of Pomfret.

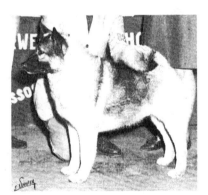

Ch. Vin-Melca's Howdy Rowdy.

Vin-Melca's Huck Finn.

Loki of Stormy Lea.

Ch. Vin-Melca's Happy Hour.

Ch. Vin-Melca's Matinee Idol.

Titanic's Porcupine Pie.

The Seventh NEAA Specialty was dedicated to Mr. Olav Wallo, a Norwegian who immigrated to the United States from Norway in 1922 and remained in the United States for the remainder of his life. A noted environmentalist and conservationist, he was well known as an authority on the elghund and the author of several breed books.

Dr. Arthur E. T. Sneeden of Scotland accepted the invitation to judge the specialty which was hosted by the Northeastern Illinois Norwegian Elkhound Association in Chicago. The show, held on June 23, 1978, drew an entry of 256. *Titanic's Porcupine Pie*, bred by Buzz Sodeman and owned by Joel and Nan Tessin, was BIS.

NEAA president was Thomas Braly, shown chairman was Lori Jelinek and chief ring steward was Bob Coleman.

The Eighth National Specialty was held June 20, 1980, in Denver, hosted by the Columbine Norwegian Elkhound Club. An English judge, Mrs. Mary Jarman, judged an entry of 247. She chose *Ch. Vin-Melca's Matinee Idol* as her BIS. The breeder was Robert Maddox and the owners were Patricia V. Craige and Peter Eckroat.

Mary Sue Schumann was president of NEAA at the time. Connie Britt was show chairman and Ingebord Hayden was chief ring steward.

The NEAA Ninth Specialty was dedicated to Florence Palmer, known not only for her Torvallen Kennels but for her work with NEAA and the Norwegian Elkhound Minutemen Association. The specialty was held May 6/7, 1982, in Attleboro, Massachussetts, hosted by the Minutemen Association. The BIS was *Karin's Yogi Bear*, bred by Barbara A. Innes and owned by Gary Proudfoot. There were 219 entries judged by Baroness Susan Van Boetzelaer of Holland. Show chairman for the event was Cotton Silverman, aided by chief ring steward, John Prentiss. Edward Hall was NEAA president.

It was back to Anaheim for the Tenth NEAA Specialty, June 14/15, 1984. The NEA of Southern California hosted the show and Norwegian Judge Jakob Petter Holsing judged the 273 entries. He chose *Windy Cove Chief Cochise* as the BIS. Cochise was owned and bred by Mrs. Marie Peterson. NEAA president was Lori Jelinek. Ed Schlesinger was show chairman and John Prentiss was chief ring steward.

The Eleventh NEAA National Specialty was held April 17/18, 1986, in Houston, Texas. It was hosted by the Norwegian

Elkhound Club of Greater Houston. The judge, Mrs. Mary Newton, from England, chose *Ch. Kirkssted Olav* as BIS. Owners of the winner were T. and C. Reese and Robert Ness. Harold Shew was NEAA president at the time.

Christian Vole, a judge from Norway, judged the Twelfth NEAA Specialty on America's north shore, Cleveland, Ohio. The show was held May 5/6, 1988, with Mrs. Cecilia Frye as show chairman. Chief ring steward was John H. Prentiss. Harold Shew was NEAA president. The specialty was dedicated to Edna Mae Beiber and Doris Phillips.

Out of the 376 dogs entered in the show, Mr. Vole chose *Ch. Roundel's Gizmo of Vikiro* as BIS. The breeder was Bonnie Turner and owners were Robert and Victoria Lawton. The winner's dam, Ch. Misty Tara Trogan Khya Kodiak, was bred by Paul and Nina Ross.

From Lake Erie, the specialty moved to the Northwest and Portland, Oregon, June 12/14, 1990. The Thirteenth NEAA Specialty was won by *Ch. Norelka's Surfs Up At Ardon's*. Breeders were Kathy and Albert Carter and the owner, Arlene M. Aliano. The judge, Oyvind Dahl, from Norway drew 243 entries.

NEAA president was Mrs. Camille LaBree. Mr. Pete Eckroat was show chairman. Donald Moss was chief ring steward. The show featured the first futurity to be held by NEAA at an independent specialty. Mrs. Pat Philipp was futurity chairman. The show was dedicated in honor of Mr. John H. Prentiss.

NEAA returned to Chicago for its Fourteenth National Specialty, hosted by Northeastern Illinois NEA. Mrs. Ann Heward from England judged 293 Elkhounds to find BIS *Ch. Norelka's Sky Gazer For Trekin*. Breeders were Valory Wood and Kathy Carter. Owners were Sandi Peterson and Roberta Jean Sladeck.

The show was dedicated to the memory of Harold Shew, past president, breeder, exihibitor, editor and delegate. Mrs. Joan Brennan was president, show co-chairmen were Leslie Forrest and Patricia Viken and chief ring steward was Betty Claus.

Once again, the NEAA membership, under the leadership of President Joan Brennan, voted to invite a judge from Norway to choose a BIS at its Fifteenth National Specialty. Rolf Frostad accepted the call. Once again, it was Norwegian Elkhound Minutemen Association's turn to host the event. Show chairman was Chris "Tina" Gonsalves.

Karin's Yogi Bear.

Windy Cove Chief Cochise.

Ch. Kirkssted Olav.

Ch. Roundel's Gizmo of Vikiro.

Ch. Norelka's Surf Up At Ardon's.

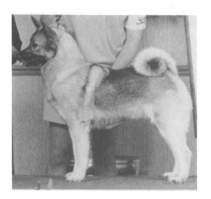

Ch. Bona Jade's Leggs Diamond.

Ch. Norelka's Sky Gazer For Trekin.

Ch. Hludaelf's Loki.

Orion Av Norden.

There were 318 Norwegian Elkhounds entered at the specialty show with a total entry of 460, including 50 obedience entries. Frostad chose **Ch. Bona Jade's Leggs Diamond** HD751671 (Ch. Vikiro's Jenuine Jade x Ch. Vikiro's Velvet Kisses Av Bond) as BIS. Breeder was Christine M. Gonsalves who was co-owner with Jane Lally.

NORWEGIAN ELKHOUND ASSOCIATION OF AMERICA NATIONAL OBEDIENCE HIGH-IN-TRIAL WINNERS

The first obedience trial held in conjunction with a national specialty was at the Anaheim show in 1974. There were 18 entries, all judged by Miss Jane Eberhart of Pasadena, California. High-in-trial was won by Stanley A. and Joan M. Green's **Orion Av Norden** HB856421 (Draco Av Norden CD x Frieda of Asgard CD) with a score of 195 from the Novice B class.

The obedience entry at the Sixth National Specialty in Washington, D.C., was judged by Mr. John Ward of Arlington, Virginia. High-in-trial from the 13 entries was won by **Ch. Hludaelf's Loki** HC26622 (Mr. Bips Tovar Tolstoy x Mr. Bips Jeanna Betts) with a score of 193 1/2 from the Novice A class. Owner was Edward R. Smith Jr.

Camalot's Bella Tigra.

Jack Daniel's Old Number Seven CD.

Can. Ch. Hammerfest's Jente To, Am. Can. CDX.

Marbran's Athena, UD.

Ch. ThomThom Jup-Don Big Guy.

Mrs. Aldythe Comstock of Sun City Center, Florida, judged the obedience classes for the Seventh NEAA Specialty in Hillside, Illinois, in 1978. Of the 42 entries, high-in-trial went to **Camalot's Bella Tigra** HC475151 (Trogen x Bella) from the Novice B class with a score of 195 1/2. Tigra was handled by Donald Rotier.

Mr. Harry L. Taylor, Denver, Colorado, judged obedience trial classes at the Denver specialty in 1980. Of the 33 entries, **Jack Daniel's Old Number Seven CD** HC291884 (Ch. Stillehavet's Jack Daniels x Skau's Kris Elka) scored 193 1/2 to go high in trial from the Open A class. Owners were John B. and Susan Murphy.

Gerard and Irene Feeley judged the obedience classes for the Ninth Specialty in Attleboro, Massachussetts, in 1982. There were 21 entries. **Can. Ch. Hammerfest's Jente To, Am. Can. CDX**, HC584575 (Inu Vi-King Av Eriksen x Hammerfest's Lite Jente) entered in Open B, Utility and Versatility, was high-in-trial with a qualifying score of 191.

The 22 obedience entries in 1984 at Anaheim, California, were judged by Mrs. Betty Mae Regan. **Marbran's Athena, U.D.**, HC473578 (Ch. Windy Cove Jr Bicentennial x Ch. Marbran's Piccadilly), shown in Open B, Utility and obedience brace class,

Ch. ThomThom Jup-Don Big Guy.   *OTCH Camalot Trulle Ayla.*

Ch. Midnight Sun Heartlight.

Ch. Liseldun Solv Sterjne Vinsja, UD.

was high-in-trial with a score of 197. Owners were Harry and June Bryan.

Highest scoring Elkhound in the Eleventh National Specialty held in Houston, Texas, was **Ch. Thomthom Jup-Don Big Guy** HC861435 (Ch. ThomThom Acer Tab Jupitor x Ch. Windy Cove Madonna Oburre, C.D.) with a score of 196. Owner/handler was Harry Beggs.

Ch. ThomThom Jup-Don Big Guy, C.D., continued his winning ways at the Twelfth National Specialty in 1988 in Cleveland, Ohio, with a score of 195 1/2 from the Open B class. Mr. Harold McConnell judged the 46 entries.

Portland, Oregon, the scene of the 1990 Thirteenth National Specialty had 37 obedience entries. Mrs. Jill Jones of Brownsville, Oregon, awarded high-in-trial honors to **OTCH Camalot Trulle Ayla** HC856409 (Ch. Windy Cove Tara's Nimbusson x Ch. Camalot's Trulle av Bella) for a score of 198. Ayla was shown in Open B and Utility B by Donald Rotier.

The Fourteenth National, held in Rolling Meadows, Illinois, drew a record 51 obedience entries. Miss Betty Graettinger judged the classes. **Ch. Midnight Sun Heartlight CD** HD514480 (Ch. Ronans Cupcake Prince x Ch. Vin-Melca's Fancy Flair), owned by Barbara A. Drake, scored 195 1/2 to earn high-in-trial from the Open A class.

Mr. George Davis from Granby, Connecticut, judged the 47 obedience entries at the Fifteenth National Specialty held in Boxborough, Massachusetts, in 1994. Highest score in trial went to **Ch. Liseldun Solv Sterjne Vinsja, UD**, HD730439 (Ch. Statton's Jaded Watters, UD x Ch. Liseldun's Frieda) owned by Steven and Renee Schmidt. He scored 196 1/2 from the Open B class.

SUMMARY

Enthusiasm and insightful training have fostered an increase in Norwegian Elkhound obedience entries across the country. Participants in agility and versatility claim their Elkhounds look forward to the new exercises with delight. As Donald Rotier wrote: "Do not accept the notion that an Elkhound cannot win in obedience competition." The scores of the winners of the national specialty competition attest to that!

National breed specialties give Elkhound aficionados an opportunity to compare, to learn, to find a dog to complement a proper bitch for a planned breeding, to see a puppy from a breeding of an available sire and dam, to attend seminars and to talk about strengths and problems in the breed. It is a joy to watch class after class of happy, independent, animated, self-confident Elkhounds in the ring. It is pure bliss to watch the ones that move correctly, front and rear; the ones that are well-balanced, with the proper head, neck, body, leg and tightly curled, center set tail; the ones with pure color, proper coat, scissors bite, dark eyes and small, dark ears—everyone's dream of the perfect Norwegian Elkhound.

CHAPTER FOURTEEN
IN CONCLUSION

The history of the Norwegian Elkhound has been set in print through the eloquence of writers such as Julia Rands, Kitty C. Heffer, Olav Campbell, Olav Wallo, Swanson and Franciose, Anne Roslin-Williams and others. Extensive coverage has lent to the credibility of the existence of the Elkhound in ancient times, his virtues as a hunter, as an obedience dog and as a utility dog. The books provide a detailed chronology of Elkhounds produced since the first stud books were opened in Norway a hundred years ago. Putting all that aside, however, exposes a silver thread running through all that has been written, a thread that binds together all the information about the Norwegian Elkhound—the preservation of the beauty and the character of the breed.

What Julia Rands said in 1938 in *Scandinavian Invasion* might just as well be said today: "It is very interesting in studying family trees and pedigrees to notice how few are the producers of first rate stock even among the best animals and how slender the lines of descent. Of course, I expect many good elkhounds have been wasted, many potential breeding animals have been sold as pets and lost sight of; but even so, it is surprising to find from how few individuals our present show dogs are descended." She goes on to say: "It seems to me as a looker-on, that the show ring has tended, of recent years, to encourage the smaller, lighter type of elkhound and also those of undesirable temperament: the aggressive and the silly ones are generally the best showers. The sensible wise, well-behaved elkhound knows that there is nothing to get excited about at a show and often doesn't make the best of himself. And so the type of dog that learns good manners easily and is such a delightful sporting companion in the country is discouraged. Faults of character are very, very difficult to breed out and if our dogs are left uneducated and wild from one generation to another they will in time become untrainable and we shall wake up to find that the breed has lost its good name and nobody wants elkhounds..." This was England in the 1930s. It could be America in the 1990s.

The number of Elkhound litters registered with the AKC has steadily increased over the years. The Elkhound has not gained the distinction of being the most or the least of anything but, because of the continued increase in litter registrations, it can be surmised that the Elkhound has continued to function satisfactorily with no gross exaggeration of faults of his character.

Animals, like man, have acclimated to an ever-changing environment since day one. Fig leaves, sermons from atop mountains and cave dwellings were a crucial link in man's descent through time. However, jeans, television and condominiums dominate the scene, for the most part, in today's western civilization. Elkhounds, by the same token, are no longer the primary guardians of the farm and family or providers of meat in a subarctic climate as they were in their descent through time. As a result, there have been subtle changes in their appearance—coat, bone density, angulation—just as man's appearance and behavior have changed.

Minor modifications in the standards reflect the need to change among the countries that recognize the Norwegian Elkhound as a breed. The characteristics that have not been altered in the standards are those that pertain to the preservation of the beauty and the character of the breed.

Kitty C. Heffer took up the cross in England from Miss Rands. She reiterates the same sentiments from a different perspective in *The Elkhound* in 1969: "Visiting and judging shows, both in this country and abroad I am struck by the fact that, though I have spoken and written in praise of so many Elkhounds, the ones I have really looked on with covetous eyes have been something less than a dozen. In each case it was something about their character that struck a chord. To me character is the first requisite I look for." This is yet another instance of a breeder reiterating the importance of character in preserving the Norwegian Elkhound as he was meant to be.

There was a time when Elkhounds could be identified with a kennel by slight variations in breed characteristics. Kennels in one area may produce dogs with darker coloring, short on leg, low-set tails or a combination of the many breed characteristics. The reason was that the gene pool within the given area was limited.

The economy improved. Travel became easier. More people traveled farther and farther to dog shows. It was almost a case of *veni, vidi, vici.* Owners began breeding their Elkhounds to dogs from other areas, thus increasing the gene pool and combining the telltale traits of kennels of other areas..

Another reason for the disappearance of kennel identification by traits was that the NEAA nationals were given every two years instead of three, beginning with the 1976 specialty. More people were able to attend. When they liked what they saw, they either purchased puppies or bred to dogs from those kennels, again combining the traits of several kennels.

Air travel made it possible to ship dogs all over the country for breeding and showing. Elkhounds were being campaigned for the purpose of winning one of the many top dog awards or being number one in the ratings. It became fashionable to breed to the top dog or number one Elkhound. Breeders concentrated on breeding for show quality instead of breeding for the preservation of breed character and beauty.

A worthwhile project undertaken by NEAA and spearheaded by Harold Shew, a past president, was the breeder/judge critique. A questionnaire was sent to each Norwegian Elkhound breeder/judge who had judged at least three shows with Elkhound entries during the course of a year. The questions on the form concerned the quality of Elkhounds being shown, obvious faults and an overall critique of the breed. Results of the survey were published in the NEAA Newsletter. The project was terminated because of lack of participation by our breeder/judges!

A breeder, judge and writer, at times considered controversial—ever outspoken—was Mary O. Jenkins. She served as chairman of the Standard Committee for the 1973 revision. Other members were Karen Elvin, Jeanne Smolley and Susan Phillips as ex-officio member. During the last few months before completion of the revision, Dr. Robert Indeglia replaced Jenkins as chairman although she continued working with the committee. In one of her last critiques she wrote: "Bold and energetic are probably the two most important words in our standard when one is evaluating the purpose of the dog. He must have these qualities to be a true representative of the breed." The silver thread remained unbroken.

It is common to hear someone parrot, "The perfect dog has yet to be born." Perhaps the statement should be rephrased:

The perfect dog has not yet made an appearance in the show ring, and would he be recognized as such if he did? Show rings are filled with cookie-cutter Elkhounds, all possessing the unmistakable, prepotent breed characteristics that burst forth on any dog even remotely related to an Elkhound. They are undeniably nice dogs. But what about the dog with the correct ears of good leather and dark color, the centered tail that is tightly curled, the strong, arched neck of good length, the short loin, correct movement coming and going as well as from the side; the dog that moves at a moderate speed to exhibit his correctness; the dog that shows his true character and beauty without a hunk of liver being thrust in his face; the dog that is too often placed at the end of the line because he is different from the others. Take a good look at him because he may be close to being the perfect Norwegian Elkhound.

The single, most powerful determinant of breed type is the dog show—not the Elkhound standard. Elkhounds are judged against the winning dog, not against the standard. A person wanting to breed his bitch goes to the winning dog with total disregard for the standard. Nothing breeds success like success. Much of the time, the winning dog is the best dog. That is not the point. The point is that the standard, and only the standard, is the ideal toward which to breed.

The pedigrees of the most promising Elkhounds in the written history of the breed are like a blueprint—a map joining the past, the present and the future. The names of the great dogs of the past will span the pedigrees of the great dogs of the present. Their names will grace the pedigrees of the great dogs of the future—generation after generation, the silver thread of breed character and beauty. Great names do not assure great dogs, however; but unknown names certainly assure unknown gene combinations and therein lies one of the problems.

Any of the several well-written books on genetics point out the unknown factors in breeding. Any knowledgeable breeder keeps notes on dogs in a pedigree: overshot bite, loose tail, light eyes and poor hips are examples. Even though the progenies do not portray a weakness, the breeder knows the possibility or probability that exists and takes that factor into account when planning a breeding. Breeding to a dog on the basis of a show win is venturesome, at best. Just as imprudent is the owner of the show dog who breeds it indiscriminately. Would there be as many litters of any breed, for that matter, if there were no dog shows? Probably not.

Madam Judge.

A dog with a lackluster pedigree should not be discounted if it is correct. The main consideration to his disadvantage is having to contend with the unknown hereditary factors he is carrying. If he is bred to a mate with a well-documented pedigree according to a plan to identify good and undesirable genes, the waif could well become an asset to any kennel. A breeder can detect many of the recessive traits in a dog after the third generation but is never surprised when the unusual crops up.

Many Elkhound owners breed one litter a year or every two years—just often enough to have something to show. Some will provide their Elkhounds for stud service or at lease in return for a puppy. Others will buy a puppy when they need something to show. For the most part, Elkhound owners are not big breeders. They leave that to someone else. Serious breeders know that it is difficult to impossible to breed out undesirable traits with a limited number of breedings.

The old stereotype of an owner taking on the characteristics of his dog can be portrayed of the Elkhound owner as well. Just take a look at the long-time breeder: silver-gray hair (with shades of blue), spectacles (with bifocals), beautiful scissors bite (store bought), arched neck (arthritis), short loin (obscured by coat) and tightly curled tail (sitting on it). Elkhounds are proud and independent and so are their owners.

The stoneware clay sculpture in the picture was created by Canadian Artist Marion Fralick Bartlett. She is well known for her imaginative animals that evoke human-like personalities. Her tongue-in-cheek sculpture of the Norwegian Elkhound was presented to Judge Nina P. Ross at the Canadian Norwegian Elkhound Specialty in Kars, Canada, in 1993.

As a Norwegian Elkhound breeder/judge of many years, I had the privilege of judging regional specialties and supported entries in the United States and Canada. I was honored in Norway with an impromptu gathering of 57 Elkhounds—gray, black, white and jamthund. My conclusion is that we can be pleased that our generations have preserved the character and beauty of the breed. Lest we become complacent, let me say, "There is work to be done." Of all the Elkhounds I had the privilege of examining, there have been five—four bitches and one dog—that I, like Kitty Heffer, looked on with covetous eyes. The silver thread, howbeit fragile, perseveres.

BIBLIOGRAPHY

Campbell, Olav P. *My 60 Years With Norwegian Elghunds*. Hopkins, Minnesota: Show Quality Publications, 1988.

Franciose, Helen E. and Nancy C. Swanson. *Your Norwegian Elkhound*. Fairfax, Virginia: Denlinger, 1974.

Great Gray Dogs. The Norwegian Elkhound Factbook. 1974 Edition. Little Rock, Arkansas: Great Gray Dogs, 1974.

Great Gray Dogs. The Norwegian Elkhound Factbook. 1980 Edition. Little Rock, Arkansas: Great Gray Dogs, 1980.

Heffer, Kitty C. *The Elkhound*. Twyning, Tewkesbury, 1969.

Norwegian Elkhound Association of America. "Interpretive Comments on the Norwegian Elkhound and the Standard," N.E.A.A., 1989.

Onstott, Kyle. *The New Art of Breeding Better Dogs*. Rev. Philip Onstott. New York: Howell Book House Inc., 1968.

Ritchie, Anna. *Viking Scotland*. London: B. T. Batsford Ltd., 1993.

Rosenberg, Frantz. *Big Game Shooting in British Columbia and Norway*. London: Martin Hopkinson & Co., Ltd., 1928.

Roslin-Williams, Anne. *The Elkhound in the British Isles*. London: Witherby & Co. Ltd., 1993.

Ross, Nina P. *Of Gods and Dogs, Norse Mythology*. Memphis, Tennessee: Towery Publishing Co., 1994.

Ross, Nina P. "The Norwegian Elkhound Structure and Function," N.E.A.A., 1994.

Ross, Nina P. *PUC, Gray Dog of Norway*. Pelham, AL: The Best of Times, Inc., 1995.

Wahlgren, Erik. *The Vikings and America*. London: Thames and Hudson Ltd., 1986.

Wallo, Olav O. and William C. Thompson. *The Complete Norwegian Elkhound*. Middleburg, Virginia: Denlinger, 1957.

Wallo, Olav O. *The New Complete Norwegian Elkhound*. New York: Howell Book House Inc., 1970.

Wallo, Olav O. *The New Complete Norwegian Elkhound*. 3rd ed. New York: Howell Book House Inc., 1987.

Glossary

Agility: An AKC-approved competition for dogs involving exercises other than those required in traditional obedience training, i.e., tunnels, seesaws, walking a plank. Numerous titles are offered.

Afterbirth: The placenta attached to the sac in which the fetus develops into a puppy.

American Kennel Club (AKC): A governing and registration body for purebred dogs.

AKC Field Representative: AKC's official representative on site at dog shows. Interprets and monitors adherence to rules. Evaluates judges, administers judge's tests and answers exhibitor's questions.

AKC Gazette: A monthly publication of the AKC containing articles, statistics about shows and registrations and official and proposed actions of the AKC.

All-Breed Club: A club devoted to the showing and breeding of purebred dogs. Membership is open to breeders and exhibitors of all breeds. Holds championship shows.

All-Breed Show: An AKC-approved show in which all AKC-approved breeds can be exhibited.

Angulation: Angles formed by the meeting of bones, i.e., stifle, hock, shoulder, upper arm.

Artificial Insemination: Impregnating a bitch with frozen or extended sperm.

Back: That portion of the topline starting just behind the withers and ending where the croup and loin join.

Backcrossing: To cross a first generation hybrid with one of the parents.

Baiting: Keeping a dog alert in the ring through the use of food or a favorite toy.

Balance: Overall fitting of the various parts of the dog to give a picture of symmetry and correct interaction.

Bay: A hunting dog's prolonged barking or voicing.

Bench show: A dog show that requires dogs that are competing to be leashed on benches.

Best Of Breed: Best of that breed in an all-breed or specialty show. In the all-breed show it goes on to compete for higher awards.

Best In Show: Top award in an all-breed show.

Best In Specialty Show: Top award in a show for one breed.

Best Of Variety: Top award for breeds that are divided by variety based on coat, color or size.

Best Of Winners: Defeats winner of the other sex. Captures that sex's points if greater than its own on that day.

Bitch: A female dog.

Bite: Position of upper and lower teeth in relation to each other. Various breed standards call for different kinds of bite often based on function.

Bloodline: A specific strain or type within a breed.

Breech Presentation: Puppy born feet first rather than head first. Can cause whelping difficulties as puppy may get turned sideways in the birth canal.

Breed Ring: Exhibition area where dogs are judged by breed.

Breeder: A person who breeds dogs.

Brucellosis: A sexually transmitted disease or infection.

Brush: A bushy tail, heavy with hair.

Bulbus Glandis: A portion of the penis closest to the testicles that fills with blood to three times its size during the sexual act. It serves to "tie" the male and female together while the male ejaculates sperm.

C.D.: Companion Dog; a title earned as a result of winning prescribed scores in novice classes at a specified number of AKC-licensed or member obedience trials.

C.D.X.: Companion Dog Excellent; a title earned as a result of winning prescribed scores in open classes at a specified number of AKC-licensed or member obedience trials.

Caesarean Section: Removing puppies from the womb surgically.

Campaigning A Dog: Seriously exhibiting a champion to compete for top honors in his breed, group and top 10 all-breed honors.

Canine Herpes Virus: An infection in puppies caused by an infected dam. A leading cause of puppy mortality.

Canine Parvovirus: Myocardial forms attack only puppies. Severe, often fatal reaction. Cardial form attacks older dogs.

Championship: A title earned by winning 15 points under AKC rules, including two major awards of 3, 4 or 5 points under two different judges.

Championship Points: Awarded on the basis of the number of dogs competing by sex and breed. Each part of the country has a different point rating based upon previous year's entries. Maximum number of points per show is 5. Fifteen are needed for a championship, with two major awards among them.

Choke collar: A dog collar fitted so that the degree of tension exerted by the leash holder can either tighten or loosen it.

Chromosomes: Cell nucleus of all multicell organisms that contain DNA. Comprising the genes of that species.

Coat: Hair covering of a dog, usually an outercoat and an undercoat.

Cobby: Compact, short bodied

Colostrum: A part of the bitch's milk which provides puppies immunity from many viral and bacterial diseases.

Conformation: The form and structure of the various parts to fit a standard.

Congenital: Acquired during development in the uterus and not through heredity; present at birth.

Coupling: Loin; the part of the body between the ribs and the pelvis.

Cow-hocked: Hocks turned toward each other.

Crabbing: Moving with body at an angle with the line of travel like a land crab. Also called sidewinding.

Croup: Tail end of the back.

Cryptorchid: A male dog with neither testicle descended. Ineligible to compete at AKC shows.

Dam: Mother of a litter of puppies.

Degeneration: Used in reference to inbreeding. After primary generations, stock shows reduction in size, bone and vigor.

Dehydration: Loss of body fluids—may lead to death.

Dentition: Number of teeth and their arrangement in the jaws.

Developmental Phases: Stages through which puppies grow.

Dew Claws: Hardy nails above pastern. Most breeds have them removed. In many breeds they are not present.

Dewlap: Loose skin hanging under the throat.

DNA: Deoxyribonucleic acid—genes are made up of DNA. They are regarded as the building blocks of life.

Dominant: Color or characteristic that covers up all others which are recessive to it.

Double coat: Having a weather-resistent outercoat that is protective against brush and brambles and an undercoat of softer hair for warmth and waterproofing.

Down in pastern: Pastern is weak or faulty and set at an angle from the usual desired vertical.

Eclampsia: An attack of convulsions during and after pregnancy.

Egg: A female reproductive cell.

Estrus: Period of bitch's heat cycle when she is ready to breed.

Fallopian Tubes: Conduits for eggs from ovary to uterus.

Fetus: The growing puppy within the womb.

Filial Regression: The tendency of offspring to regress toward mediocrity if controlled breeding is not carried out.

Flank: The side of the body between the last rib and the hip.

Fluid Pressure: Pressure caused by pumping action of the heart as the blood flows through the veins and arteries.

Forechest: The point of the thorax that protrudes beyond the point of the shoulder.

Foreface: That part of the muzzle from just below the forehead to the nose.

Gait: The speed and manner in which an animal moves.

Gene: The smallest unit of hereditary information.

Genetics: The study of the science of heredity.

Genotype: Genetic term meaning the unseen genetic makeup of the dog.

Gestation: The organic development of the puppy within the uterus.

Get: A collective noun denoting either the entire representation or a sample of the progeny of a given sire or dam.

Groom: To comb, clip and brush a dog.

Guard hairs: Longer, smoother, sometimes stiffer, hairs of the outercoat that grow through the undercoat and conceal it.

Gun shy: Being afraid of the sight or sound of a gun.

Handler: Person showing the dog.

Heat: A bitch coming into season so she can be bred. Usually twice a year.

Heredity: The sum of what a dog inherits from preceding generations.

Hetrozygous: Non-dominant for a trait or color. Carries both dominant and recessive genes for a variety of traits.

Homozygous: Dominant for a trait or color. Carries no recessive for that characteristic.

Hybrid: Dogs who have gene pairs—non-dominant.

Inbreeding: Very close familial breeding, i.e., brother X sister, father X daughter or son X mother.

Judge: A person approved by AKC or UKC to judge various breeds.

Layback: The angle of the shoulder blade in comparison with the vertical.

Lead: A strap or cord fastened around dog's neck to guide him. Also called leash.

Lead Training: Teaching the dog to walk and trot properly so as to best exhibit his conformation. May also be used for control.

Line Breeding: Breeding closely within a family of dogs, i.e., grandfather to granddaughter.

Litter: The collective group of young born of one whelping.

Match Show: A practice show that serves as a training ground for young dogs, prospective judges and members of the dog club holding the show.

Malnutrition: Lacking the proper nourishment to provide normal healthy growth.

Meiosis: Reduction division; cell division occurring in the germ cells that reduces the chromosome count by one-half.

Mendel, Gregor: A monk in 19th Century Czechoslovakia who discovered the mathematical formulas for the inheritance of color and size in sweet peas and launched the science of genetics.

Metritis: A uterine infection in the dam that can transmit bacterial infection to an entire litter.

Mitosis: Process of cell division when the chromosomes split lengthwise, resuslting in daughter cells that may each possess the full diploid number of chromosomes.

Monorchid: A male dog with only one testicle descended. Ineligible to compete in AKC shows.

Muzzle: The foreface or head in front of the eyes.

NEAA: Norwegian Elkhound Association of America; parent club for the Norwegian Elkhound; an AKC member club.

Natural Selection: Charles Darwin's theory of how species evolve.

Neonatal: Newborn.

Neonatal Septecemia: An infection in newborn puppies picked up by staphylococcus germs in the dam's vaginal tract.

Nucleus: The center of a cell. Contains chromosomes and is essential to all cell functions, such as cell division for reproduction.

OFA: Orthopedic Foundation for Animals.

OTCH: Obedience Trial Championship; an obedience championship title first offered July 1, 1977.

Outcrossing: Matings of animals that are somewhat inbred to unrelated animals to reinstate vigor and substance.

Ovulation: The female process of creating eggs for reproduction.

Ovum: An egg ready for sperm to fertilize it.

Parasites: Infestations of lice, ticks or fleas as well as internal infestation of various worms.

Pastern: The body's shock absorber. Located at the juncture where the paw meets foreleg.

Pedigree: Hierarchical listing of ancestors. Best used when combined with photos and anecdotal data.

Phenotype: The actual outward appearance as can be seen—opposite of genotype.

Placenta: A vascular organ that links the fetus to the dam's uterus. Nourishes and mediates fetal change. Also known as an afterbirth.

Postpartum: After birth.

Prepotent: Strong tendency of an animal to pass its characteristics on to its offspring.

Prick ears: Carried erect and usually pointed at the tips.

Proestrus: First part of heat cycle.

Professional Handler: A person paid to show and train dogs.

Proportion: Relationship, ratio of one body part to another.

Proven Sire: Male dog that has enough offspring to judge his potency.

Puppy Septicemia: Bacterial infection caused by a mastitis infection in the dam. Often fatal if not treated immediately.

Purebred: A dog whose sire and dam are of the same breed and whose lineage is unmixed with any other breed.

Quarantine: A period in which a dog is isolated from other animals while being observed for communicable diseases.

Recessive: Color or trait which is not dominant and must link up with another recessive for expression.

Reserve Winners: Dog or bitch that is runner up to the winner. May gain points if winner is ineligible or is disqualified.

Ribs: The thorasic vertebrae that surround the heart and lungs.

Ring Stewards: Persons assisting the judge by assembling classes, giving out armbands, arranging ribbons, and in general, being an assistant for the judge.

Ruff: Thick, longer hair growth around the neck.

Sac: Membrane housing puppy within uterus.

Scrotum: Housing for male dog's testicles.

Show Pose: Setting a dog in a position to exhibit its conformation. Also called stacking.

Showmanship: The bravura exhibition of a dog.

Show Superintendent: A person (organization) hired by club giving show to manage and run the show.

Sire: Father of a litter.

Soundness: When all mental and physical aspects of a dog are complete and functioning in a normal relationship.

Specialty Club: A club devoted to fanciers of one specific breed of dog.

Specialty Show: An AKC-approved show for members of a single breed only.

Spermatozoa: Motile sperm from male dog.

Standard: An official description of the breed developed by that breed's parent club and approved by AKC.

Structural Design: The blueprint from which the originators of a breed sought to create a dog for the task at hand.

Stud dog: A male dog used for breeding purposes.

Subcutaneous Muscle: The type of muscle that lies directly under the skin.

Symmetry: A pleasing balance of all parts.

T.D.: Tracking Dog title.

T.D.X.: Tracking Dog Excellent title.

Test Breeding: A mating usually of a parent of unknown genotype and one of a known genotype to reveal what characteristics the unknown one will throw.

Tie: The locking together of the dog and bitch during mating caused by the swelling of the Bulbis Glandis just behind the penis bone.

Topline: That portion of the dog's outline from the withers to the set on of the tail.

Toxic Milk Syndrome: Toxic bacteria in dam's milk having a toxic effect on nursing puppies.

Tube feeding: Inserting a tube down the esophagus into the puppy's stomach to release milk formula slowly.

Type: Characteristics distinguishing a breed.

U.D.: Utility Dog title.

Umbilical cord: A cord that connects the fetus with the placenta attaching at the puppy's navel.

United Kennel Club (UKC): A governing and registration body for purebred dogs.

Vaccinations: Shots administered to ward off certain diseases.

Vulva: External parts (lips) of bitch's genital organs.

Wean: Gradually changing puppies to solid food away from mother's milk.

Whelp: To give birth; a puppy or young dog; in whelp; to be pregnant.

Winners (Dog & Bitch): Best from all the competing classes. Wins points toward championship.

Withers: Highest point on the shoulder blades.

Zoology: The branch of biology that deals with the study of animals.

Zygote: Cell and resultant organism resulting from the union of the ovum and spermatozoon.

Appendix

ILLUSTRATIONS

Chapter 1:
English Ch. Llychlyn Morgan
Malm, Norway.
Viking Ship: Oseberg.
Gamle Bamse Gram.
Tortasen's Jakko.
Comparing Black and Gray Elkhounds.
Finnish Spitz, the Barking Bird Dog.
Swedish Jamthund.
Swedish White Elkhound.

Chapter 2:
Camalot Tyra Av Vinsteren.
Ch. Camalot Ruff's Trogan Av Bella.
Ch. Camalot Ruff's Tryste Av Bella.
Ch. Camalot's Trulle Av Bella.
Ch. Camalot Tryste's Totally Hot.
Ch. Camalot Bella's Trykk.
Ch. Camalot's Total Celebration.
Ch. Camalot's Rebel yell.
Caren Showing Ch. Camalot's Final Deliberation.
Pedigree: Ch. Crafdal Trygvie Vikingsson.
Am.Can.Ch. Crafdal Trygvie Vikingsson.
Irish Am. Ch. Crafdal Thor Mhor.
Ch. Crafdal Tryg 'n Thor's Thunder.
Ch. Crafdal Tryg 'n Thor's Tufsen.
Ch. Crafdal Tryg 'n Thor's Rollo.
Ch. Crafdal Lillabo Kvinna.
Glenna Crafts, NEAA Twelfth National Specialty.
SBIS Am.Can.Ch. Kamgaard Kit N' Kaboodle.
Ch. Kamgaard Kingfish.

SBIS Ch. Kamgaard Kiss Me Kate CD.
Am.Can.Ch. Kirkssted Kamgaard Kelly.
Ch. Kamgaard Klear Impression.
Ch. Kamgaard Kermette of Pelstad.
SBIS Am.Can.Ch. Kamgaard The Kissing Bandit.
SBIS Ch. Kamgaard Knave of Hearts.
Ch. Kamgaard Klear Skies Ahead.
Am.Can.Ch. Kamgaard Korniche.
Am.Ber.Ch. Kamgaard Kiss-Ka-Dee.
Ch. Vikiro Tara's Adventurer.
Ch. Vikiro Tara's Macho Man.
Ch. Roundel's Gizmo of Vikiro.
Ch. Vikiro's This Gun for Hire.
Ch. Vikiro Ruby's Ghostdancer.
Pedigree: Ch. Vin-Melca's Rebel Rouser.
Ch. Vin-Melca's Rebel Rouser.
Ch. Vin-Melca's Vikina.
Ch. Vin-Melca's Valley Forge.
Ch. Vin-Melca's Vickssen.
Ch. Vin-Melca's Howdy Rowdy.
Ch. Vin-Melca's Vagabond.
Ch. Vin-Melca's Happy Hour.
Ch. Vin-Melca's Nimbus.
Ch. Vin-Melca's Last Call.
Ch. Vin-Melca's Marketta.
Ch. Windy Coves Sweda.
Ch. Windy Coves Rowdy Ringo.
Ch. Windy Cove Wendy's Silver Sun.
Ch. Windy Cove Tass av Oftenasen.
Ch. Windy Cove Mona av Oftenasen.
Ch. Windy Cove Gunnar of Norway.
Ch. Windy Cove Jr. Bicentennial.
Ch. Windy Cove Tara's Nimbusson.
NEAA 1984 Nat. Spec. Bicen's Cut Krystal, Indian Maiden, Chief
Cochise.
Ch. Windy Cove Rider's Carney.
Tortasen's Bjonn O'Windy Cove.
Ch. Karin's Rolph.
Karin's Big Beaver.
Ch. Karin's Elka.
Am.Can.Ch. Karin's Yogi Bear.
Ch. Karin's Calamity Jayne.

Ch. Karin's Sir Alexander McKenzie CDX.
Am.Can.Ch. Karin's Rolph.
Ch. Llychlyn Callan.
Ch. Ravenstone Silver Gerda.
Ch. Llychlyn Llywelyn.
Ch. Llychlyn Meredid.
Llychlyn Irina.
Llychlyn Idris.
Ch. Llychlyn Talfryn.
Ch. Llychlyn Gwythr.
Ch. Llychlyn Moriah.
Pedigree: Ch. Moa.
Holsing (left) With Ch. Moa and Perponche.
Ch. Moa at Age Ten.
Ch. Tortasen's Bjonn II.
Ch. Tortasen's Ane.
Ch. Rebekka.
Holsing With Eight-Week Old Puppies.
Jakob Olav Holsing.
A Visit With Jakob Petter Holsing.

Chapter 3:
Ch. Kamgaard Klear Skies Ahead.
An Elkhound is square in profile.
Too short, too long, just right.

Chapter 4:
Author's husband, Paul, tracking Elg in Norway, August 1994.
Legs appear too long.
Head and muzzle lie in parallel planes.
A Correct Scissors Bite.
Ears set high, firm and erect. Correct eyes.
Correct Tail.
Incorrect Tail.
Proper Feet.
Legs appear straight and parallel.
Correct Bend of Stifle.
A Shedding Elkhound.

Chapter 5:
Correct Elkhound Bitch.
Pedigree.

Bitch Ready to Whelp.
An Average Litter.
Growth Chart.
Breeding for the Wrong Reasons.

Chapter 6:
A Newborn Puppy.
Nursing Newborn Puppies.
Weighing a Puppy.
Three-Week-Old Puppy.
Eating Cereal.
Ch. Kamgaard Kountry Kinsman at 8 Weeks.
Sirdal's Victoria's Morn at 12 Weeks.

Chapter 7:
NEAA Specialty Winner
Best of Breed.
Elkhound in a Crate.
Getting Expression.

Chapter 8:
Three-Month-Old Norwegian Elkhound Puppy.
Correct Position for a Training Collar.
Becoming Accustomed to a Collar and Leash.
Teaching a Puppy to Stand.
Teaching a Puppy to Sit.
Teaching a Puppy to Go Down - Step 1.
Teaching a Puppy to Go Down - Step 2.
An Elkhound Going Over the Bar Jump.
An Elkhound Going Over the Broad Jump.
Paulette in Tracking Gear.
American/Canadian OTCH Camalot's Bella Tigra.
American/Canadian OTCH Camalot's Trully Ayla.
An Elkhound in Heel Position.
Team Obedience Practice.
Ch. Midnight Sun's Grin N Berrit.

Chapter 9:
Waiting for the Hunt.
A Hunting Party in Norway.
Elkhound With Fallen Elk.
Elkhound With His Prize.

Elkhounds in Norway: Owned by Per C. Lovold.
Squirrel Hunting in Tennessee.

Chapter 10:
Basic Mendelian Theory Using Garden Peas.
Process of Mitosis.
Process of Meiosis.
Development of a Zygote.
Illustrations: A Buried Trait.
Illustration: Surfacing of a Buried Trait.
Breeding Pure Dominant to Pure Recessive.
Sex Determinants.

Chapter 11:
It's a Boy!
Eight-Week-Old Puppy.
Who's There?
Couch Potato!
Outgrowing a Baby Gate.
Learning to Hunt.
Saturday Night Bath.
Puppies Need Exercise.
Five-Month-Old Puppy.
Puppy on a Leash.
The Chewing Stage.

Chapter 12: Kennels

ARJESS
BOMARK
BRISTLECONE
CEEJAY
CHARILOR
DUNHARROW
EIDSVOLD
EIKHUND
GRASTEIN
HAYFIELDS
HOMESTEAD
JANBERTS
LINVICTA
LISELDUN

LONGSHIPS
MAELSTROM
MIDNIGHT SUN
MISTY TARA
NORD-VANN
NORELKA
NORGREN
NORMARK
NORTHMOOR
NORTHWIND
NYNORSK
OSHIMA
PAM-IDA
PEBBLEBROOK
PEER GYNT
POLESTAR
QUIQUEN
RAI-MAI
REDHILL
RIVERWIND
ROB-LYN
ROUNDEL
SANGRUD
SATUIT
SCANDIA
SHARALO
SIRDAL
SOMERRI
STATTON
TANTALUM
TARROMA
THOMTHOM
TIOKA
TIRO
T.N.K.
TRAVELAS
TUNGSTEN
VALDEMAR
VALIMAR
VIKREST
VINLAND
VIN-MELCA

VIN-MELCA ALASKA
VOM BREE
WINDSHADOW

Chapter 13:
Ch. Gladjac Royal Oslo
Arctic Storm of Pomfret
Ch. Vin-Melca's Howdy Rowdy
Vin-Melca's Huck Finn
Ch. Vin-Melca's Happy Hour
Loki of Stormy Lea
Titanic's Porcupine Pie
Ch. Vin-Melca's Matinee Idol
Karin's Yogi Bear
Windy Cove Chief Cochise
Ch. Kirkssted Olav
Ch. Roundel's Gizmo of Vikiro
Ch. Norelka's Surfs Up At Ardon's
Ch. Norelka's Sky Gazer For Trekin
Ch. Bona Jade's Leggs Diamond
Orion Av Norden
Ch. Hludaelf's Loki
Camalot's Bella Tigra
Jack Daniel's Old Number Seven CD
Can. Ch. Hammerfest's Jente To, Am.Can.CD
Marbran's Athena
Ch. ThomThom Jup-Don Big Guy
Ch. ThomThom Jup-Don Big Guy
OTCH Camalot Trulle Ayla
Ch. Midnight Sun Heartlight
Ch. Liseldun Solv Sterjne Vinsja, UD.

Chapter 14:
Madam Judge

AMERICAN KENNELS AND OWNERS

ACTONDALE	William A. Hoops
ALACAZAM	Amy and Debbie Walker
ALPHA	Richard and Susan Hamilton
APPIAN	Alma P. Peterson
ARDON	Mr. & Mrs. Don Aliano
ARJESS	Roberta Jean Sladeck
ARTICA	Michelle L. Burns
ARVAKEN	Sam and Pam Reitsma
ASHLING	J. T. Kelly & D. Tenzi
ASGAARD	Mr. & Mrs. Tom Balder
ATOKA	Riley Thompson
AV KRISTIN	Dr. and Mrs. Henry Fortna
AVOGGARD	Mr. & Mrs. Ludwig J. Yttergaard
BAADKARLS	Mr. & Mrs. L. C. Boatman
BARNA	Mary Holmes
BEAR MOUNTAIN	Mr. & Mrs. W. W. Wright
BEAUX-JACQUE	Mr. & Mrs. Don Robinson
BIFROST	Mr. & Mrs. Mike Wilkes
BJORN-LASS	Richard Gamsby
BLACKBROOKE	Barbara Coffland
BLAFJELL	Mr. & Mrs. Floyd Cox
BLE TRUE	Barbara Plant
BOMARK	Mr. & Mrs. Robert Smolley
BONA	Chris Gonsalves
BRANSTOCK	Mrs. Georgia M. Cole
BREEZY ACRES	Blanche Abbott
BRISTLECONE	Sharon Burson
BRIXTON	Walter Clhanning
CAMALOT	Mari Misbeek Kater
CAR-BOB	Mr. & Mrs. Bob Streiff
CASA DEL RIO	Mr. & Mrs. O. L. Leu

CEDAR'S	Mr. & Mrs. Tom Conant
CEDARSTONE	Thelma J. Heyworth
CEEJAY	Carla S. Catalano
CHARILOR	Bob and Lori Machacek
CIBOLA	Mr. & Mrs. Henry Hemphill
CIMMERIAN	Nancy Fruzzetti
COMERA	Ray and Merle Beathard
CRAFDAL	Mr. & Mrs. Robert Crafts
CRAIKA	Mr. & Mrs. Craig Ausse
CRICKLEWOOD	Jane E. Stubblevine
DANDEE	Daniel and Doreen Bates
DELGADA	Dawn Fee
DENMAR	Marti Kincaid
DENZIL	Mr. & Mrs. Ed Schlesinger
DIABLO	Mr. & Mrs. Al Schoenstein
DORIDE	Mr. & Mrs. Richard Deimel
DRAGONDELL	Elsie E. Healey
DRAGON'S END	Karen D. Allen
DUNHARROW	Judith Reichenbach-Silker
DYRE VAA	Dr. & Mrs. E. Thorsland
EIDSVOLD	Nancy Torbet
EGERSUND	Mr. & Mrs. Terry E. Ege
EIKHUND	Mr. & Mrs. Robert Anderson
ELKHOUNDS OF ELKINS	Doris Phillips
ELKRIDGE	Fred and Margie Sharis
ELK VALLEY	
ELLYKA	Ned and Toni Welkes
ENVILLA RANCH	Mrs. Edwin B. Kulbeck
ERICSGAARD	Sue Ann Erickson
ER SUE	Mary C. Potter
EVENTYR	Mike & Sue Tweddell
EXCALIBER	Mr. & Mrs. Jim Ewen
FAIN'S	Michele Fain
FOREST HILLS	Arnold and Fern Keszler
FOWLERSTAD	Mr. & Mrs. H. T. Fowler
FOXY	E. J. and Mary Anne Ammann
FRAN-VAN	Mr. & Mrs. Louis Franciose/Susie Van Vleet
FREDRIKA	Mr. & Mrs. Fred Hart
FROMAR	Frank W. and Rose Martino
FUROR	Kim A. Sorenson
GALAXY	Mr. & Mrs. John Brownson

GALENA CREEK	Rick and Sally Berger
GALSKAP	Mr. & Mrs. Richard Rytter
GRA VAL	Grace Vail Frazier
GRAAFELL	Anne C. Sutton
GRAAFIN	Chris DeBell/Ginger Leeuwenburg
GRAAFJELL	Mr. & Mrs. Edward Forsyth
GRAAVIN	Susan M. Gereng
GRASTEIN	Ginger Lawson
GRAUHAUS	Mr. & Mrs. David Gray
GRAYHUND	Nina Gray
GREEN MEADOW	W. Scott Kluett
GREENWOOD	Mrs. Winston Scott
GREYCOTE	William D. Liles
GUNNARD	Mr. & Mrs. Bill Strong
GYLEFS	Mrs. Fred Calhoun
GYNTIANA	Mr. & Mrs. Todd Zuehike
HALFRED	Thomas H. White
HALJEN	John H. Prentiss
HARKA	Harry and Kay Hawn
HAYFIELD	Mary New
HEI-MOR	Mr. & Mrs. James M. Heifort
HESTSKO	Dorothy Wallace
HOMESTEAD	William Totten
HYONA	Carol Loitfellner
ISBJORN	Graham and Juliet Movitz
JANBERTS	Bert and Janice Halsey
JARES	James Rugila
JETOSH	Mr. & Mrs. Tim Sandhoff
JO-CALA	Jon and Camilla LaBree
JOYWOOD	Miriam C. Phillips
KcK	Ray and Sandy Kozub
KAMGAARD	Margaret Mott
KARAJON	John & Karen Haferbier
KATRINE GLEN	Mr. & Mrs. Henry M. Glasgow
KEEN-ACRES	Mr. & Mrs. Steven Keenan
KEJEN	Martin and Barbara Uhler
KETTLE COVE	Amory Coolidge
KEYPORT	Mrs. Halvor Hoff
KIMUR	Mr. & Mrs. Roger DeSaele
KIRE	Mike and Sue Formisano
KIRKSSTED	Robert and Ruth Ness
KONFEKT	Jo Anne Tichenor

KONGSBERG	Robert P. Koenig
KRYS-LYN	Mr. & Mrs. Wm. N. Mesloh
KVILTORP	Mrs. Robert J. Stuwe
LADY Q'S	Shirley Quigley
LA HABRA HILLS	Mr. & Mrs. Louis Schleimer
LAND O'LAKES	Ralph Helland
LEDGE-ROCK	Mr. & Mrs. Frank N. Mazzaro
LENANS	Les & Nancy Moser
LINDVANGEN	Mr. & Mrs. Laurence L. Litchfield
LINDTVEIT	P. L. & J. P. Brannen
LINVICTA	Ken & Judy Strakbein
LISELDUN	Barbara D. Roby
LITTLE ACRES	Sandy Groleau
LONG GULCH	Phyllis I. Beach
LONG HOUSE	Linda Gibbons
LONGSHIP	Kari Olson
LU PER	Luke Perry
MAELSTROM	Mr. & Mrs. John King
MANOR	Ron & Maureen Rook
MARBRAN	Mr. & Mrs. Tom Braly
MAR-VER	Verle & Mary S. Rice
MELREVA	Mrs. A. M. Matthews
MIDDENSTED	C. Christensen
MIDNIGHT SUN	Dick and Barbara Budny
MIDWEST	Sven and Jackie Gufstasen
MIL-MAR	Mr. & Mrs. Milton Forsythe
MISTY TARA	Paul E. and Nina Ross
NARVIKWOOD	Florence Wood/Virginia Hubbard
NEL VON	Mr. & Mrs. Nelson R. Huber
NORDEN	Mr. & Mrs. Stan Green
NORD STJERNE	Thomas E. & Beverly J. Evans
NORD-VANN	Jane S. Morris
NORDSVAAL	Don and Bettye Duerkson
NORELKA	Buzz and Kathy Carter
NORGARD	Chuck and Enid Gardner
NORGREN	Grenville and Virginia Sawyer
NORJER	Jerrie M. Schweizer
NORLANDER	Scott and Kim Tilander
NORMARK	Robert and Diane Coleman
NORPEAK	Mary M. Schaub
NORSEMEN'S	Mr. & Mrs. Harold Hobson
NORSKE	Roger and Kay Bramson

NORSKBURY	Mr. & Mrs. David Tewksbury
NORSKOGEN	Nancy C. Swanson
NORTH GATE	Mrs. Borger O. Lien
NORTHMOOR	Michael J. Welch PhD
NORTHWIND	Dennis and Cecilia Frye
NORWOOD	Kathy Paquito
OAKHAVEN	Mr. & Mrs. Arthur Oakley
OSHIMA	Tom and Betty Ricks
OSTRARN	Alan and Susan Nash
PAM-IDA	Michael and Patricia Bolyard
PEBBLEBROOK	Mr. & Mrs. Fred Philipp
PEBBLE POINT	Mr. & Mrs. Chuck Pryor
PEER GYNT	Mr. & Mrs. Gary Oliver
PINE TREE	Mr. & Mrs. Victor A. ..heiro
PITCH ROAD (WESTVIEW)	Mr. & Mrs. A. Wells Peck
POLESTAR	Janet Maier
POMFRET	Mrs. Susan Phillips
QUACHITA	Harold A. Shew
QUIQUEN	Paul Woito
RAI-MAI	Ronald R. and Sandi Peters
REBEL RIDGE	Mr. & Mrs. Robert D. Maddox
REDHILL	Mr. & Mrs. Freeman Claus
REPUBLIK	Frank and Maureen Kenton
RIKKANA	Mr. & Mrs. Rick Hall
RINGESTEAD	Dr. Margaret Ascher Beach
RISING SUN	Ruby L. Torvinen
RIVENDELL - LISELDUN	Barbara Roby
RIVERWIND	Elizabeth A. Parmer
ROB-LYN	Bob and Lynn Backer
ROCKHEIM	
ROLFHOLM	Joel and Lynn Clark
ROMAR	Mr. & Mrs. Robert A. Kemph
ROMSDAL	Alice O'Connell
ROOKWOOD	R. D. Williams
ROUGHACRES	L. E. and J. J. Burton
ROUNDEL	Victor and Bonnie Turner
ROVIK	Mr. & Mrs. Robert Smolley
ROYAL CROWN	George and Vicki Zumwalt
RUNEFJELL	Olav O. Wallo
RUSKAR	Russ and Karen Weir
SACHEMS	Paula Milnes
SANGRUD	Karin V. Elvin

SANRAY	Mr. & Mrs. Raymond Wenig
SATUIT	Janet Kaplan
SCANDIA	John and Georgia Shipley
SCHNEIDERGAARD	Gustave Schneider
SEACREST	Margaret Williamson
SENYAH	J. B. Haynes
SHARALO	Ray & Lois Mills
SHONLEH	Sharon Curry
SIERRA	Mr. & Mrs. John Montgomery
SILVERLANCE	Mr. & Mrs. Philip A. Buscemi
SIRDAL	Mr. & Mrs. Lee Korneliusen
SOLV STERJNE	Steve and Renee Schmidt
SOMERRI	Beatrice A. Hall, Edward Hall, Laura Hall Lewis
SORVESTGAARD	Mr. & Mrs. Ralph Jones
STATTON	Stan and Cotton Silverman
STERLING HILL	Shelley and Sal Ferrito
STILLEHAVET	Mr. & Mrs. John B. Murphy
STONYLEA	Mr. & Mrs. Lawrence F. Smith
STONEWALL	Mrs. Barbara Thayer Hall
STRANALUND	Alena B. Stranahan
SVENTRE	Mr. & Mrs. Leland Smith
TALPINES	Marian Casen
TANRYDOON	John P. and Sharon C. Henschel
TANTALUM	Ruth Blackburn D.V.M.
TARROMA	Mr. & Mrs. Rudy Lux
TEJANS	Mary K. Harris
TELEMARK	Mark Ingraham
TEKDAL	Dr. & Mrs. Robert A. Indeglia
THISTLEDON (BALMACAAN)	Mr. & Mrs. H. Bradley Martin
THOMTHOM	Chris and Gayle Thomas
THORNBECK FARM	Mrs. Edna May Bieber
TIOKA	Lori Webster
TIRO	Joan and Terri Brennan
TITANIC	Buzz Sodemann
TNK	Mr. & Mrs. Tom Krena
TOLANDIA	Thomas B. Toland
TONIAN	Sharon Poulin
TORDENDAL	John G. Hollister
TORVALLEN	Mrs. Florence Palmer
TOVA	Bud and Audrey Henderson
TRAVELAS	Mr. & Mrs. David Gleaves

TROLAN	Phyllis A. Smith
TROLLHEIMEN	David and Eva Bergesen
TROLLWOOD	Mr. & Mrs. Mark Bjorke
TRUELGAARD	Mr. & Mrs. Truman Veach
TUNGSTEN	Joe and Jan Wood
TUSEN BRA	Jean D. Schroeder
TYKEN	Beverly Ricci
VADSTENA	George G. Brooks Jr.
VALDEMAR	Mr. & Mrs. Nelson Huber
VALGTOR	Mrs. Alice Swanson
VALIMAR	Dr. Katherine Ellis
VALLEY HILLS	Dr. & Mrs. Henry Von Deilen
VANGAARD	Mr. & Mrs. Charles Hooper
VEGRID	Howard D. Campbell
VEL-J-NIC	Mr. & Mrs. W. Nick Nichols
VIEW PARK	Mrs. Kathy Heade
VIGELAND	Norman Vig
VIKESLAND	Mr. & Mrs. Anthony Wilson
VIKING ROAD	Dr. & Mrs. Charles Truax
VIKIRO	Bob and Victoria Lawton
VIKNA	Mr. & Mrs. J. E. Farmer
VIKREST	Leslie Forrest and Pat Viken
VINDARNE	Greg and Dee Queen
VINDSVAL	Bayard Boyesen
VINE HILL	Stanley and Mary O. Jenkins
VIN-FRIK	Lorna Nailon
VINLAND	Molly Patterson
VIN-MELCA	Patricia V. Craige
VIN-MELCA ALASKA	Dody Froehlich
VOM BREE	Dee Holloway
WABETH	Mr. & Mrs. Walter D. Moore
WHITPORT	Lynn and Donna Davenport
WILDWOOD	Mr. & Mrs. Louis Hofmann
WILLOWBROOK	Tammy and Ann Marie Greeley
WINDY CITY	Susan Kaplan
WINDY COVE	Mr. & Mrs. Joe Peterson
WINDSHADOW	Lee Ann Breading
WOODHILL	Nellie B. Wood Hilsmier
WOODSPRINGS	Marietta Hodges Jones
WYNTERHAWK	Brenda Nunez

CANADA

DORON PERM. REG.	Ron and Sherry Anderson
KARIN REG. PERM.	Barbara A. Innes
NYNORSK REG. PERM.	Randall and Elizabeth Sykes
OVERSCAIG	Allen and Nina Tate
WOLFSHEIM	Jan and Maria Van Dyck
WRATHWOOD	Lynda Tarnowski

NORWEGIAN ELKHOUND ASSOCIATION OF AMERICA: REGIONAL CLUBS

Greater Cleveland Norwegian Elkhound Association

Norwegian Elkhound Club of Greater Houston

Norwegian Elkhound Association of Southern California

Norwegian Elkhound Minuteman Association

Columbine Norwegian Elkhound Club

Northeastern Illinois Norwegian Elkhound Association

Norwegian Elkhound Club of the Potomac Valley

Norwegian Elkhound Association of Minnesota

Garden State Norwegian Elkhound Club, Inc.

Norwegian Elkhound Association of Northern California

Puget Sound Norwegian Elkhound Association

Greater Milwaukee Norwegian Elkhound Association

NORWEGIAN ELKHOUND
AKC-Approved: BREEDER/JUDGES

Richard Berger
Sally Berger
Joan Brennan
Robert Caricofe
Kathy Carter
Betty Claus
Freeman Claus
Don Duerkson
Dody Froehlich
Fred Froehlich
David Gleaves
Edward W. Hall
Nelson R. Huber
Robert A. Indeglia
Mary O. Jenkins (deceased)
Cam LaBree
Jon R. LaBree
Marie Peterson
Nina P. Ross
Paul E. Ross
Kenneth Strakbein
Patricia Craige Trotter
Robert J. Wunderlin

Orthopedic Foundation for Animals:

Norwegian Elkhound Registration Numbers

Registered Name	OFA No.	Rating	Age	Sex	Reg. No.	Owner
	NE-0447					
	NE-0448					
	NE-0452					
	NE-0456					
	NE-0458					
	NE-0464					
	NE-0468					
	NE-0480					
	NE-0485					
	NE-0488					
	NE-0490					
	NE-0491					
	NE-0492					
	NE-0493					
	NE-0494					
	NE-0495					
	NE-0499					
	NE-0500					
	NE-0502					
	NE-0504					
	NE-0507					
	NE-0508					
	NE-0511					
	NE-0514					
	NE-0522					
	NE-0525					
	NE-0528					
	NE-0532					
	NE-0534					
	NE-0535					
	NE-0537					
	NE-0547					
	NE-0548					
	NE-0550					
	NE-0551					
	NE-0552					
	NE-0554					
	NE-0558					
	NE-0562					
	NE-0563					
	NE-0567					
	NE-0568					
	NE-0569					
	NE-0571					
	NE-0572					
	NE-0573					
	NE-1461					
Abby-J	NE-1238		28	F	HC-811017	
Actondale Tryglikk Cindy	NE-0574		73	F	HB-017200	
Adam of Nordika	NE-0954					
Adelsmann Av Trebarn	NE-0745		45	M	HB-705967	
Adonis Silver Paw Donahue	NE-2219	F	30	M	HM33815802	Karen Donahue
Aevie	NE-0868		24	F	HC-310367	
Ahola's Nemaia Av Solbakken	NE-1006		29	F	HR-008713	
Aksel of Glitnir	NE-0653		48	M	HB-888638	
Al Shain Av Norden	NE-0956					
Alacazam's Color My World	NE-2061	G	41	F	HD-653640	James M. Reeder & Debra Walker
Alacazam's Westminster Abbey	NE-1818	G	48	F	HD-335526	Amy & Debbie Walker
Alpha's Decorum	NE-2092	G	26	M	HD-863647	Karyl J. Parks
Alpha's Fare Thee Well, CH	NE-1798	F	28	F	HD-506859	Richard & Susan Hamilton
Alpha's Madam I'm Adam, CH	NE-2188	F	42	M	HM35891607	Richard L. & Suzanne J. Hamilton
Alpha's Smokey Ewen	NE-1704	F	24	M	HD-436791	B. & J. Ewen

Registered Name	OFA No.	Rating	Age	Sex	Reg. No.	Owner
Alpha's Stone Pony	NE-1804	G	24	M	HD-553334	Richard & Susan Hamilton
Amanda of Brentwood	NE-0214					
Andrea of Glitnir, Can CH	NE-0582		36	F	HB-906058	
Andy's Viking King	NE-1161		36	M	HC-566104	A. Aliano
Anne Karene	NE-1175		54	F	HC-623252	A. Snow
Appian Lojal Axell Faithsson	NE-1972	G	24	M	HD-740766	James W. Hayes, Jr.
Appian Lucky Strike Talpine	NE-1865	G	29	F	HD-565388	Mark A. & Donna V. Jones
Ardee's Soote Gypsy of the Snow	NE-0351					
Ardon Denmar Quick Silver	NE-1982	G	27	M	HD-767111	Marti Kincaid
Ardon's Cash And Carry, CH	NE-1418	G	25	M	HD-114913	Arlene M. Aliano
Ardon's Holocaust, CH	NE-1527	F	27	F	HD-275400	Aecta Leach
Ardon's Innocent Taboo	NE-1690	F	28	M	HD-426238	Steve Meeker
Ardon's Quiet Riot	NE-1953	G	24	M	HD-767110	Arlene M. Aliano
Argus King	NE-1400	G	35	M	HC-948969	Dr. Eugene Purmell
Arjess Call Me Silverado, CH	NE-2176	F	26	M	HM34022403	Roberta J. Sladeck/S. Peterson
Arjess Doc Holliday	NE-1681	G	38	M	HD-289989	Sladeck & S. Peterson
Arjess Flight Commander	NE-1574	E	33	M	HD-384653	Payne & Sladeck
Arjess Gunnar's Flying High	NE-1397	E	26	M	HD-027715	Roberta J. Sladeck
Arjess She's A Gold Digger	NE-2166	G	26	F	HM34022402	Roberta J. Sladeck/S. Peterson
Arjess Sit'n On A Gold Mine	NE-2165	F	26	M	HM34022401	Roberta J. Sladeck/S. Peterson
Arjess Tambourine Man	NE-1304		25	M	HC-933366	Roberta Jean Sladeck
Arlars Tass' Storm	NE-0344					
Arlars Tass' Tari	NE-0384					
Armel Sirrus Thona	NE-1230	G	39	F	HC-706462	Dan Ketterer
Arnald Laird Av Telggren	NE-2180	G	37	M	HD-859247	Sandra B. Smith
Arne O Tass Av La Habra Hills, CH	NE-0105					Robert Caricofe
Arvaken's Miss Motor Mouth	NE-2114	G	27	F	HD-903291	Pam Reitsema
Asgaard's Hot Time Tonight	NE-1620	G	31	F	HD-255710	Kimm Balder
Asgaard's Own Trade Mark, CH	NE-1542	G	28	M	HD-233022	Reitsma & Balder
Asgaard's Rave Review, CH	NE-1754	G	25	M	HD-492751	Kimm Balder
Asgaard's Springtime Mist	NE-1645	G	34	F	HD-270565	J. & M. Nelson
Asgaard's Time To Remember, CH	NE-1561	G	25	F	HD-274226	R. & S. Peters
Asgard U Ain't Seen Nothin Yet	NE-0963	G	26	F	HU-488156	Chris & Gayle Thomas
Askeladden Ibd Eric	NE-0943		33	M	HC-234962	
Asmark Tor, CH (Norway)	NE-0379	E		M		Millie & Fred Cotteral
Astr's Rosina Av Satuit	NE-1288		34	F	HC-803072	John C. & Deborah Sherr-Ziarko
Atilly The Hund	NE-1479	G	28	F	HD-164975	Geraldine Chell
Augustus Ragnar Lodbrok	NE-2083	F	41	M	HD-713519	Mr. & Mrs. James L. Young, Jr.
B T Anneke Av Stran	NE-0556					
B. H. Baard	NE-0195					
BB's Blue Boy Av Meri Da	NE-0938		63	M	HB-896710	
Baalu of Vine Hill	NE-0035					
Baldier's Kriston	NE-0753		31	F	HC-020666	
Baldur's Viking Chief	NE-0618		35	M	HB-768095	
Bamse's Lars Av Ulnar	NE-0707		26	M	HB-971439	
Bangaard's Texas Tuffy	NE-1152		30	M	HC-637968	C. Hooper
Barad Nimrus Av Meri Da	NE-1407	F	63	F	HC-709588	J. O. & Jane Palmer
Bare Cove's Maia Serrelinda	NE-1655	G	26	F	HD-457873	T. Greeley & M. Gould
Baron Olaf Timberdal	NE-0677		28	M	HB-842367	
Barqua's Hunz' Helga	NE-0405					Mary Bartlett
Barskimming Sonda, CD,CH	NE-0295					LaBree
Bart's Elsker Av Oakhaven	NE-0079					John & Carole Boyd
Bart's Valking Av Oakhaven	NE-0043					Marie Oakley
Bath Sheba	NE-1361		24	F	HD-004092	Dr. John Herr
Bear Sabastian Viknorski	NE-1057		36	M	HC-435483	
Bearberry Thor, Can CH	NE-0850		38	M	FE-000985	
Bel-Doks Bruin Bear Vangaard	NE-0831		27	M	HC-133126	
Bengal Boy, CH	NE-0401					
Beowulf Son of Olek	NE-0498					
Beowulf's Mischevious Angel	NE-1035		24	F	HC-475029	
Beowulf's Tempest Av Ramm	NE-0979		48	F	HC-172244	
Berclair Quiquen's Delirium	NE-2088	G	24	M	HM37681101	J. Paul Woito
Bergen Dagmar	NE-0972		25	F	HE-350204	

Registered Name	OFA No.	Rating	Age	Sex	Reg. No.	Owner
Bergen's Nordic Elke	NE-0928		36	F	HC-441883	
Bermarba's BJ Brynde, CH	NE-1429	G	98	F	HC-514636	Gamsby & Transue
Bermarba's Elske Tara	NE-0969					
Bermarba's Trina	NE-0856					
Berry's Stormy Cloud	NE-0818		40	M	HB-917905	
Berryhill Frisor Venn Hesser CD, CH	NE-0959					
Berutjiel	NE-0062					Edwin Kaufman
Betanna of Fie-Dell	NE-0337					
Bethel Farm's Gray Ghost	NE-0932		31	M	HC-474441	
Bifrost Lovin' Spoonful, CH	NE-1198		42	F	HC-614597	S. Green
Bifrost's Starlight Love	NE-1116		25	F	HC-588517	S. Green
Bifrost's Topsider	NE-1052		26	M	HC-484557	
Big Boy Dallas	NE-1181		29	M	HC-668038	J. Hawkins
Bill	NE-0158					Mrs. C. H. Clarke
Binna of Vigeland	NE-0205					
Birchwood's Breezy Trynka	NE-0673		27	F	HB-873021	
Birchwood's Patty Cake	NE-0785		24	F	HC-114563	
Birchwoods Frozen Assets	NE-0549		70	M	HB-803278	Putnam
Bjarna Suendatter Avnorjer	NE-2229	G	53	F	HD-806879	Jerri Schweizer
Bjorn Av Tusentak	NE-0611		32	M	HB-728875	
Bjorn Lass Keira	NE-0097					James & Connie Hillestad
Bjorn Lass Valkyrie II	NE-1775	F	47	F	HD-296665	Michael & Jeanne Siergiej
Bjorn-Lass Aurora, CH	NE-1359		41	F	HC-915493	
Bjorn-Lass Brita	NE-1736	G	25	F	HD-625307	Richard Gamsby
Bjorn-Lass Brynde's Asset BJ	NE-1607	G	40	M	HD-215309	Richard Gamsby
Bjorn-Lass Elsket Trixie	NE-1735	F	31	F	HD-454704	Barclay Hills, III
Bjorn-Lass Fro's Son Asset, CH	NE-1433	G	26	M	HD-099960	Richard J. Gamsby
Bjorn-Lass Froda, CH	NE-1609	F	52	F	HD-099959	Richard Gamsby
Bjorn-Lass Frodo, CH	NE-1293		37	M	HC-915366	Richard Gamsby
Bjorn-Lass Frolic, CH	NE-1845	F	24	F	HD-625310	Richard J. Gamsby
Bjorn-Lass Katie, CH	NE-1726	G	51	F	HD-285292	J. Movitz & R. Gamsby
Bjorn-Lass Mickey Moose, CH	NE-1844	G	24	M	HD-599996	Richard J. Gamsby
Bjorn-Lass Molla	NE-0015					
Bjorn-Lass Morgenstjerne	NE-1432	F	31	F	HD-024712	P. Brunner-Walsh
Bjorn-Lass Nauti Cal Navaad, CH	NE-1592	G	25	M	HD-281483	Wanderer & Gamsby
Bjorn-Lass Polestar Storm, CH	NE-2022	G	39	M	HD-804496	Richard J. Gamsby
Bjorn-Lass Rinne, CH	NE-1925	F	27	F	HD-703259	Richard J. Gamsby
Bjorn-Lass Rinta Av Bermarba, CH	NE-1846	F	64	F	HD-215307	Richard J. Gamsby
Bjorn-Lass Thornbeck Freyja	NE-1734	F	61	F	HD-341552	Barclay & Sharon Hills
Bjorn-Lass Thoryn, CH	NE-1362		25	M	HD-088182	Richard Gamsby & Michael Meyer
Bjorn-Lass Tom's Silver Aura, CH	NE-1924	F	79	F	HD-215308	Richard J. Gamsby
Bjorn-Lass Tyr	NE-1488	G	47	M	HD-091431	M. & J. Siergiei
Bjorndal's Big Bold Barney	NE-1732	F	26	M	HD-509657	Margaret Brooks
Bjorndal's Julhund	NE-1498	F	46	M	HD-072859	M. & R. E. Brooks
Bjorndal's Kaila	NE-1723	G	55	F	HD-181539	M. Brooks
Bjorndal's Mountain Mist	NE-1370		67	F	HC-683143	Margaret Brooks
Bjornheim's Bjart	NE-0505					
Black Bart's Eric Av Onion CD	NE-0617		93	M	HA-893453	
Black Bart's Gidget	NE-0040					Marie Oakley
Blackbrooke Charisma O Brut	NE-0530					Barbara Coffland
Blackbrooke Lady Gwynne O'Guy	NE-0462					Barbara Coffland
Blackbrooke Lady Tara O Tass	NE-0237					
Blackbrooke Lady Trela O Tass	NE-0248					
Blackbrooke Lady Trina O Tass	NE-0162					Barbara Coffland
Blackbrooke Sir Galahad O'Guy	NE-0450		33	M	HB-929074	
Blackbrooke Sir Treveo Tass	NE-0129					B. Coffland
Ble Tru Star Elsa Av Malaca	NE-1385		28	F	HD-000667	
Ble True Crystal Sta	NE-1553	G	27	F	HD-221287	Barbara Plant
Ble True Dano Daroc Roughsea	NE-1094		32	M	HC-504207	
Ble True Lir Loki	NE-1354		31	M	HC-915270	
Ble True Rolo's Frodo	NE-1183		37	M	HC-655266	B. Plant
Bobb of Pitch Road, CH	NE-0072					Mr & Mrs Wells Peck
Boetzke of Riverland	NE-0022					Mr & Mrs W. R. Torrance

Registered Name	OFA No.	Rating	Age	Sex	Reg. No.	Owner
Bohren Home's Thjodolf	NE-0184					
Bomark Bayou Bengal	NE-0934		43	M	HC-104184	
Bomark Frostfire	NE-1201		26	F	HC-762199	R. Smolley
Bomark Hi Ho Silver	NE-1921	F	41	M	HD-524012	Wendy Gerjets & Mrs. Robt Smolley
Bomark Kandykiss Av Kiki	NE-1233		38	F	HC-713898	
Bomark Kandyman Av Kiki	NE-1062		31	M	HC-456719	
Bomark Tryg N Thors Disa	NE-0173					James Ogg
Bomark Tryg N Thors Kinta	NE-0063					Bob & Jeanne Smolley
Bomark Tryg N Thors Minka	NE-0256					O. D. Barkley
Bomark Tryg N Thors Rikka	NE-0171					W. Garrison, Jr & J. Smolley
Bomark Tryg N Thors Ruff	NE-0064					Bob & Jeanne Smolley
Bomark Tryg N Thors Tara	NE-0167					James & Janalee Frei
Bomark Tryg N Thors Tatina	NE-0151					Teresa Burrell
Bomark Tryg N Thors Traveler	NE-0168					Mrs. Robert Smolley
Bomark Tudor Rose	NE-1043		24	F	HC-527436	
Bomark's Tamara	NE-0705		29	F	HB-849485	
Bona Jade's Ebbulient Boy	NE-2060	E	33	M	HD-751502	Robert Gonsalves
Bona Kisses Little Southpaw, CH	NE-2113	G	39	F	HD-751500	Robert L. Gonsalves
Bona's Jenuine Mr Goodwrench	NE-2029	G	29	M	HD-751501	Jacalyn McManus & C. Gonsalves
Bona-Cimmerian Valkyrie	NE-1975	G	24	F	HD-748345	Marian & Edward Szymanski
Borellan Ingar	NE-0271					
Borg Av Eureka En Elghund	NE-1285		32	M	HC-849102	Brad & Michelle Smith
Borg of Thorin	NE-1195		43	M	HC-608324	M. Bittinger
Brakka Bra's Varg	NE-1967	E	25	M	HD-782903	Jean Schroeder
Brandy Juno	NE-1896	F	28	M	HD-595978	Patty Thanas
Branstock Jorek of Brubak	NE-0314					
Branstock's Bard	NE-0333					
Branstock's Baron	NE-0083					
Branstock's Sigrid	NE-0315					
Branstock's Tailormade	NE-0322					
Branstock's Tema of Tyrrells	NE-0598		33	F	HB-686408	
Brenke Patagonia	NE-2198	G	25	F	HM35364204	Brenda & Kevin Williams
Brenna's Gustau Av Orange	NE-0595		26	M	HB-690674	
Briarpatch Little Love	NE-0857		37	F	HC-129103	
Bristlecone Starlite Express	NE-2063	E	28	F	HD-798284	Sharin K. Burson
Bristlecone's I'm A Rebel Too	NE-1952	F	27	M	HD-729929	Carl & Marguerite Burson
Bristlecone's M & M	NE-1748	F	35	F	HD-389284	Sharin Burson
Bristlecone's Mega Bucks	NE-1949	E	24	M	HD-748581	Sharin K. Burson
Bristlecone's Pirate's Booty	NE-2038	G	44	F	HD-614573	Robert A. & Maureen E. James
Bristlecone's Wee Petite	NE-1308		29	F	HC-885697	
Bristlecones Ted-E-Bear	NE-1332		28	M	HC-924705	
Brite Victory Av Silver Shawl	NE-0884		24	F	HC-209624	
Britta Ingrid Hyder	NE-0628		38	F	HB-781845	
Britta's Kristi of Eldsvold	NE-1034	E	25	F	HC-453037	N. Torbet
Brodir of Sanray, Ch	NE-0096					Raymond & Sandra Wenig
Brut's Kiall Av Oakhaven	NE-0542					
Bruts Britta of Eidswold	NE-0820	G	25	F	HC-080417	N. Torbet
Buckcreek's Freyja Bjelle	NE-1556	G	26	F	HD-256781	Susan Gerena
Buckcreek's Olaf	NE-1570	G	41	M	HD-125941	Fred Rink
Buckcreek's Ridge Runner	NE-1610	G	24	M	HD-334259	Shirley Quigley
Buckey Boy CD, Ch	NE-0045					Henry Glasgow
Buddie Weiser Weaver	NE-1347		39	M	HC-839551	
Bueskytter Gabel of Trollwood	NE-1930	E	24	F	HD-812300	Diane Bjorke
Bura Av Dakaal	NE-0629		25	F	HL-558831	
Buxtehude Av Norjer	NE-0720		29	M	HC-021540	
Byorndal's Middensted Pika	NE-1186		62	F	HC-409424	M. Brooks
Callisini's Shea of St. Helena	NE-0343					
Calma Beowulf N Binna's Thora	NE-1207		39	F	HC-692354	L. Mango
Camalot Bella's Trykk, CH	NE-1001		27	M	HC-482800	
Camalot Elske Noelsske	NE-1546	G	28	F		Leila J. Noel
Camalot Juniors Sweet Surrender	NE-0893		25	F	HC-215171	
Camalot Rebel's Dragon Song CD	NE-1727	G	24	F	HD-454028	Karen Allen
Camalot Ruffs Trogan Av Bella	NE-0792		31	M	HC-111750	

Registered Name	OFA No.	Rating	Age	Sex	Reg. No.	Owner
Camalot T.H.'s Winter Finale, CH	NE-1895	G	35	F	HD-551470	Mari Misbeek
Camalot TH's Winter Wonder	NE-1936	G	33	M	HD-570629	George & Lori Parry
Camalot Trulle All Ours	NE-1216		43	F	HC-617988	
Camalot Trulle's Dancing Mist, CH	NE-1180		32	F	HC-528838	M. Tweddell
Camalot Trulle's Hot Stuff	NE-1185		37	M	HC-622710	G. Misbeek
Camalot Trulle's Spec'l Delite, CH	NE-1203		27	F	HC-740506	C. Ausse
Camalot Trulle's Wind Dance	NE-1104		30	F	HC-514940	D. Loidhammer
Camalot Tryk's Windrow Tapper	NE-1162		27	M	HC-644878	R. Phelps
Camalot Trykk Moa Av Gravind	NE-1093		25	F	HO-546985	
Camalot Trykk N TH's Finesse	NE-1318		25	F	HC-937786	
Camalot Trykk's Code of Love	NE-1571	G	52	M	HD-116830	Katherine Ellis
Camalot Tryste's Talisman	NE-1247		42	M	HC-706219	
Camalot Tryste's Thaddeus	NE-1188		29	M	HC-670393	H. Greathouse
Camalot Trystes Miracle Babe	NE-1167		25	F	HC-724921	B. Plant
Camalot Voltan of Dragon's End UD	NE-1384		24	M	HD-036834	
Camalot's Best Defense	NE-2049	G	29	M	HD-794337	Mari Misbeek & Alex Kater
Camalot's Final Deliberation	NE-2048	G	29	F	HD-794338	Mari Misbeek & Alex Kater
Camalot's Frolic in Frost	NE-1215		30	F	HC-757711	
Camalot's Lacey Frostwork	NE-1244		35	F	HC-736841	
Camalot's Rebel Yell, CH	NE-1694	F	54	M	HD-238900	Mari Misbeek
Camalot's Ruffs Tryste Av Bella	NE-0823		34	F	HC-111751	
Camalot's Tigger	NE-1002		27	M	HC-492101	
Camalot's Total Celebration, CH	NE-1908	F	24	F	HD-479363	Mari Misbeek
Camalot's Trulle Av Bella	NE-0846		26	F	HC-300751	
Camalot's Trykkster av Ardon	NE-1516	G	24	M	HD-259088	Arlene Aliano
Camalot's Tuften Av Trondelag	NE-0476					
Camalot's Tulle Tiara (Norway)	NE-1291	G	46	F	HC-891150	Carol Loitfellner
Camelot Tryst's Tracker	NE-1041					
Camelot Tuften's Toya Av Alces	NE-0754		25	F	HB-997271	
Camelot Vekke Au Sangrud	NE-1036		40	F	HC-298139	
Cannon Oak's Gunnar Revel Kika	NE-1550	G	70	F	HC-856741	M. & M. D. Palmer
Cannon Oak's Reva's Rhomulus	NE-1552	F	26	M	HD-273377	M. & M. D. Palmer
Cano's Diavolo	NE-0302					Smith
Cano's Mickey Girl	NE-0564					
Cano's Mugsey Boy	NE-0565					
Cano's Nordic Knight	NE-0659		24	M	HB-820188	
Cano's Volkyre	NE-0282					
Canon Oak's Gunnar Revel Kiva	NE-1303		37	F	HC-856740	
Canon Oak's Revel's Reva O Bicen	NE-1210		29	F	HC-734759	V. Palmer
Canon Oaks Aquarius Solus	NE-1868	G	40	F	HD-471320	Mr. & Mrs. V. Dale Palmer
Canwin Apollo's Justin Tyme	NE-1473	G	28	M	HD-121209	T. & J. Roberts
Capeheart's Storm of Greycote	NE-0838		73	M	HB-502585	
Car-Bob's Viking Star Cinnamon	NE-0415					
Carl of Vine Hill	NE-0226					
Carl-Johan Fra Herrenhof	NE-0728		44	M	HB-813517	
Cassie of Vine Hill	NE-0227					
Cedarstone's Kuppa Grog	NE-0055					
Chaffee's Ceejay	NE-2034	G	48	F	HD-548739	Mr. & Mrs. Clay C. Chaffee
Chaplin (Norway)	NE-0273					
Charilor Ostrarn's Ostara	NE-2201	F	27	F	HM34828202	Susan A. & Alan R. Nash
Charilor Sweet Home Chicago, CH	NE-1815	G	27	M	HD-530578	Robert & Lori Machacek
Charilor Sweet Magic	NE-2163	F	24	Γ	HM34828201	Lori Machacek
Charm Nor's Call Me Tuf Stuff, CH	NE-0958					
Charm Nor's Co Star I Am,CH	NE-1209		71	F	HC-353624	D. Martin
Charm Nor's Designed N'Smoke, CH	NE-1149		40	F	HC-484930	R. Anderson
Chedelins Sabrina	NE-0192					
Chewbacca	NE-1059		33	M	HC-481173	
Chindee Rugg N USA's Majesty	NE-1105A			F	HC-492983	Vicky Zumwalt
Chinook Jewel Parson	NE-0968					
Cibola Ble True Rock King	NE-1028		43	M	HC-720899	
Cibola Boomer	NE-0747		24	M	HB-994304	
Cibola Cleora of Westwind	NE-1000		24	F	HC-413760	
Cibola Kitty Mack, CH	NE-1330		25	F	HC-980206	

Registered Name	OFA No.	Rating	Age	Sex	Reg. No.	Owner
Cibola Lucky Cuss	NE-0625		26	M	HB-779500	
Cibola Modest Girl	NE-2058	F	33	F	HD-811756	Patricia & Fred Philipp
Cibola Pomeroy, CH	NE-1328		33	M	HC-895471	
Cibola Princess Alice, CH	NE-1619	G	25	F	HD-371403	Nina Gray
Cimmerian E-C Black Coast B	NE-1773	G	24	F	HD-509093	Nancy Fruzzetti
Cimmerian E-C ML's Shadow, CH	NE-1839	G	31	F	HD-538766	Edward Szymanski
Cimmerian E-J Terria	NE-1941	F	24	F	HD-716206	Jo-Ann & Wayne Goodro
Cinandas Abigail	NE-1177		64	F	HC-335637	cc
Cjardale's Mr Polaris	NE-0732		27	M	HC-020694	
Clay Snoopty Duke of Mit, CH	NE-0007					C. Gilbertson & O. Cooper
Clay Trygg Wind Sunlight	NE-0694		26	F	HB-856162	
Clay's Erick the Viking of Tass	NE-0114					Clayton Gilbertson
Clay's Mr Import April Snow	NE-0486					
Clay's Mr. Imported April Wind	NE-0422					
Clay's Viking Star of Tass	NE-0113					Clayton Gilbertson
Clover's Liten Tasses	NE-0612	G	24	F	HB-746737	R. & S. Williams
Cocalalla Julee	NE-0108					Mary Jenkins
Cogan Strawberry Shortcake	NE-1593	G	54	F	HD-478616	H & B Batchelder
Cohoe The Silver Lady	NE-0779		34	F	HC-259807	
Conan T. Barbarian	NE-1098		98	M	HB-992386	
Conray's Tryg N Thors Tyke, CH	NE-0605		39	M	HB-517559	
Corky Von Hugo	NE-2045	F	26	M	HD-769932	Peter J. & Linda M. Wallace
Corrie of Vine Hill	NE-0259					
Crafdal Bridget Av Bomark	NE-0311					
Crafdal Erik Av Bomark	NE-0170					J. Sims & G. Crafts
Crafdal Frigga Av Bomark	NE-0169					G. Bakken & G. Crafts
Crafdal Jmperator's Choska, CH	NE-1008		60	F	HC-087953	
Crafdal TNT Aloha's Cricket	NE-0721		26	M	HB-924467	
Crafdal TNT Silver Shadow	NE-0190					Pauline Nickerson
Crafdal TNT Token's Beowulf, CH	NE-0731		44	M	HB-747865	
Crafdal TNT Token's King Pin	NE-0627		27	M	HB-666602	
Crafdal TNT Vini Imp Lady Love	NE-0984		73	F	HB-844177	
Crafdal TNT Viv Imp Virtue	NE-0909		60	F	HC-804251	
Crafdal TT Mist Imp Dux	NE-0722		33	M	HB-904099	
Crafdal Thor Mhores Paulette UD, CH	NE-0194					Paul Ross
Crafdal Triglik Kirsten, CH	NE-0234					
Crafdal Troll Turi Thor Lilya	NE-0428					Roberta Sladeck
Crafdal Tryg N Thors Charmer	NE-0596		47	M	HB-522076	
Crafdal Tryg N Thors Ditto, CH	NE-0326					Paul & Nina Ross
Crafdal Tryg N Thors Grand Prix	NE-0475					Gsutoson
Crafdal Tryg N Thors Hot Line	NE-0430					Roberta Sladeck
Crafdal Tryg N Thors Livi	NE-0125					F. Adams & J. Smolley
Crafdal Tryg N Thors Njord	NE-0280					
Crafdal Tryg N Thors Ron, CH	NE-0272					
Crafdal Tryg N Thors Sundance	NE-0626		46	M	HB-542311	
Crafdal Tryg N Thors Sven, CH	NE-0467					F. Semerau & G. Crafts
Crafdal Tryg N Thors Tarek, CH	NE-0304	G	43	M	HB-167131	Chris & Gayle Thomas
Crafdal Tryg N Thors Tarn	NE-0325					
Crafdal Tryg N Thors Token, CH	NE-0376					
Crafdal Tryg N Thors Torsta	NE-0429					Roberta Sladeck
Crafdal Tryg Turi Thor Dot	NE-0349					
Crafdal Tryg's Tiara, CH	NE-0012					J. Smolley & G. Crafts
Crafdal Tryglikk Veka	NE-0153					
CrafdalTryg N Thors Rockette, CH	NE-0427					Roberta Sladeck
Craika Harka's Ritz	NE-2004	G	24	M	HD-774100	Pamela R. Norwak
Craika Sangrud Tomten's Toby	NE-1627	G	30	M	HD-252439	K & K Elvin
Craika's Carrera	NE-1430	G	35	F	HD-013822	K. Ellis & K. Ausse
Craika's Double Dare Chelsie	NE-1709	G	42	F	HD-254193	D. & R. Johnson
Craika's Main Event-Torga	NE-1725	G	45	F	HD-255068	D. & M. Dannewitz
Cricklewood Blue Star Av Marjon	NE-1386		27	F	HD-029859	
Cricklewood Buttons & Bows	NE-0890		31	F	HC-137613	
Cricklewood HG Gabriel	NE-1476	G	24	F	HD-217205	Maier & Stubblebine
Cricklewood Hi'N Mighty Liesl	NE-1281		36	F	HC-761489	

Registered Name	OFA No.	Rating	Age	Sex	Reg. No.	Owner
Cricklewood Mighty Hunter	NE-1119		24	M	HC-682853	J. Stubblebine
Cricklewood Prince Charming	NE-1693	G	27	M	HD-405727	Jane Stubblebine
Cricklewood Silver Storm	NE-0897		24	M	HC-244557	
Cricklewood Storm's Grei Lass	NE-1120		36	F	HC-521277	N. Bateson
Cricklewood Sweet Rascal	NE-1537	G	33	M	HD-159078	Jane Stubblebine
Cricklewood TNT Gigi	NE-1173		24	F	HC-743062	J. Stubblebine
Cricklewood TNT Sugar Candy	NE-1174		24	F	HC-743060	J. Stubblebine
Cricklewood TTT Sweetie's Gal	NE-0782		24	F	HC-041032	
Cricklewood Viking Krista	NE-1141		53	F	HC-810450	J. Stubblebine
Cricklewood Viking Tufsen	NE-1004		28	M	HC-429272	
Cricklewood's Gray Trysti	NE-0576		26	F	HB-631920	
Crystal Diamond Orie	NE-1745	F	31	F	HD-483746	Vickie Gilbert
Dakaal's Canasta	NE-0847		25	F	HC-186519	
Dakaal's Shadow	NE-0603		30	M	HB-801189	
Dan's Elke Av Greenmountain	NE-0296					
Dandee Cochise Sea Quest, CH	NE-1968	F	26	M	HD-731548	Doreen & Daniel Bates
Dandy Landy Av Elv Lund, C, A, Bda CH	NE-0974		51	M	FW-026091	
Daniels Dustifawn CD	NE-0510					Jelinek
Davis' Frosty Morn	NE-0600		24	F	HB-740205	
Deek of the Northwoods	NE-0253					
Deek's Kjesti Av Kaylee	NE-0416					
Dellig of Vine Hill, CH	NE-0526					
Demi Tass of Vine Hill	NE-0390					
Dena of Glitnir	NE-0708		29	F	EJ-000715	
Dengus of Denmor	NE-1040	G	58	M	HC-166717	Marti Kincaid
Denmar Little Nick Nack	NE-2256	F	57	F	HD-749380	Kim Moreno
Denmar Moore's Mystic Morning	NE-1519	G	31	F	HD-236599	Cindy Moore
Denmar's Bonnie Parker	NE-1966	E	24	F	HD-761051	Marti Kincaid
Denmar's Cactus Pete	NE-1559	G	24	M	HD-312833	Martha Kincaid
Denmar's Casino Royale	NE-1578	F	26	M	HD-312832	Marti Kincaid
Denmar's Celebration, CH	NE-1674	F	37	F	HD-312831	Martha Kincaid
Denmar's Chantilly Lace, CH	NE-1401	G	28	F	HD-061496	Marti Kincaid
Denmar's Chelsea Av Ardon, CH	NE-1256	G	32	F	HC-861946	Arlene Aliano
Denmar's Color My World	NE-1965	G	24	F	HD-761052	Marti Kincaid
Denmar's Contabile	NE-1213	G	24	F	HC-829793	Marti Kincaid
Denmar's Harvey Wallbanger	NE-1581	G	38	M	HD-170125	Marti Kincaid
Denmar's Lyrie of Westwind, CH	NE-1331	G	24	F	HC-921306	M. Kincaid & L. A. Hanson
Denmar's Pistol Pete	NE-2042	G	28	M	HD-774850	Marti Kincaid
Denmar's Saturday In The Park	NE-2234	F	25	M	HM38928604	Marti Kincaid
Denmar's The Jolly Roger	NE-2216	G	25	M	HM37651605	Marti Kincaid
Deola's Beach Charger	NE-1650	G	39	M	HD-218070	Mrs. Pat Robinson
Dittos Thiek Av Hickory Hill	NE-0912		49	M	HB-992252	
Doron Ariel's Spell	NE-2213	F	25	F	YG-940294	Marion & Clint Lee
Doups Hapie Yuanta	NE-0742		30	F	HC-066202	
Draco Av Norden	NE-0399					
Driftwood's Howdy Hot Rod, CH	NE-0334					
Driftwood's Morgan	NE-0362					
Driftwood's Premonition	NE-0232					
Driva's Miss Helmi of Vigeland	NE-0512					
Driva's Miss Hilia of Vigeland	NE-0513					
DuCharme's Drake Av Framlo, CH	NE-0134					D. Rautio
DuCharme's Dukke Av Framlo UD	NE-0127					Don Rotier
Duchess Signa Av Midnattsol	NE-0403					
Dugan	NE-1241		64	M	HC-468390	
Dunharrow's Blade Runner, CH	NE-1416	G	29	M	HD-079690	Phyllis Harris
Dunharrow's Daredevil, CH	NE-1310		29	M	HC-902450	
Dunharrow's Dazzler	NE-1279		24	F	HC-903647	
Dunharrow's Dorrian, CH	NE-1225		32	F	HC-765082	
Dunharrow's Dust Buster, CH	NE-1586	G	27	M	HD-288581	Judy Reichenbach
Dunharrow's Elvemel Dart, CH	NE-2086	G	32	M	HD-818885	Judith A. Reichenbach
Dutch Hollows Mystic Magic	NE-0699		24	F	HB-910019	
E E Smoki	NE-0798		38	M	HB-899266	
ET's Tasharea	NE-1647	F	80	F	HC-949590	David Sanders

Registered Name	OFA No.	Rating	Age	Sex	Reg. No.	Owner
Eagle's Cheri Blossom O'Vikiro, CH	NE-1389		24	F	HD-051982	
Ear Rusa Minor	NE-1037		27	M	HC-459217	
Earl of Chrisnik	NE-1066		52	M	HC-419569	
Egersund Happy Cash	NE-0320					
Egersund Happy Days	NE-0318					
Egersund Jomfruen	NE-0230					
Egersund M'Lady Em of Melreva	NE-0069					Estelle Matthews
Egersund M'Lord Steed	NE-0070					Terry & Linda Ege
Egersund Mr. O'Shea	NE-0229					
Egersund Rocca A Laurel	NE-0319					
Eidsvold Solveig Kiva' Tyll	NE-1963	G	29	M	HD-738638	William A. Trombello
Eidsvold Solveig' Kiva'Tura	NE-1927	G	25	F	HD-682670	Nancy Torbet
Eidsvold Solveig's Andrea	NE-2055	G	26	F	HD-884417	Virginia Sawyer
Eidsvold Solveig's Vika	NE-2140	F	24	F	HM33886401	Nancy Torbet
Eidsvold Solveigs Kivas Tass	NE-1923	F	24	M	HD-688526	Robert G. & Lynne E. Backer
Eidsvold Troika Av Tantalum	NE-2064	G	25	M	HD-828335	Ruth Blackburn, DVM
Eidsvold Tur-And Rokk	NE-2255	G	26	M	HM38756107	Nancy Torbet
Eidsvold Vala's Saga	NE-1547	G	25	F	HD-231617	Nancy Torbet
Eidsvold Vala's Solveig, CH	NE-1548	F	25	F	HD-231616	Nancy Torbet
Einar-Av-Timil	NE-0709		35	M	HB-838142	
Eirik of Glitnir	NE-0766		31	M	EU-000097	
Elgeland's Fram	NE-0239					
Elgeland's Vesla	NE-0328					
Eli Skronje	NE-0684		37	M	-N	
Elka Av Kjolen	NE-0245					
Elka XXXII	NE-0787		29	F	HC-089040	
Elkcrest Vika	NE-0053					Hubert & Marjorie Curtis
Elke Shana	NE-0435					
Elkie Tilberg	NE-2091	G	35	F	HD-767374	Susan J. Mesick
Elkie XV	NE-0375					
Elkridge's Eir Everlasting	NE-2211	G	25	F	HM36540401	Fred Sharis
Ellyka Stone's Throw, CH	NE-1431	F	24	M	HD-102872	Toni Welkes
Ellyka's Gangbuster, CH	NE-1922	G	24	M	HD-679948	Toni & Ned Welkes
Ellyka's Homespun, CH	NE-1591	G	69	F	HC-872174	T & J Welkes
Ellyka's Little Mohee	NE-1437	F	65	F		Pat Regan
Ellyka's Rolling Stone	NE-1289		25	M	HC-881780	Ned & Toni Welkes
Ellyka's Silver Chief	NE-2073	G	24	M	HD-852324	Charles & Susan D'Angelo
Ellyka's Silver Totem, CH	NE-2090	F	25	F	HD-854742	Ned & Toni Welkes
Ellyka's Spindrift	NE-1874	F	24	F	HD-610123	Toni & Ned Welkes
Ellyka's Spun Silver	NE-1497	G	34	F	HD-102873	Toni Welkes
Ellyka's Vanity Fair	NE-2243	G	25	F	HM39104901	Toni & Ned Welkes
Elsa XIV	NE-0533					
Elsa-Sonja	NE-0671		25	F	HB-937588	
Elsket Av Sangrud CD	NE-0135					Karen Elvin
Elvemel's A New Lief, CH	NE-1789	G	40	F	HD-355729	Kent & Lisa MacFarlane
Elvemel's Genesis of Michaux	NE-2153	G	24	F	HM35074003	Marian Siegel, VMD
Emmerich's Norwegian Pride	NE-1750	G	27	F	HD-457297	Larry & Gayle Emmerich
Eric Winston	NE-0887		24	M	HC-212414	
Erica Birget	NE-1706	G	49	F	HD-205532	James & Lisa Ragsdale
Erica of Pitch Road	NE-0388					
Ericksons Chris of Norges	NE-0590		62	M	HB-219053	
Ericsgaard Fram, CH	NE-0060					Sue Erickson
Ericsgaard Lefle, CH	NE-0156					Sue Erickson
Ericsgaard Mirkel, CH	NE-0037					Mark Hyatt
Ericsgaard Munin, CH	NE-0017					Sue Erickson
Ericsgaard Natevind	NE-0018					Sue Erickson
Ericsgaard Nordavind	NE-0157					Sue Erickson
Ericsgaard Olsa	NE-0201					
Ericsgaard Qualitet	NE-0478					Sue Ann Erickson
Erik of Keyport, CH	NE-0126					Rick & Lana Hall
Erika Nanook the Viking	NE-0769		25	F	HC-048798	
Erika's Elvenking	NE-0692		43	M	HB-672434	
Erikson Viking	NE-0601		24	M	HB-713291	

Registered Name	OFA No.	Rating	Age	Sex	Reg. No.	Owner
Eventyr's Amazon Dixie	NE-2192	G	25	F	HM36428905	Mike & Suzanne Tweddell
Eventyr's Eclipse	NE-1381		38	F	HC-986758	Michael Tweddell
Eventyr's Fantasy Ayla	NE-1703	E	29	F	HD-399742	Janice Leatherman
Eventyr's Ferrari	NE-1776	G	24	F	HD-554922	Mike & Sue Tweddell
Eventyr's I've Got A Crush	NE-1959	F	37	F	HD-680517	Mike & Sue Tweddell
Eventyr's Silver Bentley	NE-1780	F	24	M	HD-554919	Mike & Sue Tweddell
Eventyr's Silver Spirit, CH	NE-1774	G	24	F	HD-554924	Mike & Sue Tweddell
Eventyr's Silver Strike	NE-2184	G	25	M	HM36428901	Mike & Suzanne Tweddell
Eventyr's Starfire	NE-1375		37	F	HC-986757	Michael & Sue Tweddell
Eventyr's Summer Scorcher	NE-1779	G	60	M	HD-212850	Mike & Sue Tweddell
Eventyr's The Real Thing	NE-1960	F	37	M	HD-680516	Mike & Sue Tweddell
Eveton's Bozo	NE-0638		31	M	HB-806270	
Fanegjorgs Bjorn Av Bjorksyn, CH	NE-0038					Don & Betty Duerkson
Fanta's Endless Night	NE-2171	G	24	F	YG-911213	Charles D. Macinnes
Fantasy's Christian Jadan	NE-2222	G	38	M	HM32170203	Marcella Harris
Fantasy's Lothlorien	NE-2223	E	25	F	HM37716302	Janice Leatherman-Sagle
Fantasy's Midnight Sun, CH	NE-2232	G	51	M	HD-779009	Christina Elizabeth Coster
Fantasys Backscatter, CH	NE-1984	G	30	F	HD-721344	Janice Leatherman-Sagle
Fantasys Eminent Thunder	NE-2107	G	24	M	HM32170201	Daniel Sagle
Fantasys Freedom Faun	NE-2021	G	25	F	HD-761971	Joann Stahl
Fantasys Freedom Hunter	NE-1702	E	47	M	HD-284574	J. Leatherman-Sagle
Fantasys Mythical Artemis	NE-1790	G	26	F	HD-541770	Daniel & Janice Sagle
Fantasys Night Stalker, Am Can CH	NE-2017	G	24	M	HD-832920	Jeff & Karen Kaminski
Fantasys Phantom Primeval	NE-2018	G	24	M	HD-851660	Daniel N. Sagle
Fanto of Glitnir, Can CH	NE-0756		24	M	FG-000168	
Fanto's Olga of Taber	NE-1020		28	F	JH-021636	
Fenris Av Angur-Boda	NE-0926		30	M	HC-238700	
Fetter's Nikki Av Val Halla	NE-0451		24	M	HC-014207	
Finn of Pitch Road	NE-0049					Henry Glasgow
Finn's Tekla of Narvikwood, CH	NE-0090					John & Sharon Henschel
Firacres Houdini	NE-0904		58	M	HB-902213	
Flame's Ember	NE-0132					
Flynn's Bullwinkle of Sno-Ilp	NE-2028	G	58	F	ILP-74352	John & Geraldine King
Foltz' Tauni of Middensted	NE-0655		28	M	HB-785107	
Forest Hill All That Jazz	NE-2152	G	24	F	HM34059006	Jan M. Herinck
Forest Hills Arna	NE-0348					
Forest Hills Chance	NE-2062	F	32	M	HD-777763	P. Walling & F. Keszler
Forest Hills Chantelle	NE-1847	G	57	F	HD-275414	Roger & Jean Eichman
Forest Hills Comanche Victory	NE-0142					Arnold & Fern Keszler
Forest Hills DD Av Windy Cove	NE-1877	G	39	F	HD-485665	L. Breading & E. Parmer
Forest Hills Fury	NE-2110	F	37	F	HD-767841	Fern Y. Keszler
Forest Hills Ruff 'N Rendition	NE-0964					
Forest Hills Ruffan	NE-1339		47	M	HC-815265	
Forest Hills Silver Tora	NE-0246					
Forest Hills Tauno	NE-0433					
Forest Hills Tosco	NE-0289					
Forest Hills Tova	NE-1998	F	24	F	HD-782771	Dorothy E. Brown
Forrest HIlls Comanche's Loki	NE-0299					
Forrest Hills Kaci	NE-1342		24	F	HC-983534	
Fort Knox Av Katrine Glen, CH	NE-0004					Henry Glasgow
Foxy's Autumn Sun Av Touche	NE-1360		25	M	HD-007007	
Foxy's Double O Seven	NE-2044	F	28	M	HD-759911	E. J. & Mary A. Ammann
Foxy's Raider	NE-1999	G	24	M	HD-791134	Sandra Yost
Foxy's Smoke On The Water	NE-1974	G	24	M	HD-749744	Sheila & Bruce Leonard
Frederick's Mon-Ami	NE-1981	F	29	F	HD-767504	Judy Frederick
Fredrika's Eriksson	NE-0989		109	M	HB-360965	
Fredrika's Field Marshal, CH	NE-0795		29	M	HC-043189	
Fredrika's Flirt of Sharalo	NE-1224		24	F	HC-795923	
Fredrika's Friar Tuck	NE-1158		28	M	HC-634918	W. Lawrence
Fredrikas In A Good Mood	NE-0840		57	M	HB-736098	
Frey	NE-0623		74	F	HB-253682	
Freya Nordkapp	NE-0871		46	F	HB-953667	
Freya Thora Ryger	NE-0687		24	F	HB-985779	

Registered Name	OFA No.	Rating	Age	Sex	Reg. No.	Owner
Freya of Mt Carmel	NE-0852					
Freyja Av Greenmountain, CH	NE-0340					
Freyjan-Ellyka's Diva	NE-1885	G	26	F	HD-613033	Paul J. Graham
Frick Frack Frikka	NE-1831	F	121	F	HC-686381	Lorna M. Nailon
Frija Mathilde	NE-0669		39	F	HB-981087	
Frisor Ceredo	NE-0338					
Fromar Finnshavn Georgiana	NE-2172	F	24	F	1045807	Charles D. Macinnes
Fromar's Firecracker	NE-2205	F	26	M	HM36899701	Caren Martino / Ian Bergman
Fromar's Howdi Merica	NE-0469					
Frossen's Skygge	NE-1286		25	M	HC-877903	Rosemary Olive & Guy Olive
Frostvaer Av Sangrud	NE-0262					Karen Elvin
Furrer's Calashandra Av Kejen	NE-1783	G	31	F	HD-451724	Martin & Barbara Uhler
Furrer's Kodiak Brown Bear, CH	NE-1749	G	50	M	HD-280859	Randy & Robin Furrer
Galaxy's Finloper	NE-1118		38	F	HC-505907	J. Brownson
Galaxy's Jack O Tash	NE-0961					
Galaxy's Krigskip	NE-0873		24	M	HC-261322	
Galaxy's Krigsterne	NE-1061		38	F	HC-403926	
Galaxy's Natasha	NE-0668		24	F	HB-900799	
Galaxy's Regulus	NE-0828		31	M	HC-029684	
Galaxy's Stor Bjorn	NE-0642		32	M	HB-884239	
Galena Creek's Hot Pursuit	NE-1455	F	26	M	HD-175656	R. & S. Berger
Galena Creek's Hot Shot	NE-1443	G	24	M	HD-175658	Herbert Coplin
Galena's Magic Silver Lady	NE-1475	G	28	F	HD-110049	Berger & Stuart
Gareloch's Frolicing Goblin	NE-1568	E	31	F	HD-222561	Faye Lunardi
Gefjon of Middensted	NE-0213					
Geodi Little Bear	NE-0743		29	M	HB-968746	
Gilbert's Hondu	NE-0586		24	F	HB-916148	
Glede of Ada Cascade	NE-1297		28	F	HC-906421	Mary & Doug Sanders
Glintner's Haakon, Can CH	NE-0848		24	M	GJ-015972	
Glitnir Ingmar	NE-0992		41	M	GW-072637	
Glitnir Jorgen, Can CH	NE-0962					
Glitnir's Illja	NE-1023		46	F	GW-108440	
Grauhaus First Edition	NE-1054		24	M	HC-488444	
Grauhaus Limited Edition, CH	NE-1046		24	F	HC-488445	
Grauhaus Whitehaush Debate, CH	NE-1222		29	M	HC-761401	
Gravind's Eternally Hot	NE-1696	G	54	M	HD-222777	Williamson & Mohr
Gravinds Winter Knight	NE-1670	F	51	M	HD188561	Vicky Zumwalt
Grayhund's Wind Storm	NE-0657		26	M	HB-846399	
Gretta Katrin	NE-0238					
Grizzly Rex of Nordica	NE-0757		53	M	HB-655475	
Guendahl's Aces High	NE-2221	G	25	M	HM37883502	J. Fryhover
Guendahl's Heia	NE-2242	G	27	F	HM37883504	J. Fryhover
Gunnarsholm Pewter Tindre	NE-2046	G	30	F	WN-779932	Jo Anne Willman
Haar Vel's Rusken's Toki	NE-0222					
Hadad's Kia	NE-0967					
Hammerfest Lite Overlevende	NE-1680	F	30	F	HD-384592	R. & D. Dyrdahl
Hammerfest's Jente To, CDX	NE-1157		36	F	HC-584575	P. Anderson
Happy Lavena	NE-0146					Andrew & Anna Deiss
Happy Tak	NE-0604		27	M	HB-684397	
Har Vel's Rusken Av Oftenasen	NE-0075					M. Peterson & Mrs Hudlow
Harka Diablo's Gamay Rose, CH	NE-1137		27	F	HC-612644	H. Hawn
Harka's Aramis	NE-1341		30	M	HD-003807	
Harka's Bergen	NE-1746	G	70	F	HD-221716	Richard Meek
Harka's Bristol Cream	NE-1283		25	M	HC-887921	Claud Butler
Harka's Camalot Innocence	NE-2120	G	38	F	HD-787837	Harry & Kay Hawn
Harka's Cinnabar	NE-1295		24	M	HD-034099	Harry Hawn & Martin Dinning
Harka's Good Time Charlie	NE-1572	G	26	M	HD-317952	Hawn & Webb
Harka's Morning Glory CD, CH	NE-1015		26	F	HC-478556	
Harka's Northern Chinook, CH	NE-1822	G	29	F	HD-524047	Alice Hastings
Harka's O' What A Dream	NE-1494	G	35	F	HD-108504	Michelle & Brad Smith
Harka's Promised Flicka	NE-1471	G	24	F	HD-182440	Harold Swanson
Harka's Sampson	NE-1039		27	M	HC-340338	
Harka-Diablo's Gambler, CH	NE-1204		27	M	HC-789630	H. Hawn

Registered Name	OFA No.	Rating	Age	Sex	Reg. No.	Owner
Harkas Tasmanian Tasha	NE-2006	G	39	F	HD-650894	Bruce Friedman
Harwal's Finrod	NE-0902		24	M	HC-365196	
Hedda Huestis-Schenck	NE-1715	G	31	F	HD-379565	S. Huestis & C. Schneck
Hedtskos Njord	NE-1881	G	39	M	HD-618052	William Lindveit
Heidi O Tass Av La Habra Hills, CH	NE-0110					Glen & Shirley Minott
Heidi XVII	NE-0033					Henry Glasgow
Heidoo Olaf Addfus Heiskell	NE-0434					Claussen
Helke's Silver Sue	NE-0115					Fred & Hedy Keller
Hell's Skjolden of Norske	NE-1017		34	M	HC-396322	
Herka's Dynasty	NE-1717	G	39	F	HD-342865	M. & H. Swanson
Hestko's Toast Of The Town	NE-2227	G	36	F	HM32867103	Dorothy Wallace
Hestsko Elena, CH	NE-2085	G	47	F	HD-672929	Ray Beathard & Dorothy Wallace
Hestsko Hidden Acres Bonus	NE-1950	G	36	M	HD-720582	Dorothy Wallace
Hestsko's Six Pack	NE-1395	E	26	M	HD-058281	Mrs. G. W. Wallace
Hestsko's Unsinkable Molly	NE-1793	G	55	F	HD-219473	J. Landis & D. Wallace
Hestsko's Witch Doctor	NE-1719	E	24	M	HD-512921	Mrs G. W. Wallace
Highland Bagpiper, CH	NE-1729	G	65	M	HD-091683	Christina Bishop
Highland's Belle Starr	NE-0145					Bev Ricci
Highland's Shenandoah	NE-0044					Ron & Bev Ricci
Highland-Tyken Cheer For Me	NE-0606		26	F	HB-781432	
Hirtzelheim Majestic Rm, A & C CH	NE-1761	G	24	M	HD-529508	G. Kraus & C. Wadsworth
Hirtzlheim Princess Nordic	NE-1529	G	73	F	MY-228716	Diana Hirtle
Hirtzlheim's Keesta's Thor	NE-1611	G	24	M	SS-534133	K & S Kerr
Hites Noshota Bay	NE-0459					
Holbakke Kjaerlig Thorbjorn	NE-1829	G	28	M	HD-503290	Barclay E. & Sharon J. Hills
Holbakke Krystal Cave Bear	NE-1738	G	26	F	HD-503239	Pat Brunner-Walsh
Holly Av Norpeak	NE-0436					
Holly II	NE-0310					
Homestead's Lightning Bug	NE-1408	G	35	M	HD-037812	William L. Totten III
Houndhaven Nordic Raider CD, Can CH	NE-1086		24	M	KP-089001	
Houndhaven's Nordik Questa	NE-1422	G	30	F	QG-453225	Lynda Tarnowski
Houndhaven's Schamir	NE-0970					
Houndhaven's Zephyrus, CH	NE-0908	G	24	M	HC-296951	R. & L. Backer
Howdy's Carmia of Edgewood	NE-0748		54	F	HB-675060	
Howdy's Folly Av York	NE-0839		67	F	HB-629927	
Howdy's Taki Tam Tessa	NE-0730		33	F	HB-902553	
Howdy's Yum Yum Av York, CH	NE-0654		38	F	HB-609428	
Hu'Mar's Happy Boomer	NE-0165					H. & M. Curtis
Hu'Mar's Happy Cookie	NE-0164					H. & M. Curtis
Hu'Mar's Happy Honeybun	NE-0166					H. & M. Curtis
Hundhalla's Havimal, CH	NE-0812		48	M	HB-770310	
Hunter's Bond Av Little Acre, CH	NE-0901		32	M	HC-176372	
Hunter's Enoch Av Little Acre	NE-1021		30	M	HC-410251	
Hyona's Bladr, CH (Norway)	NE-1369	G	27	M	HD-035729	Carol Loitfellner
Hyona's Dame Ericka	NE-1541	G	39	F	HD-267510	B. & J. Carrier
Hyona's Gra Garth, CH	NE-1660	G	29	M	HD-387104	Carol Loitfellner
Hyona's Hemmelig Tjeneste Hauk	NE-1659	F	25	M	HD-405448	Gary Niedzwiecki & C. Loitfellner
Hyona's Kia Av Baldr	NE-1900	E	31	F	HM-170978	Carol A. Loitfellner
Hyona's Lea	NE-1901	E	29	F	HM-181689	Carol A. Loitfellner
Hyona's Odin Av Gra Garth	NE-2057	G	24	M	HD-911882	Carol Loitfellner
Hyonas Amulett Dame	NE-1300		25	F	HC-951219	Eileen G. Smith & C. Loitfellner
Hyonas Garth	NE-1682	F	32	M	HD-632252	John Canger & C. Loitfellner
Hyonas Hjerter Elske	NE-1698	F	30	F	HD-613893	Morris & Loitfellner
Hyonas Kaisa	NE-1863	G	26	F	HD-796933	Diane & Don Forsyth
Ienar's Diamond Gal	NE-1891	F	95	F	HC-999255	Martin L. & Barbara J. Uhler
Illya's Bix Av-Stran	NE-0331					
Illya's Inga Av Stran	NE-0746		51	F	HB-637844	
Illya's Jassi Scamp Av Stran	NE-0306					
Incus G. Donahue	NE-2218	G	24	F	HM37562408	Karen Donahue
Independent Lady Av Meri Da	NE-0706		30	F	HB-929100	
Ingar Freya Av Stran	NE-0539					
Ingelow Lady	NE-0380					
Ironsides of Rivanol	NE-0841		25	M	HC-147111	

Registered Name	OFA No.	Rating	Age	Sex	Reg. No.	Owner
Isbjorn Elvemel A New Romance	NE-2141	G	24	F	HM35074001	Juliet Movitz
Isbjorn Luna Moth	NE-2252	G	24	F	HM39330102	Juliet Movitz
Isbjorn Macintosh, CH	NE-1964	G	24	M	HD-752554	Juliet Movitz
Isbjorn Princess Katie	NE-2118	G	31	F	HD-834929	Victoria & William Babcock
Isbjorn Super Simonize, CH	NE-2178	F	24	M	HM35791503	David & Eva Bergsen & J. Movitz
Istindel's Bear of Ace's Image	NE-1228		24	M	HC-842917	
Ivan Ravenstone Av Kongsberg	NE-0185					
Ivarsson of Ruskar CD, CH	NE-0925		24	M	HC-276169	
Jack Daniels Pi Nada	NE-1031		40	M	HC-359848	
Jan-Arc's Kita	NE-0523					Theodore & Ann Clandening
Janbert Circuit Breaker, CH	NE-0703		36	M	HB-836558	
Jandal's All That Jazz	NE-1425	G	24	F	HD-119021	Shawna Myers
Jandal's Artic Flo Cover Girl, CH	NE-1928	F	44	F	HD-609989	Michelle Burns & J. Price DVM
Jandal's Bourbon And Branch	NE-2068	F	24	M	HD-877546	Janice W. Price, DVM & D. Brice
Jandal's Chill A Cella, CH	NE-1580	F	44	M	HD-151363	D & J Price
Jandal's I Was Here	NE-2069	G	46	M	HD-607968	Janice W. Price, DVM & G. Price
Jandal's Jenny Come Lately, CH	NE-1196		25	F	HC-741201	N. Turner
Jandal's New Year's Toast	NE-1482	G	31	F	HD-142458	Raye D. Davis
Jandal's Rapid Fire, CH	NE-1701	F	86	M	HC-751617	Dan & Janice Price
Jandal's Some Like It Hot	NE-1862	G	33	F	HD-607969	Dale Price & Janice W. Price, DVM
Jandal's Stardust, CH	NE-1579	G	32	F	HD-316579	D & J Price
Jayenn's K-Karen	NE-0374					
Jayenn's Tusen Takklik Nel's	NE-0624		26	M	DU-000740	
Jaywill's Ragnar	NE-1406	G	26	M	HD-132861	William Knudsen
Jeff's Raisondetre	NE-1688	G	45	F	HD-237841	Jeffery Cobb
Jenta Dois of Serendipity	NE-0991		26	F	HC-408698	
Jeri Kirkssted Rock Kristol	NE-1823	F	28	M		Robert K. & Ruth H. Ness
Jeri's Diamond Av Deola	NE-1772	G	24	F	HD-558330	P. Robinson & J. Breunig
Jimgem's Travis, CH	NE-1231		27	M	HC-887101	R. & L. Backer
Jo Cala's Tradewind's Promise	NE-1658	F	25	F	HD-346358	Pam Reitsma
Jo Cala's Wicked Wanda, CH	NE-1296		32	F	HC-885146	Jon & Camille LaBree
Jo-Cala's Classy Chassie, CH	NE-1255		25	F	HC-862114	
Jo-Cala's Little Panda Bear, CH	NE-1711	F	45	F	HD-247878	Kelly, Tenzi & LaBree
Jo-Cala's Ms Houdini, CH	NE-1112		29	F	HC-540491	Jon LaBree
Jo-Cala's One And Only, CH	NE-1427	F	31	F	HD-054766	LaBree & Stranahan
John John	NE-0957					
Joker's Rising Son	NE-0515					
Joywoods Bjonna av Kierkrol, CH	NE-0061					
Jumacs Sunflower	NE-1784	G	84	F	HD-332949	Judith McCauley
Juniorsson Graa Ghost, CH	NE-1229		46	F	HC-637633	
K F Vala of Eidsvold	NE-1282	G	32	F	HC-810749	N. Torbet
K F Viking of Eidsvold	NE-1240	G	26	M	HC-810748	R. & L. Backer
K J Butterball Morgan CD	NE-1590	F	36	F	ILP-61847	Kent Mitchell
KCK Felony's Grand Larceny, CH	NE-1813	F	24	M	HD-526547	R. L. & Sandra Kozub
KCK Felony's Ms Deme Anor, CH	NE-1806	F	24	F	HD-526552	R. L. & Sandra Kozub
Kahru's Heart 'N Soul, CH	NE-1796	E	39	F	HD-545114	Daven & Bonnie Heikkinen
Kamgaard Bard Av Dunharrow, CH	NE-1150		53	M	HC-401302	J. Reichenbach
Kamgaard Kamelot, CH	NE-1011		24	M	HC-404552	
Kamgaard Karbon Kopy, CH	NE-1194		34	F	HC-633516	K. Kaffke
Kamgaard Kase Lot	NE-1792	F	25	F	HD-504770	L. Gibbons & M. Mott
Kamgaard Kavalier	NE-1413	F	24	M	HD-102335	Diane Chisholm
Kamgaard Keep The Faith, CH	NE-1436	G	24	F	HD-122522	Casen & Peterson
Kamgaard Keeper's Finders	NE-1560	G	42	F	HD-112523	Mazza & Mott
Kamgaard Kentuckiana	NE-1819	F	28	F	HD-534336	S. Brackin & M. New
Kamgaard Kermette of Pelstad, CH	NE-1534	G	24	F	HD-247022	Lillian P. Kletter
Kamgaard Kermit	NE-1287		24	M	HC-931968	Lillian Kletter
Kamgaard Kermitsson	NE-1624	G	24	M	HD-340459	Marion Casen
Kamgaard Ketch The Wind MSLF	NE-2208	F	29	F	HM34640802	Cynthia A. & David M. Bundy
Kamgaard Kingfish, CH	NE-1294		27	M	HC-981582	Margaret K. Mott
Kamgaard Kiss-Ka-Dee, Bermudian CH	NE-2143	G	25	F	HM40580701	Margaret K. Mott/L. J. Gibbons
Kamgaard Kissing Bug, CH	NE-1226		24	F	HC-842109	
Kamgaard Kit N Kaboodle, CH	NE-1208		24	F	HC-785374	M. Mott
Kamgaard Klean Sweep, CH	NE-1973	G	33	F	HD-658589	Judy Silker

Registered Name	OFA No.	Rating	Age	Sex	Reg. No.	Owner
Kamgaard Klear Impression	NE-1781	G	26	F	HD-504762	M. Mott & M. Rook
Kamgaard Klear Skies Ahead	NE-2098	G	28	F	HD-861946	Sally Simmonds & Margaret Mott
Kamgaard Know It All	NE-1217		55	F	HC-533154	
Kamgaard Kome As You Are	NE-1545	G	28	F	HD-233279	S. & E. Arseven
Kamgaard Korniche, Can. CH	NE-1668	F	25	F	HD-401453	Margaret K. Mott
Kamgaard Kount Me In	NE-1340		47	F	HC-802389	
Kamgaard Kountry Kinsmsn	NE-1474	G	25	M	HD-252077	Donley & Mott
Kamgaard Kourt Marshal, CH	NE-1353		36	M	HC-847256	
Kamgaard Krona Av Briarpatch	NE-0155					
Kamgaard Kuddles	NE-1931	G	43	F	HD-508681	Marilynn D. Arsenault
Kamgaard N. Wolfshiem Kaliber, CH	NE-1841	F	31	M	HD-536902	Maria A. Van Dyck
Kamgaard Smokey Bear, CH	NE-1221		28	M	HC-785809	
Kamgaard The Kissing Bandit, CH	NE-1399	F	24	M	HD-115322	M. Mott & S. Kletter
Kamgaard The Komeback Kid, CH	NE-1211		25	M	HC-802258	C. Brockhaus
Kamgaard TrygNThors Tyken	NE-0335					
Kara of Carrollton	NE-0086					Henry & Vivienne Goebel
Karalea's Trys Av Glenlea	NE-0373					
Karhu's Chanel No. Five, CH	NE-2177	G	24	F	HM36075001	Ronald R. & Sandra M. Peters
Karhu's Heart-Throb	NE-1937	G	44	F	HD-545113	Daven & Bonnie Heikkinen
Karhu's O'Man Bojangles, CH	NE-1566	G	26	M	HD-268910	D & B Heikkinen
Karhu's Realities	NE-2195	G	25	F	HM36075003	Bonnie & Daven Heikkinen
Kari of Telemark	NE-0224					
Karin Ehli	NE-0191					
Karin's Katrina	NE-0778		54	F	HB-714800	
Karlyle's Baldr of Drgons End	NE-1163			M	HC-742441	M. Huber
Katrine Glen Fjall	NE-0100					
Katrine Glen Liten Bjorn	NE-0807		30	M	HC-027060	
Katrine Glen Netta	NE-0179					W. T. Wayland
Katrine Glen Skadi	NE-0719		67	F	HB-352114	
Kaycees Private Pepper	NE-2170	F	35	F	HD-870283	Holly Scheer
Kaylee's Heidi Lee	NE-0578		46	F	HB-351890	
KcK Felony's Rowdy Rascal, CH	NE-2119	G	40	M	HD-747519	Sandra Kozub
Keen Acres Chase Me	NE-1074		31	M	HC-468124	
Keen Acres Heatherbloom	NE-1033		24	F	HC-468127	
Keen Acres Showcase	NE-0261					
Keimah Bear	NE-0643		29	F	HB-758948	
Keiv Gray Wolf	NE-0701		27	M	HB-856168	
Kejen's Elfin Magic	NE-1666	F	35	F	HD-319566	Daniel & Doreen Bates
Kejen's For Pete's Sake	NE-1890	G	27	M	HD-649141	Martin L. & Barbara J. Uhler
Kejen's Little Corker	NE-1788	G	37	M	HD-435036	Martin & Barbara Uhler
Kejen's Revelie	NE-1507	E	25	M	HD-285672	Martin Uhler
Kejen's Tryg or Treat, CH	NE-1787	F	57	M	HD-235860	Martin & Barbara Uhler
Kejens Padimonium Delite, CH	NE-1821	F	40	F	HD-450540	Randall & Robin Furrer
Keken's Abracadabra	NE-1786	E	26	F	HD-515893	Martin & Barbara Uhler
Kenai II	NE-0283					
Kenjen's Mhyh O' My Heart, CH	NE-1724	G	51	F	HD-235861	M. & B. Uhler
Kim Von Pepper	NE-0449					
Kimur's Howdi Trygger, CH	NE-0421					Roger & Shirley DeSaele
Kimur's Mister Magnus	NE-0616		25	M	HB-790989	
Kimur's Peppermint Patti	NE-0516					Deseale
Kimur's Thorksson Thunder	NE-0143					Mrs. Roger DeSaele
Kimur's Topsy Turvey	NE-0189					Mrs. Roger DeSaele
Kincaid's Val Av Oakhaven	NE-0085					Maxine Davis
King Av Kartine Glen, CH	NE-0002					Henry Glasgow
King Elk Wendy Jo's Bjorn	NE-1205		52	M	HC-530089	M. Walton
King Elk Wendy Jo's Sno Pike	NE-1013		28	F	HC-416243	
King Gustav III	NE-0472					
Kingelk-Lady Christy	NE-0091					Betty Walton
Kirkssted Ali Charm	NE-1961	G	28	F	HD-708357	Ronald Smith & Robert K. Ness
Kirkssted Dainty Diadem	NE-1673	G	25	F	HD-382284	R. Ness & E. Smith
Kirkssted Harleigh	NE-1751	G	24	F	HD-506475	D. Mills, R. Scalzo & R. Ness
Kirkssted Ivan	NE-1460	E	36	M	HD-075716	M. & S. Butts & Ness
Kirkssted Jiminy Kricket, CH	NE-1506	F	28	M	HD-045978	Robert & Ruth Ness

Registered Name	OFA No.	Rating	Age	Sex	Reg. No.	Owner
Kirkssted Kamgaard Kelly, CH	NE-1380	G	24	F	HD-037987	Margaret K. Mott
Kirkssted Kan N Kam Kamille	NE-1569	G	24	F	HD-294949	R & R Ness
Kirkssted Kanna Lily, CH	NE-1363	E	27	F	HC-993719	Robert K. & Ruth H. Ness
Kirkssted Kate's Kabenj, CH	NE-1316	F	35	M	HC-857548	Robert & Ruth Ness
Kirkssted Kleine Schatz	NE-1942	F	26	F	HD-714967	Robert & Ruth Ness
Kirkssted Kopper, CH	NE-1421	G	24	F	HD-114460	Robert & Ruth Ness
Kirkssted Kristin Av Norgard, CH	NE-2009	F	57	F	HD-472498	C G & E R Gardner & R Ness
Kirkssted Odin	NE-1678	G	25	M		Roland Williams
Kirkssted Olav, CH	NE-1420	E	24	M	HD-121682	Robert & Ruth Ness
Kirkssted Selja	NE-1679	G	25	F		Wiste & Ness
Kirkssted Solveig	NE-1943	F	25	F	HD-714966	Robert & Ruth Ness
Kirkssted Tika Kali	NE-1677	G	25	F	HD-425052	Kessler & Ness
Kirkssted's Bloeman Van Ness	NE-2013	G	31	F	HD-803069	Ginger & Christopher Debell
Kirsten Av Fjellsyn	NE-0264					
Kirsten Av Norpeak, CD	NE-0010					Mary Schaub
Kirsten's Randi Av Geran	NE-0647		25	F	HB-843550	
Kirsti Vesla Greta Av Rob-Lyn	NE-0640	F	24	F	HB-832354	R. & L. Backer
Kjekk's Stormi of Narvikwood	NE-0011					Charles Coleman
Kjersti Bjorn of Narvik	NE-0575		27	F	HB-720846	
Knospartek's Silver Lady	NE-0911		24	F	HC-255828	
Konfekt TNT Moose's Candy Thor	NE-1805	G	51	M	HD-289695	Dale Dunn
Krisda Bell Chimes	NE-0438					
Kristan's Tristan Mischief	NE-1990	G	27	M	HD-719402	W. T. Langhorne, Jr.
Kristian of PItch Road	NE-0073					Mr & Mrs Wells Peck
Kristiansund Ladi	NE-0183					John Wolfe
Kristie Av Katrine Glen	NE-0003					Henry Glasgow
Kristin Lis	NE-0341					
Kristin's Cameo	NE-1492	F	54	F	HD-069331	Kris Fortna
Kristin's Emma Lee	NE-1644	G	33	F	HD-335123	Kris Fortna
Kristin's Huggin Blade, CH	NE-1939	F	31	M	HD-647249	Kris Fortna
Kristin's Huggin Brie	NE-1794	G	29	F	HD-491183	Kris Fortna
Kristin's Huggin Kiss Abby, CH	NE-1929	F	24	F	HD-717878	Kris Fortna
Kristin's Kid Nice Lee Done, CH	NE-2087	G	25	F	HD-885055	Kris Fortna
Kristin's Miss Scampi Lee	NE-1951	F	24	F	HD-760422	Kris Fortna
Kristin's Ruff N Tuff, CH	NE-1055		30	M	HC-479422	
Kristina Karandor	NE-1551	G	25	F	HD-363301	Margaret Mott
Krystal's Black Frost	NE-1136		30	M	HC-578393	G. Olive
La Princessa Velotta Canwin	NE-1531	G	25	F	HD-214263	June Roberts
La Sant Charra Sabrina	NE-0679		32	F	HB-819735	
Lacey De La Bel	NE-2093	G	58	F	HD-555030	Linda Belmontez
Lacy Souix	NE-1871	G	28	F	HD-586497	David & Marilyn Costar
Ladenbi of Rascal Mountain	NE-0371					
Lady	NE-1573	G	24	F	HD-300309	Doyle Huffman
Lady Anne Bristol	NE-2241	G	32	F	HM35067106	Douglas A. Beaver
Lady Elka VIII CD	NE-0607		33	F	HB-615730	
Lady Elsa Maureen	NE-0935		24	F	HC-388562	
Lady Freya of Hammerfest	NE-0489					
Lady Kelly Wyoming	NE-0589		24	F	HB-693024	
Lady Natashia	NE-0200					
Lady Nikoli	NE-0112					
Lady Q's New Attraction	NE-2254	F	58	F	HD-768736	Patrcia C. & William J. Law
Lady Q's New Connection	NE-2047	F	33	M	HD-758430	Shirley Quigley
Lady Q's Show Off	NE-1642	G	48	F	HD-220384	Cynthia Kinser
Lady Q's Somethin Special, CH	NE-1327		40	F	HC-864563	
Lady Rikka Av Kollomhaus	NE-0174					
Lady Sharene	NE-0292					
Lady Tasha Amanda Westby	NE-2145	F	42	F	HD-756794	Roald I. Westby
Laika III	NE-0065					Herb & Marie Stahl
Langmoore's Aloe	NE-0423					
Lars Friskie Av Helke	NE-0212					
Lars of Doride	NE-0006					Richard Deimel
Lars' Jenta Av Helke	NE-0176					
Larsa Sirrka of Krynn	NE-0784		37	F	HB-885520	

Registered Name	OFA No.	Rating	Age	Sex	Reg. No.	Owner
Latra Per Mare Per Terras	NE-0830		24	F	EL-037310	
Laua Lars	NE-1770	G	24	M	HD-486020	Walter Remers
Layla	NE-0772	F	25	F	HC-268161	L. Spooner
Lazer	NE-1022		61	F	HL-586114	
Ledge-Rock's Jahan of Statton	NE-0949		29	F	HC-277723	
Ledge-Rock's Wanda Heksa, CH	NE-0898		28	F	HC-182074	
Ledgerock Silver Wizard	NE-1602	F	25	M	HD-340576	Laura Wonneberger
Ledgerock's Autumn Lief, CH	NE-1604	G	24	M	HD-329670	K & L MacFarlane
Lefse Lenvik of Tykens, CH	NE-0790		34	F	HB-914896	
Leif Ode Odin	NE-0910		27	M	HC-202130	
Leifa	NE-0518					
Leka Katrina Bjorna	NE-1664	G	32	F	HD-575469	Robert N. England
Lenans Forest Hills Special, CH	NE-1636	E	36	F	HD-247567	Les & Nancy Moser
Lenans Gentle On My Mind	NE-1957	G	24	F	HD-756241	Minnie Forsyth & Nancy Moser
Leonard's Silver Harp, CDX, CH	NE-2074	F	66	M	HD-422903	Bruce Leonard & Sheila Leonard
Liebes Boo Kaisa of Wyndmoor	NE-1855	F	45	F		Charlotte Lieberman
Likkas Bjorn Av Norge	NE-0712		31	F	HB-896124	
Lillabo Grimm	NE-0944		24	M	HC-368052	
Lillian's Tanya Paulette	NE-0172					
Lilliven of Middensted	NE-1050		46	F	HC-462008	
Lindiveit's Freyja	NE-0081					S. P. Brannen
Lindtveit's Bjarni Jacmdrson	NE-0446					
Lindtveit's Elske, CH	NE-0216					Pat Brannen
Lindtveit's Erik	NE-0236					Pat Brannen
Lindtveit's Lady Kiska	NE-0693		22	F	HB-918987	
Lindtveit's Njord	NE-0217					
Lindtveit's Tina	NE-0215					Pat Brannen
Lindtveit's Tussi	NE-0409					Pam Epp
Lindveit's Laila	NE-0799		38	F	HC-039422	
Lindveit's Rykte	NE-0678		30	M	HB-827103	
Lindveits Pika	NE-0461					
Linual Eldorado Scamp	NE-1663	G	39	M	HD-234316	Carol Braegger
Linvicta Sherman Tank, CH	NE-1606	F	108	M	HC-598108	K & J Strakbein
Linvicta's Song of Keloran, CH	NE-2007	F	27	F	1037685	Lori Draper
Linvictas Prefferd Stock	NE-2136	F	26	M	HM32553803	Ken & Judy Strakbein
Linvictas Town Clown, CH	NE-1530	F	64	M	HC-932714	K. & J. Strakbein
Liseldun Solv Sternje Vinsja	NE-1962	G	25	M	HD-730439	Renee S. & Steven D. Schmidt
Liseldun's Bridget, CH	NE-2151	G	25	F	HM33750401	Barbara D. Roby
Liseldun's Cirion	NE-1166		25	M	HC-662658	S. Maquire
Liseldun's Frieda	NE-1452	G	24	F	HD-169424	Barbara D. Roby
Liseldun's Imladris Elladan	NE-1144		37	M	HC-535007	B. Roby
Liseldun's Imladris Linn	NE-1132		33	F	HC-535005	B. Roby
Liseldun's Lisbet	NE-1824	G	24	F	HD-533604	Barbara D. Roby
Liseldun's Panache	NE-1866	F	24	F	HD-619781	Mrs. Janet P. Kaplan
Liseldun's Petra, CH	NE-2065	F	24	F	HD-850069	Barbara D. Roby
Liseldun's Remi	NE-1306		24	M	HC-915808	Fred W. Sharis
Liseldun's Steffen	NE-1876	G	30	M	HD-533605	Anne Carstensen-Joy
Liseldun's Trykk	NE-2066	F	24	M	HD-847472	Peter Chesnulevich
Liseldun's Viktor	NE-1349		24	M	HC-994299	
Little Acre's Bicentennial, CH	NE-0978		31	F	HC-267995	
Little Bear's Volla	NE-0365					
Little Kristi of P B	NE-0864		28	F	HC-138439	
Little Nobs Rascal Loki	NE-1859	E	36	M	HD-472930	Rob & Carol Hoffman
Little Wapiti	NE-0588		34	F	HB-686369	
Llewellyn's Minnesmerke Noel	NE-1095		26	F	HC-565798	
Lloyd's Mist-N-Pitch Chelsea	NE-1653	G	49	F	HD-557536	Michael Taylor
Lobi's Supernatural, CH	NE-1487	G	25	M	HD-170409	Billy & Lona King
Lobi's Superstition	NE-1643	G	44	F	HD-170644	N. Annis & L. King
Loki Av Valhalla	NE-0178					
Loki Prestehund	NE-0279					
Loki of Stormy Lea	NE-0800		32	M	HB-985228	
Long's Peaches	NE-0274					
Lor Lyn Katrinka	NE-0159					

Registered Name	OFA No.	Rating	Age	Sex	Reg. No.	Owner
Lord Tufsen Av Norvegr, CH	NE-0729		25	M	HB-949837	
Lordan's Sweet Gypsy Rose	NE-0835		40	F	HB-929574	
Lordan's Sweet Melody	NE-1393		24	F	HD-034692	
Lordan's Sweet Sasha, CH	NE-1284		31	F	HC-810979	Annette M. Colucci & L. Jelinek
Lordan's Sweet Syn-O-Min	NE-1485	F	24	F	HD-152873	Reardon & Jelinek
Lordan's Titan Saturnac	NE-1409	G	39	M	HC-921170	K. & P. Menzel
Lordan's Trail Blazer, CH	NE-1243		26	M	HC-811054	
Lordan's Viken Warrior, CH	NE-1232		24	M	HC-812113	Pat Viken
Lordan's Viking Storm	NE-1315		24	M	HC-923741	
Lordans Norskburg Caroller	NE-1445	G	24	F	HD-105334	D. & D. Tewksburg
Loveable Bandit	NE-1710	F	31	M	HD-407833	Myra Anne Bachman
Loyen's Janik	NE-0353					
Loyen's Road Runner	NE-0257					
Lu Per Canssom Mo's Major Girl, CH	NE-0952		24	F	HC-321744	
Lu Per Canwin Candor Tufson	NE-1355		24	M	HC-992005	
Lu Per Moldor Candorsson	NE-1014		39	M	HC-320327	
Lu Per Northwind Av Norwin, CH	NE-0744		28	M	HB-953832	
Lu Per Tryg N Thor's Torron, CH	NE-0844		49	M	HB-890682	
Lu Per Tryg N Thors Aleta	NE-0752		34	F	HB-892107	
Lu Per Tryg N Thors Candor	NE-0755		34	M	HB-892106	
Lu Per Tryg N Thors Reina	NE-0413					
Lu Per Tryg N Thors Silver Mist	NE-0867		25	F	HC-183846	
Lu Per Tryg N Thors Theron	NE-0946		43	M	HC-146904	
Lu Per Tryg N Thors Trina	NE-0716		32	F	HB-890455	
Lu Per Wayward Traveler, CH	NE-0981		33	M	HC-316061	
Lu per Delway Sventre Timber, CH	NE-1123		35	F	HC-605517	S. Smith
Lu per Noreen Av Nor-Way, CH	NE-1089		36	F	HC-449799	
Lucy	NE-1899	F	44	F	HD-510924	Dr. Joan Eccleston
Lurich Sasste Kim O'Kamgaard, CH	NE-0404					M. Kampish & R. Wunderlin
Lurich Sasste Prince of Hoy, CH	NE-0496		27	M	HB-591348	R. & L. Backer
Luv's Mistake Av Hei-Mor, CH	NE-0382					
Ly-Den's High Country	NE-0656		24	M	HB-842342	
Ly-Den's Little Dickens	NE-0350					Spiegel
Lynriks Tuf's Ienar, CH	NE-1489	G	99	M	HC-525783	Martin Uhler
Lyon (Norway)	NE-0056					Herb & Marie Stahl
Lyra Av Norden	NE-0815		27	F	HC-061130	
M-Y Lady	NE-1383		51	F	HC-860237	
MJR Buffalo Bill Cody	NE-2012	G	24	M	HD-786850	Ronald Smith
MJR Maximas Bandit Queen	NE-2043	G	28	F	HD-786849	Ron Smith
Mageroy Ailsa	NE-0816		27	F	HC-118903	
Magic Morning Mist	NE-1071		28	F	HC-567342	
Malaca Elsie Bandit's Buddy	NE-1576	G	27	F	HD-266244	M & A Brooks
Malaca Milton	NE-1892	G	55	M	HD-342456	Peter F. & Helen Long
Mandi Surprise	NE-2070	F	27	F	HD-854997	Daryl Strike
Mandy Pandy Doerr	NE-0975		27	F	HC-453387	
Manor's Trouble Stone	NE-1524	G	29	M	HD-200328	M. & K. Rook
Many Penny	NE-0186					
Marbran's Mariah of Tass	NE-0071					Joyce Poe
Marbran's Tass Peppermint	NE-0460					
Marit of Eidsvold	NE-0540	E	20	F	HB-686465	N. Torbet
Marjon's Christy Av Kara	NE-1129		33	F	HC-543029	C. Eyck
Marjon's TNT Muffin	NE-1073		38	F	HC-573609	
Marjon's Windy Shadowmist, CH	NE-1010		25	F	HC-463063	
Marko of Eidsvold	NE-0541	E	20	M	HB-686462	Floyd Cox
Marta Av Cedarholm	NE-0133					Mr & Mrs Fred Lathe
Martrick's Tartek Trollvenn	NE-0858		28	M	HC-109236	
Martrick's Tuf N Dux Ruffrenn	NE-0998		41	M	HC-266552	
Marvale's Great Love	NE-1632	G	25	F	HD-351364	Ronald A. Smith
Maximillian Rex	NE-2108	G	25	M	HD-895631	Dan Denlinger
Maya's Silver Shawl	NE-0529					
Maylepp's Hallucination	NE-0881		43	F	FC-000344	
Maylepp's Krishelle	NE-0880		43	F	FC-000952	
Mayo's First Loki Beowulf	NE-0580		24	M	HB-721097	

Registered Name	OFA No.	Rating	Age	Sex	Reg. No.	Owner
Melissa Av Jumac	NE-1672	G	88	F	HC-853404	Judith E. McCauley
Melreva Bamse Lady Dinka	NE-0400					
Melreva Knut	NE-0036					George Gill
Melreva Rik's Lord Carlo	NE-0263					
Meri Da's Wolf	NE-0951		29	M	HC-312336	
Merica Taeü's Delaney	NE-1133		67	F	HC-485585	G. Delaney
Michaux's Gandalf The Gray	NE-1558	G	39	M	HD-126633	J. & S. Koziol
Michaux's Misty	NE-1509	G	34	F	HD-154018	Jane Stanton
Middensted Diamondgill Rolf	NE-1165		31	M	HC-625261	G. Gill
Middensted Tauni's Fieste	NE-1131		24	F	HC-642676	C. Christiansen
Middensted's Fin Jeordie	NE-0393					
Middensted's Image of Tauni	NE-1833	F	44	M	HD-424282	Ann C. & Charles C. Christiansen
Middensted's Lady of the North	NE-0715		37	F	HB-915030	
Middensted's Mighty Mopar, CD	NE-1528	G	48	M	HC-979586	C./A. Wadsworth
Middensted's Vidar	NE-0392					
Middensted's Wholly Tyr	NE-0269					
Midgard ThomThom B-Jup Wulf, CH	NE-1292	F	25	M	HC-917776	Chris & Gayle Thomas
Midwest Ace In The Hole, CH	NE-1837	F	39	M	HD-424492	Barb & Dan Jelinek
Midwest Cricklewood's Sassy	NE-0836		24	F	HC-156028	
Midwest Grand Prix's Brandy, CH	NE-0788		31	F	HC-017254	
Midwest Grand Prix's Happy Hooker	NE-1126			F	HC-570781	J. Gustafson
Midwest Grand Prix's Hi Steppe	NE-0837		25	M	HC-152087	
Midwest Grand Prix's Holly, CH	NE-0783		30	F	HC-004239	
Midwest Grand Prix's Legacy	NE-1117		48	M	HC-380523	J. Kocol
Midwest Grand Prix's Princess	NE-1503	G	48	F	HD-056314	Gustafson & D Jelinek
Midwest Grand Prix's Puffin	NE-1368		26	F	HC-984462	David & Pat Gleaves
Midwest Grand Prix's Rocky, CH	NE-1504	G	48	M	HD-056313	Dan & Barb Jelinek
Midwest Grand Prix's Tanya, CH	NE-1499	G	24	F	HD-249567	Gustafson & D Jelinek
Midwest Lordan's Sweet Charity, CH	NE-1090	F	25	F	HC-418306	Dan & Lori Jelinek
Midwest One Tough Cookie	NE-1934	G	25	F	HD-688099	Dan & Barb Jelinek
Midwest Tania	NE-0440					
Midwest Tassa	NE-0531			F	HB-838168	Sven Gustafson
Migan Rebel's The Shooter	NE-1453	G	24	M	HD-202226	Michele & Gary Fain
Migar Dynastar Wind-Dancer	NE-1625	G	24	M	HD-403524	Gidu & Camilla Shroff
Migar Rebel's Doc Holiday, CH	NE-1344		29	M	HC-998221	
Migar Rebel's Dynamohum, CH	NE-1343		29	F	HC-998222	
Migar Rebel's Sure Shot	NE-1451	G	24	F	HD-202799	Michele & Gary Fain
Migar's China Doll, CH	NE-1626	F	24	F	HD-367560	Michele & Gary Fain
Migar's Jasmine Jade	NE-1852	G	24	F	HD-658452	Michele V. & Gary D. Fain
Migars Miss T	NE-2025	F	43	F	HD-676374	Dean Hanley & Michele Fain
Migars The Color of Money	NE-1722	G	24	M	HD-507394	M. & G. Fain
Migars The Coming Of Thunder	NE-2079	G	24	M	HD-897698	Michele & Gary Fain
Mika's Amazing Grace	NE-0832		24	F	HC-022712	
Mike's Elke Summer	NE-0301					
Mikes Heidi Rexdatter	NE-0834		34	F	HC-059899	
Mil-Mar's Buttons-N-Beau	NE-1600	G	36	F	HD-224426	M & M Forsythe
Mil-Mar's Sassy Sadee Sue	NE-2019	G	42	F	HD-611556	Anthony Hanson
Mil-Mar's Too Hot To Handle	NE-1849	F	26	F	HD-572362	Jeff & Sabine Russell
Miss Chiff	NE-1237		52	F	HC-589116	
Miss Delia	NE-1912	E	25	F	HD-797499	Sharon Walsh & Carol Loitfellner
Miss Mitzi	NE-0408					
Miss Silver Lefse	NE-1249		34	F	HC-791441	
Mister Imported Nyka Av Oakhaven	NE-0363					
Mistress Renea	NE-0937		66	F	HB-907887	
Misty Berg	NE-0005					Henry Glasgow
Misty Bonz Skylar	NE-1248		24	F	HD-024283	
Misty Eryka Av Pebble Point	NE-1083		33	F	HC-450379	
Misty Tara Kyriemhor Tuf	NE-0863		38	M	HC-039388	
Misty Tara Lillabo Jhoni	NE-1143		30	F	HC-631919	G. Murphy
Misty Tara Lillabo Paula, CH	NE-0921		60	F	HB-872454	
Misty Tara Thor Mhora Khya	NE-0903				HC-	
Misty Tara Thor Mhora Lhora CDX, CH	NE-0940		43	F	HC-141110	
Misty Tara Thor Mhora Mhynka, CH	NE-0920		37	F	HC-141109	

Registered Name	OFA No.	Rating	Age	Sex	Reg. No.	Owner
Misty Tara Trogankhya Kodiak	NE-1056		24	F	HC-564751	
Misty Tara Tryglikk Kris, CH	NE-0290					Earl Gossard
Misty Tara Tryglikk Kyrie, CH	NE-0255					Paul Ross
Misty Tara Tryglikk Tyka	NE-0300					D. Carne & D. DeSantis
Misty Tara Tryglikk Valiant, CH	NE-0367					Mr & Mrs Charles Robb
Misty Tara Tryglikk Valla, CH	NE-0432					
Misty of Christopher Creek	NE-1214		28	F	HC-754023	
Misty of Norway II	NE-1069		58	F	HC-227474	
Mittag Av Willowbrook	NE-0473					
Moon Maiden Av Hei Mor	NE-0160					
Morke Av Tusentak	NE-0609		32	F	HB-736212	
Mr Bips Ja	NE-0477					
Mr Imported Bjorn Av Oakhaven	NE-0346					
Mr Inported's Renka Av Helke	NE-0559					
Mr. Imported Keija Av Oakhaven	NE-0457					
Ms Rag-A-Dee Muffin	NE-0758		48	F	HB-727186	
Ms Yogi Bear	NE-1562	F	29	F	HD-214178	Marilyn Giles
Munsons Norger Saber	NE-1661	G	24	M	HD-355628	Milt & Rita Munson
Nadia's Nordic Nova	NE-0030					James & Nadia Powers
Nancy's Northern Cotton	NE-1087		61	F	HC-248948	
Nanna Freya Av Skien	NE-0584		30	F	HB-595773	
Narnia's Gandalf Av Von Kugler	NE-0686		27	M	HB-886752	
Natascha Av Ida	NE-0501					
Natasha Urus	NE-1940	G	50	F	HD-507827	Denise Hall
Natasha of Rutherford	NE-0649		27	F	HB-806469	
Nel-Von's Cinderella	NE-0444					Raymond & Lois Wilson
Nel-Von's Jeni Av Kaylee	NE-0988		43	F	HC-238948	
Nel-Von's Norja Flame, CH	NE-0577		42	F	HB-440212	
Nel-Von's Storm Doll, CH	NE-0196					
Nel-Von's Tass My Lass of Clay's	NE-0177					Sylvia Sizemore
Nelly MC	NE-0615		33	F	HB-664483	
Nichol of Bjonndale	NE-0583		24	F	DG-000202	
Nickoleena Av Fellyord	NE-2159	G	57	F	HD-644332	Carrie Roanes
Nikkis Kristi of Heard Grove	NE-2146	G	32	F	HM30007401	Charles & Martha Hutchings
Nikks Illya Av Grove Hill	NE-0109					
Njords Oscar of Ingelow	NE-0660		25	M	EC-000332	
Nor-Lan's Little Snop	NE-0412					
Nord Stjerne's Bitabrit Bo	NE-1563	F	24	F	HD-273098	Diane Bjorke
Nord-Vann's Lara Of Roundel	NE-1979	F	25	F	HD-786788	Diana & Lee Korneliusen
Nord-Vann's Lura, CH	NE-2094	F	37	F	HD-743344	Jane Morris
Nord-Vann's Magnum of Roundel, CH	NE-2040	G	30	M	HD-752047	Patricia & H. Fred Philipp
Nord-Vann's Sage	NE-1946	G	33	F	HD-649641	Jane S. Morris & B. M. Turner
Nord-Vann's Sentra	NE-1955	G	24	F	HD-730416	Barbara Ewen & Jane S. Morris
Nord-Vann's Shana, CH	NE-1500	F	25	F	HD-210739	Jane S. Morris
Nord-Vann's Zeus, CH	NE-2096	F	37	M	HD-747389	Jane Morris
Nord-Vanns Leela	NE-2023	F	30	F	HD-726807	Ted & Lissa Jackson
Nordak Chelsa's Hannel	NE-1730	G	25	M	HD-496160	Duane & Kristi Olson
Nordbo Nanna	NE-0316					D. L. & P. A. Epp
Nordbo Natasha	NE-0317					D. L. & P. A. Epp
Norden's Starlight Saber, CH	NE-1449	E	30	M	HD-068305	Stanley A. Green
Norden's Summer Mandolin	NE-1838	G	30	F	HD-533484	Jennifer C. Ennis & J. M. Oliver
Nordika's Stian Sloane	NE-1178		28	M	HC-697987	J. Sloane
Nordika's Jeni	NE-0955					
Nordika's Jodi Of Michaux, CH	NE-1577	G	90	F	HC-690535	M Siegel & J Sloane
Nordly's Thorburn Hi Inga	NE-1364		25	F	HC-994424	Harry W. & Martha G. Kerr
Nordlys I'm a Proud Missy	NE-1700	G	26	F	HD-423787	Wm. & Pat Law
Nordlys M & M Sweet Dreaming	NE-1508	G	25	M	HD-258925	W. & P. Law
Nordlys M & M Sweet Insperation	NE-1511	F	24	M	HD-258924	W. & P. Law
Nordlys MNM Frigg Av Freygus	NE-1648	F	39	F	HD-402538	C. Loadman-Copeland
Nordlys Thorawulf Morwenna	NE-1223		29	F	HC-805735	
Nordlys Thornburn Hi Darby	NE-1481	F	43	M	HD-001778	Wm. J & Pat Law
Nordsvaal's Bissel Schatzie	NE-0249					
Nordsvaal's Esquire Av Scandia	NE-0414					

Registered Name	OFA No.	Rating	Age	Sex	Reg. No.	Owner
Nordsvaal's Howdy Vykktir, CH	NE-0521					Friend
Nordsvaal's Kipen Vinne	NE-1012		28	F	HC-426417	
Nordsvaal's Mean Joe Green, CH	NE-0947		39	M	HC-301513	
Nordsvaal's Playboy	NE-0439					
Nordyls M & M Candied Darth	NE-1540	F	27	M	HD-224759	K. & B.Knicely
Norelca's Do Ya Wanna Dance, CH	NE-1737	G	25	F	HD-546530	Gamsby & Brunner-Walsh
Norelka N Lenans Night Games	NE-2246	G	26	F	HM38437404	Roberta Jean Sladeck
Norelka's Dance Hall Dolly	NE-1601	E	28	F	HD-266674	A & K Carter
Norelka's Limited Edition, CH	NE-1612	E	24	M	HD-311716	J Maier & K Carter
Norelka's Love Dance	NE-1762	G	27	F	HD-468854	Robert & Katherine Hussey
Norelka's Major League, CH	NE-2245	G	26	M	HM38437406	N. Moser / A. & K. Carter
Norelka's Sky Gazer For Trekin, CH	NE-1978	F	31	F	HD-686258	Sandi Peterson & Roberta Sladeck
Norelka's Special Edition, CH	NE-1623	G	25	M	HD-307250	Albert & Kathy Carter
Norelka's The Color Purple	NE-2251	G	42	F	HD-894316	Albert & Kathy Carter
Norelkas Surfs Up At Ardon's, CH	NE-1886	G	24	F	HD-647078	Arlene M. Aliano
Norgren Jubilees Wild Robbin, CH	NE-2071	E	30	F	HD-833158	Ann Price
Norgren Kiva Snow Flury	NE-1903	F	26	F	HD-638444	Wanda Adams
Norgren's Son of a Witch, CH	NE-1239		27	M	HC-880578	
Norgrens Bugsy Malone	NE-1191		26	M	HC-785851	W. Totten
Norgrens Emblem Of Pride, CH	NE-2015	E	29	F	HD-789848	Virginia Sawyer
Norgrens Frighten Lighten	NE-0994		36	F	HC-302761	
Norgrens Juniorsson, CH	NE-0872		36	M	HC-079442	
Norgrens Kostejig Jenta	NE-0637		29	F	HB-764364	
Norgrens Kountry Bumpkin, CH	NE-1501	F	35	F	HD-139062	Dorothy Wallace
Norgrens Limited Edition, CH	NE-1067		30	F	HC-483823	
Norgrens Loki Of Takkdahl, CH	NE-1947	G	32	M	HD-651251	Robert & Donna Dyrdahl
Norgrens Pasayten Warrior, CH	NE-2126	G	24	M	HM32552303	Sheila Renwick
Norgrens Ravishing Ruby, CH	NE-0776		24	F	HC-051038	
Norgrens Solv Dama	NE-1127		27	F	HC-617969	A. Fuquay
Norgrens Solv Thor	NE-1456	F	28	M	HD-154050	R. & B. Vandercook
Norgrens The Prides Inside, CH	NE-1834	G	30	M	HD-544327	Grenville Sawyer
Norlander's Sha Sha Sirdal	NE-2162	G	32	F	HD-891859	John & Jo Ann Christiansen
Norlund Jet Set	NE-1140		34	M	HC-585430	K. Brandt
Norlund Jon-Steiner O Vinland, CH	NE-1082	G	40	M	HC-463177	C. Brown & K. Brandt
Norlund Rigel	NE-1345		34	F	HC-954811	
Norlund Titan	NE-1459	G	42	M	HC-956722	E. & R. Sykes
Norlund's Kestrel, Can. CH	NE-1539	G	62	F	HC-925955	E. & R. Sykes
Norlund's Phantom, CH	NE-1495	F	61	M	HC-954069	C. Ashley & E. Ashley
Norlund's Tevia, CH	NE-0987		24	F	HC-459930	
Normark Logo of Nynorsk, C, Am CH	NE-1718	G	24	M	HD-478505	E. Sykes & D. Coleman
Normark Moose's Legacy, CH	NE-1769	G	29	M	HD-478923	Diane & Robert Coleman
Normark Moose's Legend	NE-1830	G	35	M	HD-478924	Diane & Robert E. Coleman
Normark TNT Promise's Lic Rish	NE-1075		27	F	HC-532810	
Normark TNT Promise's Moose, CH	NE-0874		24	M	HC-272292	
Normark TNT Steady As A Rock	NE-1378		25	M	HD-067574	K.C. Estes
Normark Tevia's Topp	NE-1525	G	26	M	HD-242308	D. & P. Gleaves
Normark Tevia's Torden, CH	NE-1502	F	24	M	HD-242309	Wallace & Coleman
Normark Tiara's Treasure	NE-2100	F	38	F	HD-780511	Diane E. Coleman
Normark's Special Angel	NE-2224	F	53	F	HD-797875	David & Pat Gleaves
Norox's-Smokey-Cinder	NE-1441	F	64	F	HD-142447	Roxann Straw
Norse Viking of Mossy Rock CD	NE-1114		46	M	HC-388522	D. Jeffries
Norske's Double Trouble	NE-1064		25	M	HC-535463	
Norske's Vallie of Vadheim	NE-1063		25	F	HC-535462	
Norskies Troy Youngen	NE-1124		26	M	HC-610453	H. White
Norskogen Frosti Av Vippo	NE-0181					
Norskogen's Jenebel	NE-0990		25	F	HC-378898	
Norskogen's Uffe Bjarnison	NE-0861		34	M	HC-087815	
Norskogen's Way Out Wendi	NE-0862		34	F	HC-087814	
Norsled Hal 1	NE-0767		30	F	HC-088801	
North Oak's Valor CD	NE-0639		24	M	HB-875021	
Northface Tarka's Bjorn	NE-0865		25	M	HC-167523	
Northwind's Crystal Fox, CH	NE-1638	F	27	F	HD-313233	Ammann & Frye
Norway's Ashley Celik	NE-1817	F	24	F	HD-559311	Danisa Pewatts

Registered Name	OFA No.	Rating	Age	Sex	Reg. No.	Owner
Norwood Timber's Caedmon	NE-1826	G	30	M	HD-540743	James Joyce
Norwood's Keeta	NE-1639	G	31	F	HD-259822	Hebert & Politoff
Norwood's Krystal Of Mistalyn	NE-1442	G	37	F	HC-988516	Kathy Paquito
Norwood's Trinka Av Mistalyn	NE-1373		24	F	HD-043754	Grover De Marinis & K. Paquito
Norwoods Timber Av Mistalyn	NE-1396	F	30	M	HD-047929	S. & J. M. Devine
Noste of Kotofjell	NE-0014		15	I	HB-072276	Nancy Torbet
Nykke Of Bjorndal	NE-1402	G	25	F	HD-062571	J. & S. Kinnamon
Nykker TNT Howdy Hoyden	NE-0610		31	F	HB-700711	
Nykker TNT Silver Jerzy Belle, CH	NE-0945		32	F	HC-252143	
Nykker TNT Silver Skyrocket, CH	NE-1235		37	M	HC-777946	
Nykker TNT Silver Star Dust, CH	NE-1322		26	F	HC-962099	
Nykker's Tryg Tempest	NE-0095					Pauline Nickerson
Nynorsk Fileur De Cartes	NE-2014	F	27	M	WL-777635	Linda Wilcott & Richard Mercier
Nynorsk Here Comes The Son, CAN CH	NE-1919	G	27	M	VU-735552	Marion & Murray Hogan
Nynorsk Literary Air, CAN CH	NE-1894	G	24	F	VS-739743	Elizabeth & Randall Sykes
Nynorsk Literary Innovation	NE-2135	G	24	F	HM40312801	Elizabeth Sykes
Nynorsk Quiquen Silver, Can CH	NE-1526	F	44	F	HD-248401	E. & R. Sykes
Nynorsk Steinerdottir Signe	NE-2167	G	27	F	HM37825301	Charlotte L. Brown
Oakwood's Rokki Robb	NE-0808		32	M	HB-004634	
Oakwood's Romeo	NE-0997		32	M	HC-365246	
Oakwoods Bewitched	NE-0619		24	F	HB-788299	
Oakwoods I'll Fly-Away, CH	NE-1068		33	F	HC-477727	
Oden of Valhala	NE-1029		118	M	HB-602062	
Olaf Av Katrine Glen	NE-0046					Henry Glasgow
Olympia Olav Leigh	NE-0885		25	M	HC-226192	
Onyks Gyger of Middensted	NE-0391					
Orion Polaris Rivendell	NE-0324					
Oseberg Alette (England)	NE-1212	G	25	F	HC-794803	Bob & Lynne Backer
Oshima's All That Love	NE-2139	F	40	F	HD-793354	Thomas & Betty Ricks
Ostrarns Kristin Kaptaviken	NE-1246		31	F	HC-795413	
Ouachita Ils N Brevik Mirage, CH	NE-0941		30	F	HC-249912	
Ouachita's Justinian	NE-1101		25	M	HC-570828	
Ouachita's Ziegfield	NE-1102		24	M	HC-563926	D. Loidhammer
Ouachua's Boulevardier	NE-1105B		25	M	HC-586962	G. Scott
Our Turkey Erikka	NE-1685	G	31	F	HD-450676	Lorna M. Nailon
Overscaig N W Bux's Freya	NE-2020	F	28	F	WL-784654	Erik Enochsen
Oxboro's Wind Song	NE-1134		43	F	HC-488917	K. Knoll
Paixao's Shebaniah Av Viking	NE-1652	G	25	F	HD-344945	R. & A. C. Sutton
Pebble Point Acemis Fanarok	NE-1193		25	M	HC-699777	C. Harmon
Peer Gynt Act I Solveig's Song	NE-1168		28	F	HC-669217	D. Stordahl
Peer Gynt Act II Mountain King	NE-1491	G	28	M	HC-947962	Sara E. Meyer
Peer Gynt Bitabrits Gyntiana, CH	NE-1771	G	25	F	HD-468896	D. Zuehlke & M. Oliver
Peer Gynt Going In Circles, CH	NE-2257	G	26	F	HM39033003	Marlene Oliver
Peer Gynt's Trib To Teodor	NE-2164	G	41	F	HD-798235	Marlene Oliver
Peer Gynt's Trib To Trav'lr	NE-2101	G	30	M	HD-798236	Carol Harmon & Marlene Oliver
Pelstad's Elfin Magic	NE-1605	G	32	F	HD-242581	Sharon Hershberger
Pepper Freska La Croix	NE-1985	G	57	F	HD-433625	Arthur & Rosemary Lacroix
Pepper Lee Ann	NE-0796		26	F	HB-993192	
Pepperjoe	NE-0919		26	F	HC-408003	
Peppi of Langport Valley	NE-0759		28	F	HB-957002	
Phantom Lady	NE-1827	F	30	F	HD-500756	Jean Wilkens
Piek of Hoved Havgen	NE-0342					
Pinheiro Mosca Lily Jayenn CDX	NE-0581		48	F	HB-383670	
Pinheiro's Inga of the Pines	NE-0150					Larry & Pat Fetter
Pinheiro's Mosca Lily Jayenn	NE-0267					
Pinheiro's Rum Lars	NE-0180					
Pinheiro's Rum Mina	NE-0286					
Pitch Road Taske Av Hestehov	NE-0013					Ralph Nichols
Poland's Freya	NE-0355					
Polestar Kelsean Icy Lite	NE-1631	G	26	F	HD-307108	Ronald A. Smith
Polestar Wynter Storm	NE-2084	G	33	M	HD-767584	Harry Beggs
Polestar's Charger of Wales	NE-1358		24	M	HD-093016	
Polestar's Cornerstone	NE-1051		53	F	HC-217146	

Registered Name	OFA No.	Rating	Age	Sex	Reg. No.	Owner
Polestar's Dark Crystal	NE-1486	F	43	F	HD-017952	Shultz & Maier
Polestar's Diva	NE-1585	G	25	F	HD-306736	Janet Maier
Polestar's Endora	NE-1263		26	F	HC-864183	
Polestar's Free Flight, CH	NE-1869	G	24	F	HD-630433	Janet C. Maier
Polestar's Jet Stream	NE-1870	G	24	M	HD-648365	Janet C. Maier
Polestar's Preferred Edition	NE-1880	G	25	F	6414526888	Karen Weir
Polestar's Protege, CH	NE-2010	F	24	F	HD-898480	Robert L. & Janet C. Maier
Polestar's Sirius	NE-1262		26	M	HC-875675	
Polestar's Solar Flame, CH	NE-1712	G	26	F	HD-447729	Janet Maier
Polestar's Solar Flare, CH	NE-1251		24	F	HC-864184	
Polestar's Spiritt of Uppsala	NE-1257		25	F	HC-912645	
Prin-Ruhadi-Dondi-of-Norway	NE-0842		29	F	HC-083637	
Prince Arne Av Cha'Ru	NE-0879		25	M	HC-185944	
Prince Baron Av Meri-ba	NE-1267		35	M	HC-767417	
Prince Elgernon of Fie-Dell	NE-0359					
Prince Norge Av Von Kugler	NE-0939		24	M	HC-295778	
Prince Pretty Boy Gregg	NE-0845		24	M	HC-179499	
Princess Christiana	NE-0381					
Princess Erika Av Faarway	NE-0658		72	F	HB-220212	
Princess Erika of Paulson	NE-1388		27	F	HD-021214	
Princess Freska Tally-Ho	NE-0636		41	F	HB-733649	
Princess Leigha Robbins	NE-1414	F	27	F	HD-155747	Robyn & Ken Robbins
Princess Lobinas Pollyanna	NE-1164		25	F	HC-661659	J. Barone
Princess Natacha of San Ann	NE-2137	F	24	F	HM33258003	Robert R. Hall
Princess Rainier Whipple	NE-1825	G	26	F	HD-696478	William Ian Whipple
Princess Sonja of Alkcrest, CH	NE-0352	G	73	F	HA-727565	Chris & Gayle Thomas
Promises Big Deal	NE-1444	G	33	M	HD-065864	Janice Leatherman
Quiquen Anda	NE-1107		27	F	KU-129726	Sykes
RGM Poland's Rowdy Rebel CD	NE-0899		34	M	HC-133249	
RM Middensted Lazer Tag	NE-1991	F	30	M	HD-703615	Gerlad E. & Nancy Brewer
Ragnhilde Ave Sjøsterne	NE-0106					
Rai Mai's Petticoats 'N Lace, CH	NE-1405	E	27	F	HD-039921	Heikkinen & Peters
Rai-Mai's American Anthem, CH	NE-1851	G	24	M	HD-595413	Ronald R. & Sandra M. Peters
Rai-Mai's Brandy Alexander, CH	NE-2016	F	31	M	HD-723989	Ronald R. & Sandra M. Peters
Rai-Mai's Gambler's Paradise	NE-1520	G	24	F	HD-224683	C. D. Davenport
Rai-Mai's Mint Julep, CH	NE-1954	G	25	F	HD-717773	John & Karen Haferbier
Rai-Mai's Rawhide 'N Leather, CH	NE-1410	G	24	M	HD-113553	R. R. & S. M. Peters
Rainbow's Akeit	NE-1731	G	24	M	HD-548354	Louise Richert
Ramayana Av Vinland, CH	NE-0313	G	50	F	HB-84778	Molly Patterson
Ramsele's Pandora	NE-0420					
Ramsele's Sea Raider	NE-0419					
Rasin Kiva	NE-1621	G	40	M	18741/84	Mrs Joe Peterson
Rautio's Tam	NE-0128					Ron & Chris Rautio
Raven	NE-1902	F	40	F		Nancie & Robaire Bozeman
Raven of Weminuche	NE-2233	G	42	F	HM30450701	Bill Parker
Ravenstone Milord	NE-1463	G	26	M	HD-189852	Jane S. Morris
Ravenstone Rainbow	NE-1535	G	24	F	HD-370400	Margaret Mott
Ravenstone Rebel Yell	NE-1549	E	26	M	HD-372100	S. & E. Arseven
Ravenstone Rolls Royce	NE-1533	G	24	M	HD-340202	Margaret Mott
Ravenstone Teodor, CH (Am & Eng)	NE-0244					Rick & Lana Hall
Raymin's Bartender's Special	NE-1843	F	24	F	VA-678136	Ray & Minnie Forsyth
Raymin's Classic Caddilac	NE-2054	G	27	M	WW-812023	Diane Hales
Raymin's Classic Corvette	NE-2059	F	28	F	WW-812028	Minnie Steer
Rebel	NE-1125		46	M	HC-489791	M. Widvey
Rebel Ridge's Amethyst, CH	NE-1088		31	F	HC-549877	
Rebel Ridge's Viking Ceaser	NE-1169		37	M	HC-596569	M. Kincaid
Rebel Ridge's Waco, CH	NE-0291					
Rebel Ridges Cisco	NE-0666		55	M	HB-452857	
Reeves Lady Cassandra Heard	NE-0869		34	F	HC-396606	
Reidar CD	NE-0675		49	M	HB-582560	
Rendition's True Rhythm	NE-1986	G	24	M	HD-809534	Kathi Boyd & Joan & T. Brennan
Renegade's Brutus	NE-0308					
Riiser Guy's Lisa Av HuMar	NE-0424					

Registered Name	OFA No.	Rating	Age	Sex	Reg. No.	Owner
Rikkana's Free Wheeler, CH	NE-0644		24	M	HB-861794	
Rikkana's Hip Hugger, CH	NE-0621		50	F	HB-425961	
Rikkana's Independence, CH	NE-1111		79	M	HC-040882	Jon LaBree
Rikkana's Look At Me Now, CH	NE-0810		30	F	HC-024863	
Rikkana's Outa Sight	NE-0210					Rick & Lana Hall
Rikkana's Pooh Bear, CH	NE-0833		59	F	HB-696113	
Ringo II	NE-0067					Willie & Patricia Dishman
Rinna of Elkridge	NE-1656	G	24	F	HD-356405	Margaret B. Sharis
Rising Sun's Kasjmir Bouquet	NE-2186	G	53	F	HD-719969	Karen Carnathan
Rising Sun's Pride av Norgren	NE-2128	G	24	M		Ruby Torvinen
Rivendell's Astria av Satuit, CH	NE-1045		27	F	HC-466400	
Rivendell's Brand	NE-0676		31	M	HB-780359	
Rivendell's Flicka of Gylef	NE-0739		29	F	HB-967034	
Rivendell's Liv, CH	NE-0814		32	F	HC-002724	
Rivendell's Thorin Oakenshield	NE-0995		33	M	HC-367300	
Riverdell's Brutus	NE-0749		30	M	HB-967033	
Riverwind Falcon Au Tafeta	NE-2237	F	26	F	HM38703001	Lee Ann Breading
Rob Lyn's Head Of The Class	NE-2157	G	24	F	HM34869908	Robert G. Baker/Lynne E. Backer
Rob Lyn's Ka-Ndy	NE-2024	F	26	F	HD-842443	Jack & Betty Gordon & L. Backer
Rob Lyn's Kaia	NE-1329	F	24	F	HC-970543	L. & I. Graf
Rob-Lyn's Bjorn	NE-2175	G	31	M	HM32941302	Anna Kane Laird
Rob-Lyn's Brave Lars Anderson	NE-2210	G	29	M	HM34870101	Christine & Joe Dokken
Rob-Lyn's Dagmar O'Gorman	NE-1744	F	30	F	HD-553683	Patrick & Cathryn Gorman
Rob-Lyn's Flicka Av Kragsbyn	NE-2075	G	25	F	HD-847444	Pamela J. Ryan & Lynne E. Backer
Rob-Lyn's Freya Shadow	NE-2230	G	36	F	HM32941301	Mary Dunlop
Rob-Lyn's Frosted Pink Lady	NE-1121	G	33	F	HC-520269	E. Leider
Rob-Lyn's Grey Lord	NE-1695	G	24	M	HD-502257	R. & L. Backer
Rob-Lyn's In Like Flint	NE-2183	F	31	M	HM32941402	Robert B. & Lynn E. Backer
Rob-Lyn's Jag Alskar Gunnar	NE-1883	G	24	M	HD-672292	Pamela Ryan & Lynne Backer
Rob-Lyn's Lady Rana	NE-1858	G	24	F	HD-608603	Robert G. & Lynn E. Backer
Rob-Lyn's Lil Meg Of Misti	NE-1872	F	26	F	HD-607871	Pam Ryan & Lynne Backer
Rob-Lyn's Magic Genie, CH	NE-1190	F	26	F	HC-846400	R. & L. Backer & G. Thomas
Rob-Lyn's Memory Maker	NE-2003	G	24	F	HM2548701	Robert & Lynne Backer
Rob-Lyn's Milka Girl	NE-2169	G	58	F	HM20126401	Cynthia Lueck-Blank
Rob-Lyn's Misti Skei	NE-1628	G	24	F	HD-341927	David O'Brien & L. Backer
Rob-Lyn's Nordic Tasha	NE-1629	E	24	F	HD-341928	David O'Brien
Rob-Lyn's Nordik Knight	NE-2127	G	39	M	HD-767290	Lynne E. Backer
Rob-Lyn's Proud Pioneer	NE-0774	G	27	M	HC-018080	Robert & Lynn Backer
Rob-Lyn's Rough 'N Rowdy	NE-1536	G	39	M	HD-094106	Mary Nelson
Rob-Lyn's Silver Certificate	NE-1439	E	24	F	HD-181565	R. & L. Backer
Rob-Lyn's Silver Katrina	NE-1662	G	27	F	HD-563479	D. Cruse & L. Backer
Rob-Lyn's Special Tribute	NE-2089	F	25	F	HD-886568	Rosemary Somers & Lynne E. Backer
Rob-Lyn's Speculation	NE-0806	G	25	M	HC-055362	G. & P. Toman
Rob-Lyn's Tyra of Norman	NE-0891	G	29	F	HC-149864	J. Zabulski
Rob-Lyn's Weekend Warrior	NE-1893	E	25	M	HD-741356	Lynne Backer & Linda A. Graf
Rob-Ton's Trollson's Tarpen	NE-0520					
Robart's Silver Cinder	NE-0025					Diann Schiller
Robarts Smilin Tiger	NE-0009					Diann Schiller
Rohunds Macho Man	NE-1298		60	M	HC-591835	Shirley Quigley
Roki Kismit	NE-1084		30	F	HC-533564	
Rokke Bjorn Degernes (Norway)	NE-1258	G	25	M	HC-900802	C. Loitfellner & Cotterell
Rokon Misty's Christina	NE-0811		24	F	FA-000788	
Ronan's Cupcake's Prince, CH	NE-1187		25	M	HC-698921	D. Tewksbury
Roundel Necromancer	NE-1350		24	M	HC-972347	
Roundel's Gizmo Of Vikiro, CH	NE-1472	G	24	M	HD-162301	Victoria Lawton
Rowdy of the Northwoods	NE-0632		28	M	HB-791084	
Royal Crown My Grandma's Pepsi, CH	NE-1197		29	F	HC-707957	V. Zumwalt
Royal Crown's Amaretto, CH	NE-1583	F	37	F	HD-173201	Katherine Ellis
Royal Crown's Blue Diamond, CH	NE-2173	G	41	F	HM33211802	Vicky P. Zumwalt
Royal Crown's Blue Moon	NE-2104	G	48	F	HD-657933	Vicky P. Zumwalt
Royal Crown's Blue Print	NE-2077	G	46	F	HD-657933	Vicky P. Zumwalt
Royal Crown's Blue Ribbons	NE-2204	G	32	F	HM33211803	Vicky P. Zumwalt
Royal Crown's Johnny Walker	NE-1336		25	M	HC-959727	

Registered Name	OFA No.	Rating	Age	Sex	Reg. No.	Owner
Royal Crown's Lady K of Valimar, CH	NE-1768	G	39	F	HD-384270	Vicky P. Zumwalt
Royal Crown's Lord Calvert	NE-1480	F	25	M	HD-177306	Patricia J. Peterson
Royal Crown's Party Of One	NE-2196	E	32	F	HD-909091	Vicky P. Zumwalt
Royal Crown's Promenade, CH	NE-2209	G	26	F	HM36262505	Vicky P. Zumwalt
Royal Crown's Spirit Helper, CH	NE-2197	G	25	M	HM36262504	Vicky P. Zumwalt
Royal Crown's Will of the Wind	NE-1675	G	42	F	HD-217179	Vicky Zumwalt
Royal Crown's Windwalker, CH	NE-1335		42	M	HC-834491	
Runefjell Karlee	NE-0277					
Ruskar's Gold Edition, CH	NE-2125	G	53	F	HD-725420	Russell F. & Karen L. Weir
Ruskar's Quiquen Conspiracy	NE-2129	E	26	F	HM32266301	J. Pual Woito
Rutter's High Mountain Storm	NE-1809	G	24	M	HD-565327	Terrillann Rutter
Ryfjelds Driva Av Vigeland, CH	NE-0206					
Saaberg's Tanka	NE-1138		56	F	HC-379991	C. Bergerud
Sachem's Sophia of Michaux	NE-2158	F	55	F	HD-659419	Marian Siegel, VMD
Saga's Scamp of Redhill, CH	NE-0503					Johnson
Sal-Heidi of Clearview	NE-0993		25	F	HC-381803	
Samantha Bachrom	NE-1151		35	F	HC-553470	J. Paddon
San-Dee's Jinx Av Yak-Vali	NE-0825		39	F	HC-104961	
Sandride's Hi And Mighty, CH	NE-1003		24	M	HC-430307	
Sandyhill's Beautiful Bu	NE-2105	G	27	F	90/97	Carl & Coco Barringer
Sangrud Brooke's Lenke	NE-2193	G	26	M	HM35533106	Kristen E Wehking/Karen Elvin
Sangrud Kolle's Tomten, CH	NE-1301		33	M	HC-848857	Karen B. Elvin
Sangrud Toby's Bingo	NE-1887	E	26	M	HD-625750	Karen B. Elvin
Sangrud Toby's Brand	NE-2226	G	65	M	HD-625748	Karen Elvin / Kristin Wehking
Sangrud Toby's Brooke	NE-1888	G	26	F	HD-625747	Karen B. Elvin
Sangrud Tomten's Tassia	NE-1622	F	54	F	HD-097666	K & K Elvin
Sangrud Tomten's Trylle	NE-1618	F	54	F	HD-097667	K & K Elvin
Sangrud Torga's Ruffin Rulette	NE-2000	G	24	F	HD-790323	Karen B. Elvin
Sangrud's Hoken Fantasket	NE-0733		24	M	HC-012992	
Sangrud's Hugo Fantasket	NE-0849		39	M	HC-012994	
Sangrud's Tanrydoon Kolle	NE-1108		43	F	HC-415058	K. Elvin
Sangrud's Windrow Tinker, CH	NE-1649	G	80	F	HC-869199	K. Elvin & R. Phelps
Sangruds Jorrun Hontassig	NE-0916		27	F	HC-251033	
Sanray's Finnetta Be Happy	NE-0689		29	F	HB-858869	
Sasha Av Telggren	NE-1803	F	36	F	HD-423155	Sandi Smith
Sasha Tass	NE-0278					
Saski	NE-0813		36	F	FA-000789	
Sasquatch Owen Echo	NE-1016		42	M	HC-289149	
Satuit Sejariara Av Statton, CH	NE-1236		26	F	HC-837848	
Satuit's Senny of Liseldun	NE-1564	G	24	F	HD-291873	Barbara Roby
Satuits Liten Ulv Taska	NE-1654	F	33	F	HD-292650	Paula Milnes
Scandia's Budget Buster	NE-1338		24	M	HD-003752	
Scandia's Free Spirit, CH	NE-1411	G	34	F	HC-969696	Kathy M. Siftar
Scandia's Rum Runner	NE-1337		25	M	HC-887094	
Scandia's Wild Turkey, CH	NE-1404	F	36	F	HC-956846	J. E. & G. L. Shipley
Schmidt's Yogi Bear	NE-0361					
Scotch Penny	NE-0634	F	24	F	HB-834491	L. & J. Edfors
Seacrest General Admiration	NE-2250	G	24	M	HM39454504	Jennifer & Margaret Williamson
Seacrest's Gray Rose	NE-2011	F	27	F	HD-771130	Ginny Lynne Caldwell
Seacrest's Winter Heat	NE-2247	G	24	M	HM39454502	Margaret Williamson
Seafarer's Princess Sierra's	NE-2168	F	28	F	HM34070806	Donna Stankowski
Selkir's Silver Gamble	NE-1910	F	26	M	HD-685017	Darlene & Mike Stuart
Sergeant Major Wapiti	NE-0305					
Shadow's Shady Lady	NE-0860	G	29	F	HC-167535	D. Martenson
Shadowmist Ruffian Nord-Vann, CH	NE-1319		35	F	HC-884204	
Shadowmist Sparkle Plenty	NE-1468	G	56	F	HC-877736	Moore & Simpson
Sharalo's Sassy Doo Nikki	NE-1640	G	39	F	HD-209263	R. J. & L. M. Mills
Sharalo's Sparkle Plenty	NE-1227		26	F	HC-792889	
Sharalos Diamonds R Forever	NE-1989	G	29	F	HD-690421	Ray & Lois Mills
Sharalos Sassy James Bond, CH	NE-1983	G	29	M	HD-690422	Ray & Lois Mills
Sharalos Sassy Silver Ghost	NE-1691	F	55	M	HD-109935	Raymond & Lois Mills
Sharalos Silver Candy Kiss	NE-1757	F	25	F	HD-548268	Ray & Lois Mills
Sharalos Silver Paw Prints, CH	NE-1778	G	26	M	HD-538654	Raymond & Lois Mills

Registered Name	OFA No.	Rating	Age	Sex	Reg. No.	Owner
Sharalos Sterling Silver, CH	NE-1777	F	26	M	HD-516057	Raymond & Lois Mills
Sharlo's Sassy Lassy	NE-1357		47	F	HC-792888	
Sheba Von Leiba of Kay Lee	NE-0339					
Sheena Ashes Of Mo	NE-1987	G	29	F	HD-721207	Warren & Karen Plaskett
Sheera	NE-1763	E	26	F	HD-626512	Jean Vermillion
Shejac's Krystal Mountain	NE-1728	G	30	F	HD-422486	N. & M. Garrett
Sherjac's Dark Shadow	NE-1914	G	29	M	HD-706931	Brett A. & Angie C. Morgan
Sherry's Freya	NE-1637	G	24	F	HD-350398	Sherry Stone
Shubin's Shaddo	NE-0763		41	M	HB-823202	
Shubin's Ty	NE-0762		27	M	HB-991171	
Sid Stu's Nikki	NE-0265					
Sigrid of Fie-Dell	NE-0275					
Sigrid of Telemark	NE-0266					
Silroth's Rokon Ruggen, Can CH	NE-1667	G	58	M	QN-381179	Cathy & Dirk Roberts
Silroths Silver's Selja, Can CH	NE-1671	G	44	F	RQ-448143	Ray & Minnie Forsyth
Silva Peer Grob Nattens	NE-0092					
Silver Bay' Star Gazer	NE-1544	G	32	F	HD-202198	N. & E. Thompson
Silver Bay' Star Trek	NE-1543	G	32	M	HD-192153	V. & B. Rubendall
Silver Bay's High Noon	NE-1100		28	M	HC-535078	
Silver Bay's Misty Morn	NE-1103		28	F	HC-527108	
Silver Bay's TkO Av Rockwell	NE-1309		32	F	HC-851059	
Silver Bay-Tusen Bra Foxfire	NE-1366		27	F	HC-969447	Mr. & Mrs. Dick Schmidt
Silver Bay-Tusen Bra Solvfox	NE-1367		27	M	HC-979431	Dick Schmidt & Jean Schroeder
Silver Belle Av Meri Da	NE-0695		29	F	HB-840941	
Silver Bullet IV	NE-0948		59	M	HB-983438	
Silver Candy II	NE-0309					
Silver Dreams Vashita	NE-1684	F	43	F	HD-241023	Dorothy Wallace
Silver Dutchess of Varelia	NE-1278		50	F	HC-650131	
Silver Kolohe	NE-0855		28	F	HC-120748	
Silver Shawl Elke	NE-0914		28	F	HC-199786	
Silverbell Michell Edwards	NE-0633		27	F	HB-844743	
Silvercrest's Raagnar Jeru	NE-0751					
Silverlance Imp N Tass Steig	NE-0197					
Silverlance Imp N Tass Tyra	NE-0182					
Silverlance Imp N' Tass Kaisa	NE-0198					
Silverlance Knox's Odin	NE-0199					
Simba's Princess Sheba	NE-1079		32	F	JP-060969	
Sir Cado Barcus	NE-1594	G	52	M	HD-011636	Ken Hill
Sir Harley Davidson	NE-1567	E	31	M	HD-217348	T & T Ruberto
Sir Jake Gilmore Goodwin	NE-2131	F	26	M	HM32157805	Debra & Wayne Goodwin
Sir Nicholas Eric	NE-0750		33	M	HB-929074	
Sir Valient	NE-0524					
Sirdal's Class Act	NE-1797	G	28	F	HD-477691	Diana Korneliusen
Sirdal's Crystal Moon	NE-2155	F	26	F	HM34542206	Diana Korneliusen
Sirdal's J. K. Av Truevine	NE-1323		25	M	HC-965871	
Sirdal's Jesse James	NE-2041	G	62	M	1031987	Lori Baumle
Sirdal's Mae West, CH	NE-1799	G	36	F	HD-467123	Diana Korneliusen
Sirdal's Midnight Hour, CH	NE-2080	G	27	M	HD-869635	Kim & Scott Tilander
Sirdal's Morning Glory, CH	NE-2050	E	24	F	HD-869634	Diana Korneliusen
Sirdal's Pepper of Norlander, CH	NE-2102	F	24	F	HD-909168	Joy Ritter & Diana Korneliusen
Sirdal's Thunder Hawk	NE-2095	G	29	M	HD-866480	Ann Clandening
Sirdals Aldo Cella	NE-1352		29	M	HC-959386	
Sirdals Haakon	NE-1630	G	55	M	HD-078943	D. & L. Korneliusen
Sirdals Shayla	NE-1462	G	35	F	HD-078945	Diana Korneliusen
Sirdals Sonja Av Galaxy	NE-1005		31	F	HC-369662	
Sirdals Tora Lisa	NE-1351		29	F	HC-959384	
Sirius Southern Beau	NE-2202	F	25	M	HM36714107	John.& Kathleen Kafader
Sirius Southern Belle	NE-2206	G	25	F	HM36714105	Daryll and Leigh Parkinson
Sirius Southern Gent	NE-2207	G	24	M	HM36714104	Al & Laura Graham / K. Douglas
Sirius Southern Lady	NE-2190	G	24	F	HM36714106	Brian & Gina Ridgway
Sirius Southern Style	NE-2189	G	24	M	HM36714101	David L. & Jane E. Dittman
Skessa Of Asgaard	NE-1879	F	25	F	HD-623170	Dr. F. G. Weisser & Joe Fryhover
Skjolden Sooty of Norske	NE-1200		27	M	HC-736728	J. Perry

Registered Name	OFA No.	Rating	Age	Sex	Reg. No.	Owner
Skjoll's Trollfjord of Norske	NE-1199		27	M	HC-734521	K. Bramson
Skjonberg's A Min Duv Nonne	NE-1220		27	F	HC-778849	
Skol X	NE-0931				HC-	
Slov Fjell of Eidsvold	NE-0953	E	24	M	HC-358836	Nancy Torbet
Smokey Via Northwind	NE-0933		25	M	HC-340840	
Smokey of Misty Mountain	NE-0154					
Sno-Go's Gnupa of Middensted	NE-0268					C. Christiansen
Snowdust's Ragamuffin	NE-0822		30	F	HC-068191	
Snowdust's Ragnarsaurus	NE-0780		24	M	HC-068192	
So Merri Mister Chips,CH	NE-0220					B. Hall
So Merri Princess Sonya	NE-0734		51	F	HB-627240	
Solbakken's Tupio	NE-0913		50	M	HB-879238	
Solv-Kreiger av Bifrost	NE-0560					Wilkes
Solveig of Pomfret, CH	NE-0276					B. Roby
Somerri Bartletts Balki	NE-1882	F	42	M	HD-469552	Jill Walsh
Somerri Ble True Slikipinne	NE-1027		26	F	HC-431163	
Somerri El Zid	NE-0471					
Somerri Erin	NE-0786		43	F	HB-847342	
Somerri Fas Trekk, CH	NE-0883		44	M	HC-001868	
Somerri Fru Mishka, CH	NE-1842	G	81	F	HD-137343	Laura Lewis
Somerri Fru Naomi	NE-0929		33	F	HC-469404	
Somerri Fru Stingrae	NE-1747	E	26	F	HD-549480	Laura Lewis
Somerri Gentle Wench	NE-1532	F	30	F	HD-175548	Nancy Fruzzetti
Somerri Hannibal Hayes	NE-1113		26	M	HC-596642	L. Hall
Somerri His Majesty of Ellkins	NE-1024		26	M	HC-423367	
Somerri Kid Curry, CH	NE-1070		26	M	HC-520461	
Somerri Kid's Kaleidoscope	NE-1867	G	25	F	HD-684990	Roland Masse & Beatrice Hall
Somerri Lady Leda	NE-0470					
Somerri Ljosa Loki	NE-0882		26	M	HC-232341	
Somerri Margrete D'Luog	NE-1268		25	F	HC-899170	
Somerri Monashee Dawn	NE-1513	F	46	F	HD-069254	Newell & B. Hall
Somerri Oscar Winner, CH	NE-2239	E	37	M	HM32822903	Laura Lewis
Somerri Sir Lancelot, CH	NE-1398	G	27	M	HD-011690	Juliet Movitz
Somerri Torsdags Barn	NE-0219					B. Hall
Somerri Yosemite Sam	NE-1448	F	24	M	HD-287224	L. & B. Hall
Sommer's Tana of Middenstad	NE-0466					
Son Ju Bjorklund	NE-0118					
Sonja O Tass av Ringesland	NE-0760					
Sonja XXII	NE-0761		50	F	HB-726682	
Sonja of Chicago, CH	NE-0356					
Sonjarok's Silver Smoke	NE-0646		42	M	HB-594450	
Spacer Lee Sanders	NE-1657	G	68	M	HD-002418	Philip Sanders
Spitfire Kathy of Chrisnik	NE-1321		33	F	HC-850506	
Spunky Gal Av Meri Da	NE-0698		28	F	HB-968812	
Stang's Lady Elkie	NE-0894		47	F	HB-934107	
Statton Crista Jenuine Jewel	NE-1477	F	32	F	HD-087111	Sallie & Stacy Clarke
Statton Jab'bok of Shdyhollow, CH	NE-1739	F	30	F	HD-407005	Beverly Labaire
Statton Joshua Av Norgren, CH	NE-2179	G	24	M	HM36297002	Grenville Sawyer
Statton Jr Sol of Stonylea, CH	NE-1276		28	M	HC-883169	
Statton's Jaded Watters	NE-1434	F	27	M	HD-092309	Cotton Silverman
Statton's Jamalen Gray Gal	NE-2134	E	26	F	HM33110701	Kaaren & Stan Silverman
Statton's Jenna Av Kire CD, CH	NE-1447	F	34	F	HD-048603	Susan Formisano
Statton's Jesteri Av Do-T-Do, CH	NE-1290		30	F	HC-924090	Terry La Fleur
Statton's Joslin of Tekdal	NE-1467	F	37	M	HD-115764	K & S Silverman
Statton's Paws For Keljurno	NE-2181	E	24	F	HM36297004	Kaaren & Stan Silverman
Statton's Rejenerate Av Kire	NE-1857	F	25	F	HD-575132	Cotton Silverman
Statton's Silver Dan Jaren	NE-1697	G	24	M	HD-443222	K. & S. Silverman
Statton's Silver Jurnda	NE-1615	F	30	F	HD-283979	K & S Silverman
Statton's Silver Sej	NE-1179		26	M	HC-701333	K. Silverman
Steedsson Av Truelgaard	NE-0116					Bob & Carmen Streiff
Steiner's Ilse of Chrislex, CH	NE-1334		35	F	HC-866996	C. Brown
Steiner's Lars of Vinland	NE-1676	G	82	M	HC-898174	Dorothy Wallace
Steiner's Soren of Vinland, CH	NE-1325	F	34	M	HC-898173	

Registered Name	OFA No.	Rating	Age	Sex	Reg. No.	Owner
Steiner's Taril of Vinland	NE-1326	G	34	F	HC-908757	
Sterling Hill One For Scoots, CH	NE-1764	G	25	M	HD-495562	Sal & Michelle Ferrito
Sterling Hill Winnie Of Poo	NE-1926	G	31	F	HD-608335	Sal Ferrito
Sterling Hill's Brandybuck	NE-1904	G	29	M	HD-602050	Marilyn K. McCoy
Stillehavet's Jack Daniels	NE-0620		27	M	HB-783637	
Stina of Raisen	NE-0250					
Stonhedges Molde	NE-1030		48	F	HC-206503	
Stonylea's Daemon	NE-0886		27	M	HC-210033	
Stonylea's Freigha	NE-0377					
Stonylea's Nydgling	NE-0889		27	F	HC-210032	
Stonylea's Solveig Av Satuit	NE-0247					
Storuman Star, CH	NE-1641	G	47	M	HD-159809	N. & M. Garrett
Stryn-Olaf	NE-0892		84	M	HC-468233	
Stueland's Sensible Sabrina	NE-1234		41	F	HC-718045	
Styri Solbaer Toddy-Av-Stran	NE-0876		24	F	HC-256801	
Styri Solv Kongen-Av-Stran	NE-0875		24	M	HC-256802	
Sunni Av Tassajara	NE-0437					
Sunshine VIII	NE-1219		33	F	HC-719427	
Sunshine's Alpha Tory, CH	NE-0714		24	M	HB-981858	
Sunspot Vikrest Deep Trouble, CH	NE-2215	G	43	F	HD-839571	Patricia Viken / Leslie Forrest
Sunspot's Macbeth	NE-2076	G	26	M	HD-840574	Sandra L. & William J. Faut
Sunspots Great Expectations	NE-2231	G	45	M	HD-850887	Debra & David Tewksbury
Surtsey Archangel	NE-1584	E	33	M	HD-232117	Diane Chisholm
Surtsey Aubrey Was Her Name	NE-1608	G	34	F	HD-232111	Diane Chisholm
Surtsey Gee Whiz	NE-1458	F	25	M	HD-133312	Diane Chisholm
Surtsey I Dream Of Jeannie	NE-1440	F	25	F	HD-111918	Diane Chisholm
Surtsey Libby Libby Libby	NE-1705	F	26	F	HD-535899	Diane Chisholm
Surtsey Silver Freya	NE-1307		29	F	HC-876705	
Surtsey St. Andrew	NE-1555	F	29	M	HD-2232115	Diane Chisholm
Surtsey The Angel Gabriel	NE-1554	G	30	M	HD-232114	Diane Chisholm
Surtsey The Flying Dutchman	NE-1371		24	M	HD-031441	Diane Chisholm
Surtsey Up Up And Away, CH	NE-1589	G	32	M	HD-232113	Diane Chisholm
Svartur Andlit Bjorn	NE-0854		25	M	HC-169246	
Sventre-Jandal Double Play	NE-1305		30	F	HC-864439	Dale K. & Janice W. Price
Svenya of the Woods	NE-0735		25	F	HL-572930	
Sweetheart Av Meri Da	NE-0680		27	F	HB-968811	
Sylvan Haren's Dristig	NE-1808	G	29	F	HD-483934	Kenna Hoyser
Sylvanhaven's Bruser	NE-1791	G	26	M	HD-483933	Kenna Hoyser
T. C.'s Solv Tor of Mars	NE-0591		25	M	HB-698360	
TNK Beowulf Tyr Woden, CH	NE-0824		26	M	HC-083791	
TNK Cochise's Medicine Man, CH	NE-1758	G	24	M	HD-491749	Nona & Tom Krena
TNK Cochise's Shiny Wampum	NE-1760	G	24	F	HD-489068	Kent & Beverly Knicely
TNK Holiday Treasure	NE-1897	E	24	F	HD-690402	Nona P. Krena
TNK Kachina's Normark Charm	NE-2116	G	37	F	HD-767630	Diane E. & Robert E. Coleman
TNK Kachina's Sand Dollar	NE-2099	G	35	F		Doreen & Daniel Bates
TNK's Gonzo of Ardon's, CH	NE-2035	F	27	M	HD-817203	Arlene M. Aliano
TNT's Eyrekr	NE-1457	G	42	F	HC-963749	Wade Lawrence, DVM
Tack Sa My Cket	NE-0378					
Tagran of Fie-Dell	NE-0360					
Takami's Erica	NE-1651	G	24	F	HD-341210	T. Smith & A. Smith
Takkdahl Lite Cactus Flower, CD	NE-2253	G	54	F	HD-791499	John C. & Patricia L. Norgren
Taliesin's Tarn	NE-0592		27	M	HB-674528	
Tanon's Daisy Mae, CH	NE-1313		28	F	HC-899790	
Tanrydoon Imp's Fantasstic	NE-0557					Norstrom
Tanrydoon Imp's Toreadero	NE-0241					Charles & Peggy Giles
Tanrydoon Muntek Hezekiah	NE-0587		35	M	HB-543873	
Tanrydoon Muntek Jezebel, CH	NE-0474					Jon & Cam LaBree
Tanrydoon Tasscatek	NE-0221					Reuben & Eleanor Meissner
Tantalum Bermarba Bjarni Max, CH	NE-1905	G	27	M	HD-673170	Ruth Blackburn DVM &Doris Transue
Tantalum Tomten's Alpha, CH	NE-1588	G	26	F	HD-280544	Ruth Blackburn
Tantalum Tomten's Anders, CH	NE-1565	G	24	M	HD-284573	Robert & Lynn Backer
Tanya Frigga Freya	NE-0736		37	F	HB-940440	
Tanya of Pomfret	NE-0032					Susan Phillips

Registered Name	OFA No.	Rating	Age	Sex	Reg. No.	Owner
Tara of Bhorndal	NE-0965					
Tarka of Trail's End	NE-0599		61	F	HB-207466	
Tarroma N Bicen' Rebel Romance	NE-1154		24	F	HC-664754	G. Fain
Tarroma N Norflamin's Daybreak	NE-1932	G	37	F	HD-562887	Maureen Lux & Jytte Hammond
Tarroma's Hooper, CH	NE-1280		26	M	HC-874008	
Tas' Bjorn Belle Av Marbran	NE-0211					
Tasha Suncrest	NE-2082	G	31	F	HD-754940	Matthew & Gina Peska
Tashtins Olsen	NE-2244	G	25	M	YY-989384	Linda Enochsen
Taska Skada Of Brookwood	NE-1993	F	45	F	HD-550076	Lee R. Cook
Tass 'N Gemi's Maya Av Oldenhus	NE-0187					
Tass' Silver Sun Cinder	NE-0463	G	24	F	HB-569914	Chris & Gayle Thomas
Tass's Benny Beaver of Marbran	NE-0188					Dale Poppy
Tassa of Pitch Road IV	NE-0130					
Tassatrina Av Oakhaven	NE-0149					Art & Marie Oakley
Tassca Dera Askimo, CH	NE-0740		32	F	EN-000715	
Tassket Av Oakhaven, CH	NE-0455					
Tassketsunn Av Oakhaven	NE-0819		26	M	HC-090165	
Tebunah Ha-Shalom	NE-0718		31	F	HB-858014	
Tessa Bringa of Hinsdale	NE-0630	G	34	F	HB-671636	R. Calkins
Thane of the Woods	NE-0741		28	M	HC-055650	
The Duke of Jeramie	NE-0613		24	M	HB-771694	
Tho-Ma-Sans Great Ball Of Fire, CH	NE-2027	G	24	M	HD-822199	Charles & Catherine McFadden
Thom Thom Ivy Vine	NE-2162	F	40	F	HD-826889	Christine Olson/Gayle Thomas
Thom-Thom's Morning Mist	NE-2142	F	29	F	HM32287903	Charles McFadden/G. & C. Thomas
ThomThom Acer Tab Jupitor, CH	NE-1097	G	29	M	HC-594957	Chris & Gayle Thomas
ThomThom Acer Tab Mars	NE-1077	E	26	M	HC-540590	Kent Johnson
ThomThom Acer-Don Layla	NE-1252	F	37	F	HC-821204	Chris & Gayle Thomas
ThomThom B-Tiny Turtle	NE-1435	G	46	M	HD-005172	Harmon Anderson
ThomThom Berri of Lars-Doll	NE-1595	F	25	F	HD-297262	Chris & Gayle Thomas
ThomThom Cintar Hexadecimal CD, CH	NE-0924	G	24	F	HC-256362	Chris & Gayle Thomas
ThomThom Cintar Macro, CH	NE-1038	G	24	M	HC-473065	M. Pyne & G. Thomas
ThomThom Cintar Sort	NE-0922		24	F	HC-325619	
ThomThom Cintar Zap Siri	NE-0977		36	F	HC-260203	
ThomThom Cintor Ace, CH	NE-0878	E	32	M	HC-179682	Chris & Gayle Thomas
ThomThom Fadon Wizard	NE-1060	G	26	M	HC-531189	Chris & Gayle Thomas
ThomThom Freya of Lars-Doll	NE-1515	F	24	F		K Bard & G Thomas
ThomThom GJ's Tyrell Tyr	NE-1470	G	25	M	HD-167706	Andrea Sime
ThomThom Hasak of Lars-Doll	NE-1633	F	28	M	HD-297094	Ronald L. Ball
ThomThom Hextar Love Bird CD, CH	NE-1156	G	24	M	HC-661503	Chris & Gayle Thomas
ThomThom Hextar Love Bug, CH	NE-1155	G	24	M	HC-661504	Chris & Gayle Thomas
ThomThom Jup-Don Big Guy, CH	NE-1264	G	25	M	HC-861435	Harry Beggs
ThomThom Jup-Don Hello Dolly	NE-1392	G	25	F	HD-022679	Chris & Gayle Thomas
ThomThom Jup-Don Mighty Thor,CH	NE-1382	G	24	M	HD-046297	Shelley & Sal Ferrito
ThomThom Lily of the Valley	NE-1740	G	31	F	HD-483818	Chris & Gayle Thomas
ThomThom Lordan's B-Sweet P, CH	NE-1324	F	26	F	HC-921582	Chris & Gayle Thomas
ThomThom Lordan's Sweet Julip	NE-1478	G	24	F	HD-167707	Thomas & Syftestad
ThomThom Mac Genie Mina	NE-1387	G	30	F	HD-005455	Jim & Nola Skaar
ThomThom Macv Diamond Dust	NE-1390	G	24	F	HD-046296	Chris & Gayle Thomas
ThomThom Midgard B-Jup Lars, CH	NE-1377	G	24	M	HD-005456	Chris & Gayle Thomas
ThomThom Midgard B-Jup Nan, CH	NE-1379	G	24	F	HD-022676	Chris & Gayle Thomas
ThomThom Midgard BB's Eada	NE-1496	G	2	F	HD-139793	Raymond Gunderson
ThomThom Midgard BB's Norsk, CH	NE-1505	G	33	M	HD-119829	T. & K. Nichols
ThomThom Midgard BB's Toten	NE-1687	G	54	M	HD-203185	J. & J. Mosher
ThomThom Midwest Snapdragon, CH	NE-2067	F	28	F	HD-811497	D. & B. Jelinek & C. & G. Thomas
ThomThom Norwegian Power	NE-0809	E	30	M	HC-275277	D. Brubakken & G. Thomas
ThomThom Prisort Drummer Boy	NE-1109		25	M	HC-575621	Kathy Wienke
ThomThom Prisort Happy, CH	NE-1115	G	27	F	HC-576425	Doris Bolinger
ThomThom Shogun	NE-2053	G	25	M	HD-821698	Andy & Brenda Spruce
ThomThom Sigtar Doloop	NE-1189	G	62	F	HC-378758	Chris & Gayle Thomas
ThomThom Sigtar Per Hans	NE-1096	G	43	M	HC-378757	Karsten & Marlene Oldenburg
ThomThom Sigtar Tape Drive, CH	NE-1110		47	F	HC-378759	David Larson
ThomThom Sweet-Jup's Missy	NE-1469	G	29	F	HD-139748	Gayle Thomas
ThomThom T-Bird Fancy	NE-1254	G	24	F	HC-853148	Chris & Gayle Thomas

Registered Name	OFA No.	Rating	Age	Sex	Reg. No.	Owner
ThomThom's Blockbuster, CH	NE-1996	G	29	M	HD-724540	Chris & Gayle Thomas
ThomThom's Blueberry	NE-1995	G	30	F	HD-700906	Chris & Gayle Thomas
ThomThom's Chocolate Chip, CH	NE-1864	F	29	M	HD-560112	Gayle Thomas
ThomThom's Feather Duster	NE-1994	G	29	F	HD-724541	Chris & Gayle Thomas
ThomThom's Gonna Fly Now, CH	NE-1753	G	25	M	HD-470202	Sledden Malden
ThomThom's Jack-In-The-Box, CH	NE-1523	F	24	M	HD-227805	S. & S. Ferrito
ThomThom's Jokers Wild	NE-1988	G	25	M	HD-797666	Bobbie Oxley
ThomThom's Jolly Grey Giant, CH	NE-1512	G	30	M	HD-179313	Chris & Gayle Thomas
ThomThom's Miss Jane	NE-1741	F	31	F	HD-575850	Chris & Gayle Thomas
ThomThom's Nikon Micmac	NE-2212	G	38	F	HD-916489	Casey McGovern / J. Hoppinjan
ThomThom's Silver Lady, CH	NE-2123	F	27	F	HM30818801	Chris & Gayle Thomas
ThomThom's Software Wistab	NE-0851	G	35	F	HC-054158	Chris & Gayle Thomas
ThomThom's Stonebridge	NE-1873	F	24	M	HD-713806	Gayle Thomas
ThomThom's Surely You Jest	NE-1686	G	30	F	HD-349751	Chris & Gayle Thomas
ThomThom's Susie Snowflake	NE-2124	F	27	F	HM30818804	Chris & Gayle Thomas
ThomThom's Tyson, CH	NE-2036	G	25	M	HD-863792	Gayle Thomas
ThomThom's Whitney Way	NE-2037	F	36	F	HD-700905	Gayle Thomas
ThomThom's Windy Cove Wild Bird	NE-2160	G	26	F	HM3660205	Gayle Thomas
ThomThom's Winter Frost, CH	NE-1742	G	25	M	HD-564994	Chris & Gayle Thomas
Thor	NE-0431					
Thor Bjorn Vikingson, CH	NE-0426					Nina Gray
Thor of Ledge Lodge	NE-0068					Hubert Curtis
Thor's Justice II	NE-1415	G	24	M	HD-076086	Lanie K. Gallio
Thor's Liten Mjolinr	NE-0594		27	M	HB-630848	
Thorlin's Erik Av Winsome	NE-0042					Russell Guthrie
Thornbeck Frey	NE-0103					
Thornbeck Friske	NE-0102					
Thornbeck Ynde	NE-0826		28	F	HC-130700	
Thors Jostedals Breen Storm	NE-0608		38	M	HB-684251	
Thunder's Vel Glov, CH	NE-0101				HB-95340	M. Patterson
Tia Alhim	NE-0579		26	F	HB-772098	
Tigger II	NE-0877		28	F	HC-144886	
Til-Venn's Howdy Hopscotch	NE-0175					
Timbur Tass Av Oakhaven	NE-0242					
Tina Av Valhala	NE-1044		77	F	HC-504492	
Tinker Belle II	NE-0410					
Tiro's All That Glitter, CH	NE-1423	F	46	F	HC-913582	Joan & Terri Brennan
Tiro's White Lightning, CH	NE-1145		44	F	HC-501977	J. Barnes
Tiro's Windsong of Tioka, CH	NE-1424	G	24	F	HD-125746	Les & Nancy Moser
Titanic's Finest Hour O' Rob-Lyn, CH	NE-1049	E	26	F	HC-499459	R. & L. Backer
Titanic's Porcupine Pie	NE-0950		24	M	HC-332355	
Tito Bandito	NE-0345					Meyr
Tmblwds Titan V Polestar	NE-1802	G	30	M	HD-542099	J. Maier & J. Cooke
Toka Curkin's Maesa, CD	NE-0023					Mr & Mrs DeSaele
Tolandia Peak Frean Freyja	NE-1493	G	24	F	HD-175551	Betty C. Wanderer
Tonian's Bit-O-Honey, CH	NE-1275		27	F	HC-853915	
Tonian's Bjorn Bamsi Av Barna	NE-1274		26	F	HC-841525	
Tor Av Oxnard	NE-0664		55	M	HB-466865	
Tor XIV (Norway)	NE-1259	F	37	M	HC-822501	C. Loitfellner
Tor's Albin Yenta Av Stran	NE-0519					Smith
Tor's Black Jack Av Hu'mar	NE-0163					H. & M. Curtis
Tor's Freki Av Suri	NE-0536					
Tor's Geri Av Suri	NE-0570					Tewksbury
Tor's Grey Tark Av Rob-Lyn	NE-0652	G	24	M	HB-823353	R. & L. Backer
Tora of Middensted	NE-0082					Chas. C. Christiansen
Torden	NE-1907	E	24	M	HD-676100	Mary Anne Amman & Sally Ritter
Torhid Tkea Av Stran	NE-1795	G	38	F	HD-405827	Karen & Harry Eckinger
Torijls Riiser Guy Av Mardale	NE-0727		34	M	HB-883870	
Torjus Pia Av Tostig	NE-0738		28	F	HB-948919	
Torr's Lady Siri	NE-0148					
Tortasen's Ola of Windy Cove, CH	NE-1176		48	F	HC-589553	J. Peterson
Torvallen Sasha D'Luog	NE-1106		24	F	HC-598767	D. Gould
Torvallen Tavia	NE-0635		32	F	HB-767175	

Registered Name	OFA No.	Rating	Age	Sex	Reg. No.	Owner
Torvi and Token's Tokay	NE-0357					
Torvjord Augustus Av Stran	NE-0383					
Toryl Goddess of the North	NE-0395					
Tosha's Trond Heim of Norske	NE-1065		25	F	HC-535461	
Tosha's Zackarina of Norske, CH	NE-1277		26	F	HC-884355	
Totoheimen Av Tynset	NE-0117					
Toua Av Tronoheim	NE-1092		38	F	JR-024634	
Tove Av SÛkomdal	NE-0093					
Travela's Ericka C.D., CH.	NE-2228	F	27	F	HM36802403	Roberta Oxley
Trilla's Tami Crickwood	NE-0561					
Tristan's Husquarne	NE-0454					
Tristan's Riverboat Queen	NE-1076		52	F	HC-304379	
Trofast Av Suteras	NE-0099					Alena B. Stranahan
Trolan's Toryen Borghild	NE-0544					P. Smith & B. Tykosky
Trolan's Toryen Fram	NE-0543					Smith & Pittelli
Trolan's Toryen Mephesto	NE-0546					Trolan Ken. & R. Smith
Trolan's Toryen Rom	NE-0545					Trolan Ken. & R. Smith
Trolan's Waggin' Wheel	NE-1317		32	M	HC-929258	
Troll of Glitnir	NE-0104					
Trollelgen's Lebba Hyona	NE-2056	G	26	F	HD-874503	Carol Loitfellner
Trollwood Bueskytter Keela	NE-2187	G	29	F	1049048	Ms. Elsie Priddy
Trond Av Glitnir CDX, Can CH	NE-0139					Lorna Dell
Trouper of the Woods	NE-0859		25	M	HC-154632	
Truel-gaards Trail	NE-0225					
Tryg N Thors Dublin Av Stran	NE-0223					
Tryg N Thors Jasmine	NE-1047		42	F	HC-328574	
Tryg N Thors Mist Av Grove Hill	NE-0240					
Tryg N Thors Paris Av Stran	NE-0243					A. Stranahan & S Quigley
Trygg Av Suteras	NE-0330					
Tsiulikagata Kishka	NE-1202		32	F	HC-694515	D. Gray
Tsiulikagta's Avantgarde	NE-1139		30	M	HC-591863	D. Yocom
Tsiulikagta's Solveig	NE-2214	G	26	F	HM36730805	Donna Pagel-Yocum
Tsiulikagta's Trym	NE-1597	G	41	M	HD-180484	C & M Goins
Tsiulikagtas Lykke	NE-2078	G	47	F	HD-63513	Donna Pagel-Yocom
Tstulikagta Ciara	NE-1356		26	F	HC-980826	
Tuffmar's Merri Sarta	NE-0039					Arnold & Fern Keszler
Tufins Sir Thorfinn Av Stran	NE-0717		24	M	HB-966387	
Tufins Tarla Fergy Ferguson	NE-1085		26	M	HC-515825	
Tumbleweeds Ariel Rose	NE-2148	F	26	F	HM33467101	Adam P. Schultz
Tumbleweeds Aurelia Grace	NE-2149	G	26	F	HM33467102	Adam P. Schultz
Tune Av SÛkomdal	NE-0094					
Tungsten's Swiss Twist	NE-1840	E	33	F	HD-534283	Joe & Jan Wood
Tungstens Jet Stream Laika	NE-1820	G	30	F	HD-495580	Marti Kincaid
Tunsen Bra's Freyja	NE-1099		27	F	HC-560459	
Turi IV (Norway)	NE-1206	G	27	M	HC-806400	C. Loitfellner
Tusen Bra-Silverbay Elsket	NE-1365		27	F	HC-968715	Jean Schroeder
Tusen Takk Brager	NE-0936		24	F	HC-272062	
Tuula's Kirsten	NE-0294					Pierce
Tyin's Tosha of Norske, CH	NE-0905		24	M	HC-014207	
Tyken's Go-Getter	NE-0394					
Tyken's Howdi Honey	NE-0284					
Tyken's Hustler, CH	NE-0287					
Tyken's Knock 'Em Dead	NE-0397					
Tyken's Moonlight Serenade	NE-0336					
Tyken's Ramrod Av Car Bob	NE-0131					Wm. Streiff
Tyken's Superstar	NE-0442					
Tyken's Truckin' Trek	NE-0827					
Tyrjo Av Katrine Glen	NE-0047					Henry Glasgow
Unassigned	NE-0509					
Unassigned	NE-1218					
Uppsala's Dapper Dan	NE-0641		24	M	HB-868854	
Uppsala's Diamond Girl	NE-0702		31	F	HB-861365	
Uppsala's Dream Weaver	NE-1800	F	49	F	HD-296666	Judith Cooke

Registered Name	OFA No.	Rating	Age	Sex	Reg. No.	Owner
Uppsala's Hindsight	NE-0691		29	F	HB-868853	
Uppsala's Onde of Polestar	NE-2147	G	24	F	HM33977201	Judith A. Cooke/Janet C. Maier
Uppsala's Season of the Witch	NE-1909	F	26	F	HD-689665	Judith A. Cooke & Janet C. Maier
Uppsala's Starbuck	NE-1080		26	M	HC-551159	
Uppsala's Summer Breeze	NE-1081		26	F	HC-516927	
Ursa Bonny Ginkisdatter	NE-0966					
Vaken	NE-1538	G	29	M	HD-196894	Mark Allen
Vakker Bjorn Fra Wolfsheim	NE-1733	E	25	M	HD-608200	Maria Van Dyck
Vakker-Lund's Fancy Free	NE-1072		36	F	HC-595750	
Valencarro's Bamsey	NE-0028					Floyd & Martha Brownell
Valimar Amer. Maid Royal Crown	NE-2174	G	47	F	HD-775175	Vicky P. Zumwalt
Valimar's Am Beauty of Royal Crown	NE-2032	E	28	F	HD-802280	Vicky P. Zumwalt
Valimar's Blue Moon	NE-1812	F	24	M	HD-593461	Katherine Ellis
Valimar's Christmas Noel	NE-2138	G	25	F	HM33374302	Katherine Ellis
Valimar's Doant Lemme down	NE-1765	G	28	M	HD-454282	Angie G. Luna
Valimar's Duncan Av Craika	NE-1752	G	26	M	HD-536457	Katherine Ellis
Valimar's Hot Pink Lace	NE-2238	G	25	F	HM38774902	Katherine Ellis, DVM
Valimar's Ladyhawke	NE-1756	G	27	F	HD-535803	Katherine Ellis
Valimar's Moonshadow RC	NE-1811	F	24	M	HD-568106	Katherine Ellis
Valimar's Prairie Blossom	NE-1976	G	24	F	HD-778035	Katherine Ellis, DVM
Valimar's Prairie Breeze, CH	NE-1992	E	25	F	HD-778036	Katherine Ellis, DVM
Valimar's Prairie Fire	NE-1970	G	24	F	HD-778034	Katherine Ellis, DVM
Valimar's Prairie Rain, CH	NE-2030	G	29	F	HD-778031	Sandra Tawater & Katherine Ellis
Valimar's Prairie Snow, CH	NE-1969	G	24	F	HD-778033	Angie Luna & Katherine Ellis, DVM
Valimar's Prairie Summer	NE-1971	G	24	F	HD-778032	Suzanne & Dennis McFadden
Valimar's RC Sparkling Soda	NE-1854	G	28	F	HD-677540	Amy Smith & Katherine Ellis
Valimar's Red River Kado	NE-1766	G	28	M	HD-559650	Norma J. Story
Valimar's Silver Starlet	NE-1853	G	24	F	HD-597767	Stephanie Hill
Valimar's The Scoundrel	NE-1980	F	25	M	HD-778037	Katherine Ellis, DVM
Valkrie	NE-1091		24	F	KU-103510	
Valkrie of Glenneyre	NE-1184		44	F	HC-826560	M. Cox
Valkyra Tonike Bobo	NE-1270		50	M	HC-667806	
Valkyrie Ginghi-Belle	NE-0817		56	F	HB-921028	
Valords Magic Snow Angel	NE-1878	G	25	F	HD-641744	Constance S. Vaillancourt
Valsun Goliath Cassandra	NE-0370					
Valsun Thalia of Goliath	NE-0298					
Vangaard Madoros Blaz O Glory	NE-1391		41	F	HC-904021	
Vangaard's Madoros Klase Sase	NE-1142		29	F	HC-629940	M. Ross
Vanir's Freyja	NE-1042		34	F	HC-454328	
Vardetoppens Bjorn	NE-0218					
Vardetoppens Burrelson	NE-0622		36	M	HB-646858	
Vardetoppens Froya Av Vigeland	NE-0204					
Vega Antares Rivendell	NE-0321					
Vegrid's Tass Taket	NE-0078					M. Peterson & F. Campbell
Venndal BNT Vixen Vilhelm, CH	NE-1333		41	M	HC-808222	
Venndal Jen Tar Sadie	NE-1058		25	F	HC-505818	
Venndal Marta Fra Cricklewood	NE-0999		25	F	HC-393970	
Venndal Misty's Bo-Jingle, CH	NE-2001	G	31	F	HD-705948	Dolores R. Friend
Venndal Misty's Bo-Kay, Am Can Ch	NE-2185	G	54	F	HD-705947	Dolores R. Friend
Venndal Pandamonium, CH	NE-1948	G	35	F	HD-641697	Dolores R. Friend
Venndal Ro-Jen's Solv Mist	NE-1314		33	F	HC-911266	
Venndal Ro-Jen's Solv Shimmer	NE-1346		37	F	HC-911268	
Venndal Silvaura Cashdotter	NE-1009		57	F	HC-57819	
Venndal Smokey Joe Duxsson	NE-1048		44	M	HC-420729	
Venndal Trollyk Pandora	NE-0915		24	F	HC-259290	
Venndal Trollyk Solv Roque	NE-0976		28	M	HC-378187	
Venndal Trollyk Torak	NE-0843		41	M	HB-982704	
Venndal Trollyk Torda	NE-0711		24	F	HB-982703	
Venndal Trollyk Trilla	NE-0930		24	F	HC-259286	
Venndal Trolyk Unser Madchen	NE-1007		32	F	HC-340852	
Venndal V'NK Quantum Leap, CH	NE-2191	G	24	M	HM35891801	Dolores R. Friend
Venndal Vi-King Vyka	NE-0631		24	F	HB-967150	
Venndal's Echo of Cricklewood	NE-0781		33	F	HB-941087	

Registered Name	OFA No.	Rating	Age	Sex	Reg. No.	Owner
Vesle Frikk, CH (Norway)	NE-0312	E	39	M	HB-322376	Molly Patterson
Vesle Yenta Rose of Norway	NE-1128	G	24	F	HC-687403	C. Loitfellner
Vesle-Kari of Norway (Norway)	NE-1260	G	51	F	HC-687404	C. Loitfellner & Cotterell
Vest Lykke Velvet For Nynorsk	NE-2051	G	24	F	XC-825690	Elizabeth Sykes
Vestlykke's Invictus	NE-2150	G	32	M	HD-873703	Richard Smith/T. Dale Schultz
Vigeland's Binder-Bonders	NE-0690		24	M	EL-000529	
Vigeland's Chimo	NE-0771		24	M	EW-006003	
Vigeland's Driva Au Solbakken	NE-0713		27	F	EL-000377	
Vigeland's Enegutt	NE-0704		25	M	EQ-002837	
Vigeland's Lotte	NE-0358					
Vigeland's Tara	NE-0506					
Vigeland's Triggs Tass	NE-0906		25	M	GJ-042759	
Vigeland's Trygg Sigbjorn, Can CH	NE-0487					
Vigeland's Tzar	NE-0398					
Vigeland's Vagabond Keli	NE-0685		24	F	EL-000530	
Vihund's Candy	NE-2081	G	40	F	HM-223458	Walter Viga, Jr.
Vikary's Double Dare	NE-0661		26	F	HB-827822	
Vikary's Gypsy Dancer	NE-0645		24	F	HB-828167	
Vikens Runic Forrest Fire CD, CH	NE-1446	G	24	F	HD-107576	Forrest & Viken
Vikesland's Suka	NE-0663		43	M	HB-638364	
Viking Elkhounds Astrid	NE-2031	G	50	F	HM35486401	Luis Nanni
Viking Road Storm's Saga	NE-0107					
Viking Road Storm's Sindra	NE-0087					Edna Mae Bieber
Viking Star of Nankin, CH	NE-0031					Walter Krusenski
Vikinghund's Tass	NE-1159		25	M	LU-153812	H. Hillicke
Vikinghund's Trine Av Norden, CH	NE-0907		24	F	GB-000607	
Vikingsen Dolly's Katie	NE-0111					Ardyss Webster
Vikingsson's Eryk Av Meshka	NE-0866		61	M	HB-711289	
Vikiro Belle's Desert Moon, CH	NE-1557	F	25	F	HD-253356	R. & S. Kozub
Vikiro Ruby's Ghostdancer, CH	NE-1669	G	34	F	HD-273907	R. & V. Lawton
Vikiro Son of a Gun avGareloch, CH	NE-2133	F	55	M	HD-660908	Victoria & Robert Lawton
Vikiro Velvet Kisses Av Bona	NE-1807	G	27	F	HD-530657	Christine Gonsalves
Vikiro's Bright Flame	NE-2144	G	24	F	HM34433907	Kari Olson
Vikiro's Diamond Girl	NE-1836	F	31	F	HD-510958	Robert & Victoria Lawton
Vikiro's Fancy Wrappings, CH	NE-2220	G	32	F	HM34433904	Jon & Camille Labree
Vikiro's Jenuine Jade	NE-1716	F	89	M	HC-864121	C. Gonsalves
Vikiro's Saphire N' Ice, CH	NE-1376		43	F	HC-846335	Jack Rigsbee
Vikiro's Sterling Silver	NE-1720	G	35	F	HD-450772	Mrs G. W. Wallace
Vikrest Chicago Fire	NE-2235	F	44	F	HD-833142	Brad & Julie Dahlgren
Vikrest Fire Power, CH	NE-1721	G	24	M	HD-462778	L. Forest & P. Viken
Vikrest Here Comes Trouble	NE-2236	G	25	M	HM38608608	Patricia Viken / Leslie Forrest
Vikrest Julie's Heart Of Fire, CH	NE-2240	G	46	F	HD-828533	Joe & Julie Kopala
Vikrest Troublemaker, CH	NE-2249	G	26	F	HM38608607	Patricia Viken / Leslie Forrest
Vin Melcas Social Acclaim	NE-1814	F	52	M	HD-289623	Michael & Pat Bolyard
Vin-Melca's Buckhorn	NE-0481					
Vin-Melca's Country Squire	NE-0297					
Vin-Melca's Desert Fox	NE-1261	G	37	M	HC-797300	
Vin-Melca's Double Design, CH	NE-0517					
Vin-Melca's Foxy Babe	NE-1634	G	25	F	HD-357692	M. A. & E. J. Ammann
Vin-Melca's Hanya	NE-0585		25	F	HB-972557	
Vin-Melca's Happy Holiday	NE-0387					
Vin-Melca's Happy Hour, CH	NE-0207					
Vin-Melca's Harbinger, CH	NE-0651		26	M	HB-487562	
Vin-Melca's Hartford, CH	NE-0385					
Vin-Melca's Harvey Wallbanger	NE-0553					
Vin-Melca's Hector Av Satuit	NE-0672		31	M	HB-789286	
Vin-Melca's Helen Sweetstory	NE-0396					
Vin-Melca's Hello Dolly	NE-0411					
Vin-Melca's Henny Penny, CH	NE-0231					
Vin-Melca's Hey Jude	NE-0228					
Vin-Melca's Hi Mark	NE-0138					
Vin-Melca's Hi-Rigger	NE-0602		26	M	HB-702177	
Vin-Melca's High Society	NE-0152					

Registered Name	OFA No.	Rating	Age	Sex	Reg. No.	Owner
Vin-Melca's Hijacker	NE-0538					
Vin-Melca's Home Brew	NE-0417					
Vin-Melca's Homesteader	NE-0443		25.	M	HB-909474	Diann Schiller
Vin-Melca's Honesty, CH	NE-0770		45	F	HB-830889	
Vin-Melca's Hooligan, CH	NE-0252					S. Quigley
Vin-Melca's Horse Play, CH	NE-0497					
Vin-Melca's Hot Pants, CH	NE-0614		35	F	HB-652758	
Vin-Melca's Hot Toddy	NE-0386					
Vin-Melca's Howdi Heller	NE-0674		31	F	HB-826021	
Vin-Melca's Howdi Kari	NE-0670		25	F	HB-900002	
Vin-Melca's Howdy Hunter, CH	NE-0406					
Vin-Melca's Howdy Jose	NE-0777		59	M	HB-638515	
Vin-Melca's Howdy Linvicta	NE-0147					
Vin-Melca's Howdy Rowdy, CH	NE-0057					Dr & Mrs John Craige
Vin-Melca's Huck Finn, CH	NE-0208					
Vin-Melca's Hunky Dory	NE-0329					
Vin-Melca's Mainliner	NE-0293					
Vin-Melca's Margeaux	NE-0942		28	F	HC-326017	
Vin-Melca's Morning Star	NE-1026		41	F	HC-271294	
Vin-Melca's Mount Vernon, CH	NE-0688		28	M	HB-953909	
Vin-Melca's Nightcap	NE-0597		35	F	HB-652761	
Vin-Melca's Nordic Mist, CH	NE-1312		45	F	HC-822079	
Vin-Melca's Rain Sonnet	NE-1302		43	F	HC-784198	John & Susan Murphy
Vin-Melca's Ramona UD, CH	NE-0119					
Vin-Melca's Saga Av Redhill, CH	NE-0058					Freeman Claus
Vin-Melca's Sirdal Sunrise	NE-1683	G	24	F	HD-443275	D. & L. Korneliusen
Vin-Melca's Solitaire, CH	NE-0016					Rose Martino
Vin-Melca's Sugar Babe	NE-0853		34	F	HC-147921	
Vin-Melca's The Snuggler, CH	NE-1617	G	58	F	HD-117493	Marty Forsythe
Vin-Melca's Thor Av Cickssen, CH	NE-0323					
Vin-Melca's Thunderhead	NE-0566					
Vin-Melca's Toby Tyler, CH	NE-0797		42	M	HC-165249	
Vin-Melca's Vestlykke, CDX	NE-1785	G	39	F	HD-603702	P. Craige & L. Drouin
Vindame's Geronimo	NE-1514	G	24	M	HD-211241	K. & M. Browne
Vindarne's Airwolf	NE-1518	F	24	M	HD-211249	E. & R. Queen
Vindarne's Defiance	NE-1412	F	121	M	HC-017107	E. D. & R. G. Queen
Vindarne's Deliverance	NE-1032		55	M	HC-129919	
Vindarne's Determination, CH	NE-0870		26	M	HC-171073	
Vindarne's Fish 'N Chips	NE-0918		35	F	HC-129921	
Vindarne's Fizban O' Kiva	NE-1889	F	29	M	HD-573388	Maureen E. & Robert A. James
Vindarne's Gemini, CH	NE-1517	G	38	F	HD-090716	E. & R. Queen
Vindarne's Magnum Force	NE-0917		52	M	HB-937455	
Vindarne's Rough Rider	NE-0723		69	M	HB-420249	
Vindarne's Silver Girl, CH	NE-0347					
Vindarne's Sunchip Antigua	NE-1374		55	F	HC-765679	Ethel D. & Robert G. Queen
Vindarne's Sunchip Oklahoma	NE-1245		35	F	HC-744567	
Vindarne's Top Dollar 'O Hinta	NE-1515	G	24	F	HD-215449	Grable & Queen
Vinland's Bulldogger, CH	NE-2182	G	112	M	HD-166439	Molly Patterson
Vinland's Chief Dancer, CH	NE-2217	G	91	M	HD-420170	Molly Patterson
Viracocha Loki's Gur	NE-1147		94	M	HB-968624	J. Stringham
Vista Valle Houdini Mystique	NE-1053		37	F	HC-385368	
Vista Valle Howdy's Dolly	NE-0235					
Vista Valle Howdy's John-John	NE-0402					
Vom Bree Dance Hall Dollie, CH	NE-2109	F	28	F	HD-863646	Dee Holloway
Vom Bree Genuine Risk	NE-2008	G	32	F	HD-689729	Dee Holloway
Vom Bree Snow Bunny Av Lenan	NE-2248	G	24	F	HM39702901	Dee Holloway / Elaine S. Upton
Von Kugler's Elske Av Avenger	NE-0593		34	F	HB-581131	
Von Kugler's Valiant Viceroy	NE-0366					
Von Protiva Princess Anne	NE-0465					
Voyageurs Freya of the Woods	NE-0725		26	F	HB-989106	
Vulkans Nordmann	NE-0260					
Wabeths Brigand	NE-1019	G	57	M	HC-104409	R. & B. Van Der Cook
Wabeths Bryn	NE-0483					

Registered Name	OFA No.	Rating	Age	Sex	Reg. No.	Owner
Wabeths Erika B Rowdy, CH	NE-0650		47	F	HB-525913	
Wabeths Marauder, CH	NE-0254					
Wabeths Molly Vernee	NE-0285					
Wabeths Tapio	NE-0080					D. Beers
Wabeths Torva	NE-0482					
Wabeths Trygve	NE-0441					Forrest
Wabeths Vangar of Norvik	NE-0775		29	M	HC-002376	
Wabeths Windjammer	NE-0121					
Wabeths Winona Av Fowlerstad	NE-0144					Bev Ricci
Walnut Spring Loki-Tari	NE-0233					
Wamica Shamara Tamdale	NE-0900		24	F	HC-223242	
Waylz's Duchess Olga Deneuve	NE-1182		27	F	HC-653845	T. Tarr
Weidemann's Beowulf	NE-0803		28	M	DY-000234	
Wesmor Vakkre Sonja	NE-0327					
Wesmor's Lady Astrid	NE-0369					
Westvikings Fleet N Fame	NE-1266		26	M	HC-848856	
Westvikings Free Moment	NE-1265		25	M	HC-850126	
Westwind American Storm, CH	NE-1689	G	29	M	HD-377474	T. & J. M. Sandhoff
Westwind Denmars' Calypso,Ch	NE-1419	G	26	F	HC-937516	M. Kincaid & A. Aliano
Westwind So Hot of Greyplume CD, CH	NE-1490	G	24	M	HD-206049	Glenda Mott Haggerty
Westwind Song At Sunrise	NE-1250	G	45	F	HC-638219	M. Kincaid & L. A. Hanson
Westwind's Deal Me In, CH	NE-1646	E	27	F	HD-311654	Julie L. Hancock
Westwind's Elusive Spirt	NE-1271		36	F	HC-780914	
Westwind's Night Serenade	NE-1122	G	24	F	HC-618079	M. Kincaid
Whirlwind of Raingale	NE-0332					
Whiskey Ericksen	NE-0161					
Whistle's Silver	NE-0407					
White Acres Joker's Melic	NE-0418					
Whittimere Amund, Can CH (Britain)	NE-1699	F	41	M	1018100	Fred Archer
Wilderness Thor	NE-0368					Olley
Wildwest Calamity Jane, CH	NE-0896		27	F	HC-219531	
Wildwest's Annie Oakley	NE-0971		42	F	HC-233182	
Willane Djevel Pride av Norjer	NE-2225	G	24	F	HM44923301	Virginia Sawyer / J. Schweizer
Willane's Gunnarsholm Hedda CD, CH	NE-1426	F	36	F	PS-322082	Ted V. Chmielowiec
Willow Brook Alii Blue Storm, CH	NE-2033	G	27	M	HD-844418	T. & A. Greely Garvin
Willow Brook Arielle D'Loug B C	NE-2039	G	27	F	HD-844416	T. & A. Greely & C. Gould
Wiloray's Apache	NE-0791		25	M	HC-066463	
Wilpat Nora of Woodland Hills	NE-0453					
Wilson's Buster Boy	NE-0445					Raymond & Lois Wilson
Windrow Tamrac Av Tigger	NE-1713	G	105	M	HC-709329	R. & D. Phelps
Windy Cove American Flag	NE-1018		27	F	HC-276024	
Windy Cove American Heritage	NE-0986		37	F	HC-286033	
Windy Cove Autum Evening	NE-1832	F	39	F	HD-409338	Elaine Straw & Mrs. Joe Peterson
Windy Cove Autumn Breeze, CH	NE-1417	G	24	M	HD-077082	Chris & Gayle Thomas
Windy Cove Autumn Charm	NE-1454	G	28	F	HD-077088	Mrs. Joe Peterson
Windy Cove Autumn For Norlund, CH	NE-1465	G	31	M	HD-124462	Mrs. Joe Peterson
Windy Cove Autumn Winds, CH	NE-1428	G	26	M	HD-077083	Sharin Burson
Windy Cove B Mona's Steelmaker	NE-0724		25	M	HB-972900	
Windy Cove Bella Bella	NE-0527					Mrs. Joe Peterson
Windy Cove Bicen Keen Acre Ace	NE-1078		28	M	HC-489351	
Windy Cove Bicen's Cut Krystal, CH	NE-1172		54	F	HC-449099	J. Peterson
Windy Cove Bicen's Kissin Tele	NE-1135		42	F	HC-488919	B. McClanahan
Windy Cove Bicen's Tattoo, CH	NE-1146		24	M	HC-659495	C. Pryor
Windy Cove Bobella's Nishka	NE-1153		27	F	HC-658502	E. Jones
Windy Cove Breezy Snow Cone	NE-1801	G	51	F	HD-272978	Mrs. Joe Peterson
Windy Cove Breezy Snowparka, CH	NE-1587	E	25	F	HD-272976	Mrs Joe Peterson
Windy Cove Bristlecone Topaz, CH	NE-1635	G	34	F	HD-228633	Sharin K. Burson
Windy Cove Brut Silver Lining	NE-0980		26	F	HC-381153	
Windy Cove Brut's Bella Ballet	NE-1148		76	F	HC-129830	J. Stringham
Windy Cove Brut's Light Trick	NE-0973		25	F	HC-370225	
Windy Cove Brut's Lulubell	NE-0765		25	F	HB-987624	
Windy Cove Brut's Silver Monie	NE-1242		38	F	HC-730910	
Windy Cove Cadero's Mona Lisa	NE-0137					Mrs. Joe Peterson

Registered Name	OFA No.	Rating	Age	Sex	Reg. No.	Owner
Windy Cove Cadero's Romona	NE-0136					Tom & Julie Barnes
Windy Cove Carney N Kiva'Blaze	NE-1997	G	32	M	HD-657029	Chris & Gayle Thomas
Windy Cove Carney's Dakota, CH	NE-2103	G	33	M	HD-794752	Mrs. Joe Peterson & Loyce Taylor
Windy Cove Carney's White Dove, CH	NE-2106	G	33	F	HD-800694	Mrs. Joe Peterson & Mrs. J. King
Windy Cove Carney's Winter Swan	NE-2026	G	24	F	HD-800829	John King
Windy Cove Chase A Wild Bird, CH	NE-2156	G	26	F	HM33660206	Mrs. Joe Peterson
Windy Cove Chief Black Elk	NE-1484	G	46	M	HC-972590	Duane Olson
Windy Cove Chief Cochise, CH	NE-1348		24	M	HC-973268	
Windy Cove Cochise' War Bonnet, CH	NE-1521	F	34	F	HD-153099	Chris & Gayle Thomas
Windy Cove Cochise' War Dance, CH	NE-1614	G	41	F	HD-153456	D Holloway/M Peterson
Windy Cove Cochise's War Cry	NE-1483	F	25	M	HD-158708	Duane Olson
Windy Cove Cocolalla Sutton	NE-1464	G	43	F	HC-972890	Mrs. Joe Peterson
Windy Cove Country Bumpkin	NE-1898	G	37	M	HD-517205	Carol Francis
Windy Cove Country Gentleman, CH	NE-1810	F	26	M	HD-517204	Les & Nancy Moser
Windy Cove Dandy Donn	NE-0425					
Windy Cove Dawns Tasscadero, CH	NE-0021					Marie Peterson
Windy Cove EZ Rider, CH	NE-1598	F	52	M	HC-051313	Marie Peterson
Windy Cove Family Heritage	NE-1171		29	F	HC-659648	J. Peterson
Windy Cove Flamboyant Bel-Dok	NE-0983		24	F	HC-375999	
Windy Cove Forest Hills Cedar	NE-1875	G	41	M	HD-481867	Nancy Moser
Windy Cove Forest Hills Teak	NE-1918	G	47	F	HD-459472	Nancy Moser
Windy Cove Forest Hills Wilow	NE-1835	G	36	F	HD-459083	Fern Kesler
Windy Cove Garm's Gretchen	NE-0648		25	F	HB-825830	
Windy Cove Gold Medal	NE-1603	G	27	F	HD-272984	Mrs Joe Peterson
Windy Cove Goliaths Shadrack	NE-0479					
Windy Cove Golly's Folly, CH	NE-0050					Phillip Buscemi
Windy Cove Gunnar of Norway	NE-1160		26	M	HC-749504	J. R. Peterson
Windy Cove Gunnar's Bita, CH	NE-1273		24	F	HC-861047	
Windy Cove Gunnar's Huntress, CH	NE-1372		40	F	HC-861048	A. L. & Kathy Carter
Windy Cove Gunnar's Melody	NE-1272		25	F	HC-861049	
Windy Cove Gunnar's Run N Gun	NE-1450	F	53	M	HC-883689	Barbara McClanahan
Windy Cove Gunnar's Silverbell	NE-1403	E	30	F	HD-004514	Fern Keszler
Windy Cove Gunnar's Trail Boss	NE-1582	G	50	M	HD-051314	C & D Palmer
Windy Cove Gunnola	NE-1253		33	F	HC-768335	
Windy Cove Honeysuckle	NE-1935	G	45	F	HD-483102	Michelle & Larry Philpot
Windy Cove Imp O Silverlance	NE-0051					Phillip Buscemi
Windy Cove Import O Keen Acres	NE-0074					Judi & Steve Keenan
Windy Cove Indian Maiden, CH	NE-1438	G	39	F	HC-973267	Mrs. Joe Peterson
Windy Cove Joyful Jada	NE-1522	G	25	F	HD-213784	S. & S. Ferrito
Windy Cove Jr All American	NE-0696		24	M	HB-885102	
Windy Cove Jr All Conference	NE-0726		29	M	HB-885074	
Windy Cove Jr All Pro	NE-0697		25	M	HB-885073	
Windy Cove Jr Bicentennial	NE-0923		24	M	HC-269490	
Windy Cove Jr Keen Scholar	NE-0821		26	M	HC-106753	
Windy Cove Jr Miss California	NE-0700		24	F	HB-888253	
Windy Cove Jr Miss World	NE-0710		24	F	HB-914514	
Windy Cove Junior Bobbi Sox	NE-0960					
Windy Cove Kiva Heaven Scent	NE-2072	F	31	F	HD-773801	Dirk & Cathy Roberts
Windy Cove Kiva Night Hawk, CH	NE-1856	G	24	M	1026569	Minnie & Ray Forsyth
Windy Cove Kiva' Charming Miss	NE-1913	G	25	F	HD-658600	Lee Ann Breading
Windy Cove Kiva's Big Condor	NE-1850	G	24	M	HD-584861	Edward R. & Linda H. Jones
Windy Cove Kiva's Charm Magic	NE-1944	G	28	F	HD-657313	Lee A. Breading
Windy Cove Kiva's Flicka Charm	NE-1916	F	24	F	1032527	Minnie Forsyth
Windy Cove Kiva's Goldrush	NE-1977	G	26	F	HD-743342	Elizabeth Parmer
Windy Cove Kiva's Hummingbird	NE-2199	G	41	F	HD-842849	Mrs. Joe Peterson
Windy Cove Kiva's Huntin' Falcon	NE-1884	G	28	M	HD-584859	Lee Ann Breading
Windy Cove Kiva's Karisma	NE-1938	G	27	F	HD-657035	Ardell Fuquay
Windy Cove Kiva's Keepsake	NE-1958	F	30	F	HD-659862	Les &Nancy Moser & Mrs J Peterson
Windy Cove Kiva's Kissable	NE-1920	F	25	F	HD-660210	Kim A. Sorenson
Windy Cove Kiva's Marty Robbins	NE-1848	G	25	M	HD-570406	Dorothy Brown & Fern Kesler
Windy Cove Kiva's Painted Silk	NE-1911	F	24	F	HD-657312	Mrs. Joe Peterson
Windy Cove Kiva's Reider	NE-1917	G	34	M	HD-574551	Alan & Kathy Dickson
Windy Cove Kiva's Whipoorwill	NE-2117	G	31	M	HD-837871	Bud & Audrey Henderson

Registered Name	OFA No.	Rating	Age	Sex	Reg. No.	Owner
Windy Cove Kiva's Wild Heart	NE-2002	E	25	F	HD-760127	Mrs. Joe Peterson
Windy Cove Litl Bita Country	NE-2052	F	28	F	HD-784169	Les & Nancy Moser
Windy Cove Lonestar Valentin	NE-1755	F	27	M	HD-469080	Elizabeth Palmer-Hail
Windy Cove Lulu's Tyson, CH	NE-1170		35	M	HC-601060	T. Baumgartner
Windy Cove Madonna O Burre CD, CH	NE-0764	E	24	F	HC-016211	Chris & Gayle Thomas
Windy Cove Mona Av Oftenasen, CH	NE-0027					Marie Peterson
Windy Cove Mona Cadero Junior	NE-0140					Judi & Steve Keenan
Windy Cove Mona Silver Brut	NE-0270					
Windy Cove Mona Silver Chanel	NE-0288					Kristen Mesloh
Windy Cove Mona's Importance	NE-0024					Marie Peterson
Windy Cove Mona's Importer	NE-0048					Edward & Delois Forsyth
Windy Cove Mona's Miss Import	NE-0054					Marie Peterson
Windy Cove Mona's Mr. Imported	NE-0019					M. Peterson & Mrs. Keszler
Windy Cove Mona's Silver Alder	NE-0209					
Windy Cove Mona's Silver Ambar	NE-0202					
Windy Cove Mona's Silver Birch	NE-0203					
Windy Cove Mr Imported Sher'i	NE-0354					
Windy Cove N Norelka Snofire, CH	NE-1510	G	38	M	HD-103830	A. & K. Carter
Windy Cove N Norelka Snow Bird, CH	NE-1466	G	30	F	HD-092282	Mrs. Joe Peterson
Windy Cove N Norelka Snowkist	NE-1743	G	65	F	HD-104188	Randy & Robin Rhoden
Windy Cove Nikola Heardgrove	NE-1828	G	32	F	HD-477608	Jane P. & Paul W. Heard Sr.
Windy Cove Old Fashion Lace	NE-1025		24	F	HC-438012	
Windy Cove P F Brut's Bar B	NE-0793		28	F	HC-041800	
Windy Cove Radio Buckskin	NE-2130	G	27	M	HD-906711	Darcy Rosenfeld/Mrs J Peterson
Windy Cove Rider's Carney, CH	NE-1665	G	30	F	HD-338798	Mrs. Joe Peterson
Windy Cove Riiser Guy, CH	NE-0077					Marie Peterson
Windy Cove Riiser's Whirlaway	NE-0768		36	F	HB-888812	
Windy Cove Rippled Water, CD	NE-1945	F	60	F	HD-362552	Mrs. Joe Peterson & J. Baver
Windy Cove Rodeo Cowgirl	NE-2132	F	27	F	HD-906710	Mrs. Joe Peterson
Windy Cove Rodeo Queen Reba	NE-2154	G	30	F	HD-907485	Lee Ann Breading
Windy Cove Rodna's Billy Jo	NE-0484					
Windy Cove Rodna's Luna Riiser	NE-0303					William Mesloh
Windy Cove Rodna's Sun Riiser	NE-0364					Stuart & Janet Warter
Windy Cove Ruby's Fantasstic	NE-0996		27	M	HC-385136	
Windy Cove Ruffarna Forest Hill, CH	NE-0982		35	F	HC-305831	
Windy Cove Ruffen	NE-0794		26	M	HC-149002	
Windy Cove Ruffen Rendezvous	NE-0895		26	F	HC-204109	
Windy Cove Ruffen's Redi	NE-0985		32	M	HC-297708	
Windy Cove Ruffen's Revelry	NE-0927		27	F	HC-234251	
Windy Cove Silva of Norway	NE-1192		33	F	HC-749503	J. Peterson
Windy Cove Silver Sioux Fjord	NE-0307					
Windy Cove Silver Sun Missile	NE-0052					Phillip Buscemi
Windy Cove Silver Sun Sherry	NE-0029					C. Gilbertson & O. Cooper
Windy Cove Silver Sun's Luster	NE-0281					
Windy Cove Snowdrift Iceberg, CH	NE-2097	G	28	M	HD-848574	Mrs. Joe Peterson
Windy Cove Stardust Dancer	NE-1299		24	F	HC-928806	M. Webster
Windy Cove Sun Bonnet Sue	NE-1933	G	24	F	HD-701395	Mrs. Joe Peterson
Windy Cove Super Charger, CH	NE-1269		24	M	HC-861046	
Windy Cove Super O K	NE-1320		31	F	HC-861045	
Windy Cove Super Sky Rocket	NE-1616	G	51	M	HD-149752	Straw & M Peterson
Windy Cove Super Sparkler	NE-1816	E	75	M	HD-072372	Mrs. Linda Tarnowski
Windy Cove Surprise of Vardetoppen	NE-0555					
Windy Cove Sweda Silver Slipa, CH	NE-0020					Marie Peterson
Windy Cove Sweda's Silver Son III, CH	NE-0066					Tom & Marilyn Braly
Windy Cove Symantha O'Burre	NE-0789		31	F	HC-022963	
Windy Cove TNK Kachina, CH	NE-1759	E	24	F	HD-507891	Nona & Tom Krena
Windy Cove TNK Let's Twist	NE-1311		24	F	HC-932207	
Windy Cove TNK Peace Pipe, CH	NE-1861	G	24	F	HD-609773	Nona Krena
Windy Cove TNK Tribal Counsel, CH	NE-1860	G	24	M	HD-609774	Nona Krena
Windy Cove Tara's Nimbusson, CH	NE-1130		27	M	HC-630889	J. Peterson
Windy Cove Tass Av Oftenasen, CH	NE-0008					Mrs. Joe Peterson
Windy Cove Tass N Wendy's Faith	NE-0089					Barbara Coffland
Windy Cove Tass N Wendy's Love	NE-0084					Mr & Mrs Simeon Baldwin III

Registered Name	OFA No.	Rating	Age	Sex	Reg. No.	Owner
Windy Cove Tass Slipa Harmony	NE-0122					Judi & Steve Keenan
Windy Cove Tass Slipa Lyric	NE-0665		70	F	HB-273114	
Windy Cove Tass Slipa Song	NE-0141					Mrs. Joe Peterson
Windy Cove Tass's High Fashion	NE-0829		29	F	HC-095451	
Windy Cove Tass's Love Letters	NE-0804		24	F	HC-095453	
Windy Cove Tass's Natana	NE-0662		27	F	HB-779378	
Windy Cove Tass's Roda	NE-0088					Edna Mae Bieber
Windy Cove Tass's Rodna	NE-0124					Mrs. Joe Peterson
Windy Cove Tass's Rusker	NE-0076					Mr & Mrs Jeffery Mattick
Windy Cove Tass's Ruskin	NE-0098					Christine & Ronald Rautio
Windy Cove Tass's Salutation	NE-0667		28	F	HB-870617	
Windy Cove Tass's Tassafrass	NE-0120					Dr & Mrs Arthur Malin
Windy Cove Tass's Wind Song	NE-0805		24	F	HC-094884	
Windy Cove Truly Dear Tass	NE-0683		29	F	HB-838162	
Windy Cove Truly Silver Sun	NE-0193					
Windy Cove Vanilla Snowcone	NE-2121	G	33	F	HD-836417	Mrs. Joe Peterson
Windy Cove Vardetoppens Burre	NE-0681	E	31	M	HB-924452	Mrs. Joe Peterson
Windy Cove Velvet Lace	NE-2200	G	24	F	HM36792402	Mrs. Joe Peterson
Windy Cove Vom Bree Autumn Snow, CH	NE-1613	G	27	F	HD-273363	Dee Holloway
Windy Cove Vom Bree Autumn Sun	NE-1767	G	32	M	HD-409455	D. Hollaway & M. Peterson
Windy Cove Vom Bree Kiva's Kate	NE-1956	G	31	F	HD-659754	John Feichtner
Windy Cove Vom Bree War Paint, CH	NE-1599	G	34	F	HD-221520	Mrs Joe Peterson
Windy Cove Wendy's Comanche, CH	NE-0059					Arnold & Fern Keszler
Windy Cove Wendy's Golly Garm, CH	NE-0026					Howard & Fay Campbell
Windy Cove Wendy's Silver Sun, CH	NE-0389					
Windy Cove Wendy's Stormer	NE-0034					Barbara Coffland
Windy Cove Wendy's Stormette	NE-0001					Tom & Marilyn Braly
Windy Cove Wild West Jubilee	NE-1708	G	25	F	HD-409336	Linda Douglas
Windy Cove Yours Truly Tass	NE-0737		38	M	HB-825906	
Windy Cove's Cochise' Tomahawk, CH	NE-1707	F	30	M	HD-383421	Barbara McClanahan
Windy Cove's Rocky Riser	NE-0801		41	F	HB-895852	
Windy Hill's Valentine Thor	NE-2194	G	86	M	HD-482093	Sharon Munk
Winston Chamberland Buck	NE-1782	G	29	M	HD-502542	David Sanders
Wintering's Northern Breeze	NE-2005	G	27	F	HD-804101	Daniel L. Holst
Winterings Northern Mickey	NE-1915	G	24	M	WJ-764666	Mr. K. Schidtke
Wolfie Joe Coyote	NE-1692	G	33	M	HD-326080	Lorna Nailon
Wolfshiem's Jack of Hearts, Can CH	NE-2203	G	35	M	XS-879972	Irene Orosz
Wolfshiem's Premium Blend	NE-2122	F	25	M	HM38553701	Maria A. Van Dyck
Woodchuck Hill Major Storm	NE-1714	F	34	M	HD-329042	Jacob Lapp
Woodsprings Bjonna	NE-0888		32	F	HC-130976	
Woodys Mist	NE-1394		53	F	HC-823618	
Wooglin of Pine Haven	NE-0123					
Wrathwood's Fortune Hunter	NE-2115	G	29	M	HM36988501	Lynda Tarnowski
Wrathwood's Oath To Wintering	NE-2111	G	29	F	XG-840423	Jim Wright
Wrathwood's Ode To Wintering	NE-2112	G	29	M	XG-840419	Jim Wright
Wrathwood's The Rumour	NE-1906	G	27	F	VN-806372	Lynda Tarnowski
Xanthic of the Holm	NE-0372					
Yanna Av Katrine Glen	NE-0041					Henry Glasgow
Yogi IV	NE-0251					
Yontef Tannon Erichkini	NE-0682		24	M	HB-936336	
Yoseph's Jessica Ar The Ranch UD	NE-1596	F	51	F	HD-038983	Charlotte Williams
Zachary of Starranne	NE-0773		34	M	HC-002950	
Zhivago's Sabok II	NE-0802		24	M	HC-174425	
Zieg's Sur of Thora	NE-0258					P. Mikes

Index

Aalesund 50
Accessories for showing 117
Afterbirth 99
Aggression 171
Agility 137
Agressive puppies 91
AKC-sanctioned matches 135
Aliano, Arlene M. 212
Alterdalen 15
American-Bred Class 113, 114
American Kennel Club (AKC) 1, 17, 60, 96, 109, 131, 173
Appearance, general 61
Arctic Storm of Pomfret 208
Arjess 187
Bacteria 121
Bait 118, 137
Bamse 9
Bandhund 147, 155
Bar jump 137
Bartlett, Marion Fralick 226
Bath 180
Beggs, Harry 219
Benched show 111
Bergasen 15
Bergen, Museum of 6
Best of Breed 113, 115
Bimba 17
Biopsy 170
Birth, color at 101
Bitch 89
Bjorn-Lass 19
Black Elkhound 11

Blindness 91
Blue ribbons 109
Body 62
Bomark 187
Bona Jade's Leggs Diamond, Ch. 215
Borellan 50
Brace Class 117
Bransian 15
Bred-by-Exhibitor Class 113, 114
Breeders 87, 104, 162
Breeding 160
Breeding, buying for 96
Breeding stock 89
Brinchmann, Professor 6
Bristlecone 188
British Elkhound Club 16
British Elkhound Society 67
Brood bitch 117
Brucellosis 90
Brushing 181
Bryan, Harry & June 219
Buhund 11, 12
Buying a puppy 173
Buying a show dog 95
Buying for breeding 96
Camalot Trulle Ayla, OTCH 219
Camalot's Bella Tigra 217
Campbell, Olav 221
Canadian Fish & Wildlife Agcy 17
Canadian Kennel Club 69
Canine Eye Registry Foundation, Inc. 165

Car, riding in a 107
Carter, Kathy & Albert 212
Cataracts 167
Ceejay 188
Championship points 115
Championship Title 109
Charilor 188
Chart, growth 91, 100
Chest 78
Chewing 185
Chicago, International Club of 207
Choosing a dog to show 110
Christiansen, Frank 154
Chromosome 162
Clark, Glenna 23
Classes, regular 113
Clubs, obedience training 135
Coat 62, 82
Collar 124
Color 62, 84
Color at birth 101
Come 123
Companion Dog 130, 131
Companion Dog Excellent 130, 131
Conformation 109
Congenital disorders 91
Contract 96
Coppergate Dig 4
Crafdal 23
Crafts, Robert 23
Crafts, Glenna Clark 23
Craige, Dr. John 36
Craige, Patricia Vincent 41, 211
Craige, John & Patricia V. 208
Crate 107, 118
Crating 185
Culling puppies 90
Cysts, subcutaneous 170
Dam 96
Deformities 90
Diet 84, 182
Disease 121
Disorders, congenital 91
Disorders, personality 171
Disqualification 63
Dog, buying a show 95, 110

Dog, unentered 113
Dog, working 71
Dominant 162
Down command 123, 128
Drake, Barbara A. 219
Dumbbell 137
Dunharrow 189
Dwarfism 91
Dysplasia, hip 90, 95, 169
Earmites 181
Ears, floppy 95
Ears 76, 181
Eidsvold 189
Elglia Kennels 11
Elgstolen 10
Elkhome 16
Elkhound Association, Greater
Milwaukee Norwegian 137
Elkhound Association of Scotland
16
Elkhound Club, British 16
Elkhound Club, Swedish 14
Elkhound Society, British 67
Elkhund 189
Elvlund 17, 47
English Kennel Club 16
Entry forms 117, 139
Equipment 137
Erik the Red 4
Eskamere 16, 50
Estrous 89, 177
Evaluating puppies 91
Exercise 179
Exhibitor 119
Expression 120
Fanarok 7
Feeding guide 174
Feet 62, 80
Finsk-Karels Laika 11
Fish & Wildlife Agcy, Canadian 17
Fjeldheim 10
Flags, starting 137
Foerdig 16
Forequarters 62, 80
Formula, supplemental 103
Foster, Marion 50

Fourwents 16, 50
Francoise 221
Friochan 16, 50
Fun matches 111
Gait 62, 66, 84
Gamle Bamse Gram 8
Gardetorpet 15
Garrowby 16
Gene, recessive 167
Genes 160
Genetic makeup 91
Genetic origin 95
Genetics 224
Gjetemyra 10
Gladjac Royal Oslo, Ch. 207
Glitnir 17, 47
Glitre Elkhounds 19
Glitre Kennels 9
Gokstad 5
Gonsalves, Christine M. 215
Graduate Novice 136
Grastein 190
Gray Elkhound 11
Green, Stanley A. & Joan M. 215
Greenland 4
Grimm of Lifjell, Ch. 18
Grooming 83, 179
Grooming area 118
Growth chart 91, 100
Gustafson 208
Hammerfest's Jente To Am. Can.
CDX, Can. Ch. 217
Hayfields 190
Head 61, 74
Heart worm 104
Heel 123
Heffer, Kitty C. 221, 226
Hereditary factors 160
Hereditary problems 165
Hereditary traits 172
Highest Combined Score 137
Highest Scoring Dog 137
Hillman, E. A. 208
Hindquarters 62, 81
Hip dysplasia 95
Hirtzlheim 17

Hludaelf's Loki, Ch. 215
Hock, popping 170
Holm 50
Holsing, Jakob Petter 53
Homanskogen 10
Homestead 190, 191
Hot spots, 170
Hound Group 109
Houndhaven 17, 47
Housebreaking 104, 184
Hunt, preparing for the 156
Hunting 143, 151
Hunting methods 147
Hunting tests 150
Hurtzlheim 47
Hygiene 122
Hypoglycemia 172
Immunization record 174
Immunizations 104, 183
Indeglia, Dr. Robert 223
Infections, vaginal 101
Innes, Barbara 47, 211
Internal abnormalities 91
Interstitial nephrites, chronic 172
Inverailort Kennels 17
Jack Daniel's Old Number Seven
CD, 217
Jamthund 11
Janberts 191
Jarlsberg Kennels 11, 50
Jenkins, Mary O. 223
Jorvik Viking Centre 4
Jotsoma 16
Judge 119-121
Judging schedules 119, 139
Jump, bar 137
Kalagerasen 10
Kamgaard 28
Karelian Bear Dog 11
Karelsk bjornhund 11
Karin Kennels 17, 47
Karin Perm Reg'd. 47
Karin's Yogi Bear 211
Kennel Club, American 1, 17, 60,
96, 109, 131, 173
Kennel Club, Canadian 69

Kennel Club, English 16
Kennel Club, Swedish 15
Kidneys 167, 172
Kinburn 16
Kirkssted Olav, Ch. 212
Kistrand 50
Koik 17
Laila 17
Lally, Jane 215
Lawton, Victoria & Robert 33, 212
Leash 124
Lifjell 10
Liki of Stormy Lea 208
Lillabo 16, 50
Linvicta 191
Liseldun 191
Liseldun Solv Sterjne Vinsja UD,
Ch. 219
Llychlyn Kennels 50
Lofoten 16
Longships 192
Loshund 145, 155
Maddox, Robert 211
Maelstrom 192
Mageroy 50
Malator 50
Marbran's Athena UD 217
Markers, turn 137
Matches 110
Matches, A 111
Matches, B 111
Matches, fun 111
Melreva 17, 47
Mendel, Gregor Johann 159
Mendelism 159
Midnight Sun 192
Midnight Sun Heartlight CD, Ch.
219
Millarsville 47
Mindas 16, 50
Misbeek, Mari 21
Mismarkings 91
Misty Tara 193
Mott, Margaret 28
Murphy, John B. & Susan 217
Mutation 171

Myrdal 50
Narvikwood 19
National Elkhound Assoc of
America (NEAA) 17, 47, 64, 112,
135, 154, 169, 173, 207, 223
Neck 62, 77
Ness, Robert 212
Neuter 177
Nickas 16
Non-regular classes 115
Nord-Vann 193
Norelka 194
Norelka's Sky Gazer For Trekin,
Ch. 212
Norelka's Surfs Up At Ardon's, Ch.
212
Norgren 194
Normark 194
Norsk Elghundklub 9
Norsled 50
Northmoor 194, 195
Northwind 195
Norwegian Elkhound Association 1
Norwegian standard 66
Novice, Graduate 136
Novice Class 113, 131
Nursing 99
Nynorsk 195
Obedience fun matches 135
Obedience regulations 131
Obedience shows 129
Obedience titles 130
Obedience training clubs 135
Obedience Trial Champion 130,
132
Obesity 172
Of the Hollow 50
Of the Holm 16
Open Class 113, 114
Open work 130
Ophthalmologists 165
Orion Av Norden 215
Orthopedic Foundation of Animals
90, 169
Oseberg 5
Oshima 195, 196

Ostsibirsk Laika 11
Ovum 162
Pam-lda 196
Paper training 185
Parasite 121
Patellar dislocation 170
Pebblebrook 196
Pedigree 64, 96, 224
Peer Gynt 197
Personality disorders 171
Pet stores 94
Peterson, Joe & Marie 42
Peterson, Marie 211
Peterson, Sandi 212
Peyvre 50
Phillips, Susan D. 207, 208
Picts 4
Pitch Road 19
Polestar 197
Problems, common 94
Problems, hereditary 165
Progressive retinal atrophy,
generalized 165
Proportion 61, 64, 74
Proudfoot, Gary 211
Puppies 102
Puppies, aggressive 91
Puppies, culling 90
Puppies, evaluating 91
Puppies, selling 94
Puppy, training a 123
Puppy, buying a 173
Puppy Class 113
Puppy registration 90
Purven 7
Qualifying score 136
Quiquen 197
Rai-Mai 197
Rands, Julia 87, 221
Ravenstone 16, 50
Recall 131
Recessive 162
Recessive traits 162
Redhill 198
Reese, T. & C. 212
Registration paper 174

Registration, puppy 90
Regular classes 113
Regulations, obedience 131
Renal cortical hypoplasia 167
Renal disease, familial 165
Retrieve 123
Ribbons, blue 109
Riley, Brian & Lynn 208
Riverwind 198
Rob-Lyn 198
Rogersome 50
Roslin-Williams, Anne 221
Ross, Nina P. 226
Rothenborg 50
Rotier, Donald 139
Roundel 198
Roundel's Gizmo of Vikiro, Ch. 212
Russisk-Europeisk Laika 11
Sangrud 199
Sara 9
Satuit 199
Scandia 199
Schmidt, Steven & Renee 219
Scotland, Elkhound Assoc of 16
Seborrhea 170
Selling puppies 94
Sex, determining 162
Sharalo 199
Shedding 181
Shelter 177
Shew, Harold 223
Show, benched 111
Show dog, buying a 95
Show, traveling to 118
Show, unbenched 111
Shows, obedience 129
Shyness 171
Sirdal 200
Sire 96
Sit command 123, 128
Sit from Down position 129
Size 61, 73
Skogsmarken 16
Skromtefjell 10
Sladeck, Roberta Jean 212
Smith Jr., Edward R. 215

Snorri Sturluson 7
Socialization 95, 106
Sodeman, Buzz 211
Sokomdal 10
Somerri 200
Spay 177
Specialties 111
Specialty 207
Sperm 162
Spitz, Finnish 11
Sport 171
St. Germaine, Armine 207
Stand command 123, 126
Standard, Norwegian 66
Standards 59
Starting flags 137
Statton 201
Stavholmen 16
Stavsetras 10
Stay 123
Sterility 165
Steward 119
Stonewall 19
Stonylea 19
Stormfjell 17, 47
Stud dog 89, 117
Stud fee 90
Subcutaneous cysts 170
Substance 61
Suteras 10
Swanson 221
Swedish Elkhound Club 14
Swedish Kennel Club 15
T.N.K. 203
Tail 78
Tallo Kennels 11
Tantalum 201
Tarroma 201, 202
Team Class 117
Temperament 63, 86, 95
Tessin, Joel & Nan 211
Tests, hunting 150
Thingvollr 16
ThomThom 202
ThomThom Jup-Don Big Guy, Ch. 219

Tioka 202
Tiro 203
Titanic's Porcupine Pie 211
Titles, obedience 130
Toenails 180
Topline 62, 78
Torden 16, 50
Torr Kennels 17, 47
Tortasen Kennels 10, 11, 53
Tortawe 16
Tortawe 50
Torvmosehund 3
Toys 105
Toys, playing with 123
Tracking Dog 130, 132
Tracking Dog Excellenrt 130
Training a puppy 123
Traits, hereditary 172
Traits, recessive 162
Travelas 203, 204
Traveling to show 118
Trulsmoi 16
Tune 5
Tungsten 204
Turn markers 137
Turner, Fred & Lois 208
Turner, Bonnie 212
Unbenched show 111
Unentered dogs 113
Utility Dog 130, 132
Utility work 130
Vaginal infections 101
Vakker-Lund 17, 47
Valdemar 204
Valgtor 17
Valimar 204
Vandavell 50
Vardetoppen 10
Vestsibirsk Kaika 11
Vigeland 17, 47
Vikinghund 17, 47
Vikings 3
Vikiro Kennel 33
Vikrest 205
Vin-Melca Kennel 35, 205, 206
Vin-Melca's Happy Hour, Ch. 208

Vin-Melca's Howdy Rowdy, Ch. 208
Vin-Melca's Huck Finn 208
Vin-Melca's Matinee Idol, Ch. 211
Vincent, Patricia 35
Vindsval 19
Vinland 205
Virus 121
Vom Bree 206
Walk on lead 123
Walk through doors 123
Wallo, Olav 221
Wax, ear 181
Weight 73, 100, 183
Whelping 99
White Elkhound 15
Windshadow 206
Windy Cove Chief Cochise 211
Windy Cove Kennel 41, 206
Winners Bitch 113
Winners Class 113, 115
Winners Dog 113
Wolf Night 7
Wood, Valory 212
Working dog 71
Worming 104
Yokipi 17
Zygote 160, 162